Routledge Revivals

I0130589

Dollars and Borders

Originally published in 1987, *Dollars and Borders* explores the United States' government's relation to transnational capital. James P. Hawley traces the attempts of four presidents (John F. Kennedy, Lyndon B. Johnson, Richard Nixon, and Jimmy Carter) in the 1960s and 1970s to restrict international movements of U.S. capital and analyses the political and economic issues confronted by the government during this period. This title will be of particular interest to students of Politics and Economics.

Dollars and Borders

U.S. Government Attempts to Restrict Capital
Flows, 1960-1980

James P. Hawley

Routledge
Taylor & Francis Group

First published in 1987
by M.E. Sharpe

This edition first published in 2016 by Routledge
2 Park Square, Milton Park, Abingdon, Oxon, OX14 4RN
and by Routledge
711 Third Avenue, New York, NY 10017

Routledge is an imprint of the Taylor & Francis Group, an informa business

© 1987 M.E. Sharpe

All rights reserved. No part of this book may be reprinted or reproduced or
utilised in any form or by any electronic, mechanical, or other means, now
known or hereafter invented, including photocopying and recording, or in any
information storage or retrieval system, without permission in writing from the
publishers.

Publisher's Note
The publisher has gone to great lengths to ensure the quality of this reprint but
points out that some imperfections in the original copies may be apparent.

Disclaimer
The publisher has made every effort to trace copyright holders and welcomes
correspondence from those they have been unable to contact.

A Library of Congress record exists under LC control number: 86031395

ISBN 13: 978-1-138-18781-8 (hbk)
ISBN 13: 978-1-315-64288-8 (ebk)
ISBN 13: 978-1-138-18784-9 (pbk)

DOLLARS & BORDERS

U.S. Government Attempts to Restrict Capital Flows, 1960-1980

JAMES P. HAWLEY

M. E. SHARPE, INC.
Armonk, New York
London, England

Copyright © 1987 by M. E. Sharpe, Inc.

All rights reserved. No part of this book may be reproduced in any
form without written permission from the publisher, M. E. Sharpe, Inc.,
80 Business Park Drive, Armonk, New York 10504

Available in the United Kingdom and Europe from M. E. Sharpe,
Publishers, 3 Henrietta Street, London WC2E 8LU.

Library of Congress Cataloging-in-Publication Data

Hawley, James P., 1944–
    Dollars and borders.

    Includes index.
    1. Capital movements—United States—History—20th century.
2. Capital movements—Government policy—United States—History—
20th century. 3. Euro-dollar market—History—20th century. 4. Balance
of payments—United States—History—20th century. I. Title.
HG3891.H38   1987   332′.041   86-31395
ISBN 0-87332-386-6

Printed in the United States of America

For Diane, Rebecca and Jesse
and for my parents, Jane and Peter

Contents

Preface

This book is about the state's relation to transnational capital. In the chapters that follow I describe the attempts of four presidents of the United States in the 1960s and 1970s to restrict international movements of U.S. capital—attempts that brought their administrations into direct and often acrimonious conflict with U.S.-based transnational corporations and banks. I trace the political and economic priorities of the U.S. government as it confronted, first, a chronic deficit in its international balance of payments and then growing worldwide economic disorder, brought about in part by rapid transformations in banking and finance. In the process, I attempt to reveal the dynamic relationships among state actions in the global political economy, the political and economic activities of transnational corporations and banks, and developments in global financial markets.

At the heart of the book are five case studies of attempts by the U.S. government, as issuer of the dominant global currency, to rectify its balance of payments and stabilize the dollar. In 1961–62 President John F. Kennedy proposed a tax reform that would have eliminated foreign tax credits and required transnational corporations to repatriate their foreign profits annually for tax purposes. The intention was to strengthen U.S. trade and goods exports at the expense of capital export growth. Kennedy's initiative was strongly opposed by the transnationals and eventually the administration withdrew its proposal, citing improvements in the balance of payments.

In 1963 the U.S. balance-of-payments deficit was again large and the outflow of capital was increasing. The administration imposed an Interest Equalization Tax on transnational banks as a "temporary" means of minimizing capital outflows. The tax was opposed by the banks initially, and again in each renewal battle.

Faced with a still growing deficit, in 1964 President Lyndon B. Johnson established a voluntary capital-control program, which was again resisted by the transnationals, especially when it became apparent that the program was intended to last as long as there was a trade deficit. The inadequacy of the voluntary program and continued worsening of the deficit prompted introduction of a mandatory capital-control program in 1968 which, although greatly modified after the dollar was devalued in 1971, remained in effect until 1974. The mandatory program achieved its immediate goal of reducing capital exports from the United States, yet failed to accomplish its strategic goal of reducing the deficit and stabilizing the international monetary system.

Ironically, one clear, if unintended, effect of these state efforts to restrict capital movement was to encourage some dramatic innovations in international finance in the 1970s—particularly the creation of the Eurodollar market—that would enable capital to better elude state control efforts.

In 1978 the administration of President Jimmy Carter and the Federal Reserve Board, embroiled in a dollar crisis and facing continued international economic instability, proposed multilateral regulation of the Eurocurrency markets. The proposal was defeated by the efforts of transnational banks domestically and by the lukewarm responses of most of the affected states. The erosion of state capacity to implement macroeconomic policy thus continued unabated.

These five case studies tell two stories. The first is about state policy-making efforts in the face of opposition from transnational capital; the second, about financial market innovation and the creation of new markets in response to state-imposed restrictions. Even when state policy was explicitly intended not just to maintain state power in the world system, but to rationalize markets and organize capital in order to protect it, the effect of state control efforts was rather to stimulate market innovation, which thus diminished state capacity to accomplish these very goals.

Four main conclusions will emerge in this account. First, the "interests" of transnational capital are complex and contradictory, and may not even be evident to corporate and financial actors themselves. Second, the state plays a part in defining capital's interests in a process of what I call *interest mediation and formation*, in which the ideology of state managers has a role. A third conclusion is that constraints are placed on the state by its particular economic, political, and military location in the world interstate system. Finally, it becomes clear in this account that there is a dynamic relationship between state intervention in financial markets and ongoing global financial innovation, which occurs, in part, to counter state efforts at control.

As will be discussed in the final chapter, these conclusions have relevance to the contemporary debates concerning various theories of the state (neo-Marxist, statist, and neo-realist), all of which posit some degree of state autonomy from capital. I am persuaded that most of these theories do not adequately explain the dynamics that underlie the persistent structural divisions between state and capital and in particular, the influence of the international political economy on this relation. In general, many neo-Marxists have examined state–capital divisions but have taken the individual nation-state as the unit of analysis. Those who take statist, neo-realist, and world system perspectives have avoided this pitfall but on the whole have not been centrally concerned with the dynamics and structure of class formations within the nation-state. Furthermore, most of these otherwise diverse perspectives take class "interest" to be objective rather than problematic.

PREFACE xi

To understand the divisions between state and capital, one must appreciate the role that money plays in the global economic system and in nation-states. Most contemporary neo-Marxist theories and many Marxist-influenced world-systems theories that do not directly deal with the state neglect the question of money in an effort to move away from economic-determinist explanations of state action. What is lost is the *social and political character* of monetary and financial relations. By contrast, both Karl Marx and Max Weber examined monetary relations as fundamental aspects of social organization. Marx described money as a "social relation of production," a part of the larger relations of capitalist society. In the same vein, Weber wrote: "any act of exchange involving the use of money . . . is a social action simply because the money used derives its value from its relation to the potential action of others."

In this spirit, and much indebted to the perspective developed by Karl Polanyi in his classic work, *The Great Transformation*, I seek in the chapters that follow to illuminate the social aspects of some of the major monetary and financial events and institutions of our own day.

During this work's too-long gestation period many people read all or part of the manuscript, made innumerable criticisms and suggestions, and provided moral sustenance. In particular, a deep intellectual and editorial debt is owed to David Plotke, with whom I discussed the grand themes of *Dollars and Borders*—the relation between financial and economic institutions and states, politics and social structures. David's attention to careless formulations, gaps in argument and evidence, and too many run-on sentences proved tremendously helpful and challenging. Dorie Klein also read the entire manuscript with great care and under the pressure of time, providing much intellectual and editorial assistance. Many others read all or part of the work. In particular I owe thanks to Mitch Abolafia, Robert Alford, Fred Block, James O'Connor, Peter Evans, Albert Fishlow, Peter Katzenstein, Art MacEwen, Charles Noble, Ben Orlove, Immanuel Wallerstein, and Alan Wolfe. Patricia Kolb, my editor at M.E. Sharpe, proved very skillful in suggesting changes in some of the chapters and in the order of presentation, as did Roger Hayden, editor of the journal, *International Organization*, whose suggestions improved an earlier version of chapter 7 which appeared in that journal. Needless to say, I alone bear responsibility for all opinions expressed, as well as any errors of fact.

Over a period of what now seems a number of lifetimes, Diane Ehrensaft, my wife, has given me encouragement and love. My children, Rebecca and Jesse, put up with closed doors while their father worked. To my family I owe many thanks and much love.

JAMES P. HAWLEY

DOLLARS & BORDERS

1. The Erosion of U.S. Hegemony

In the twenty years between 1960 and 1980, the world economic system and the relations between governments and capital within that system underwent nearly constant change. The 1960s marked the high point of the global power of the U.S. and U.S. transnational capital. In the 1970s the Bretton Woods fixed-exchange-rate monetary system collapsed, global economic competition increased, and worldwide depression threatened. The events of this period fatally strained domestic political coalitions in the United States. Things did not work as they once did, and, accordingly, individuals and institutions had to seek new ways and means of achieving their goals.

The economic crisis of the seventies was not a result of spontaneous economic forces and their effects; rather, state actions in the global and domestic political economies were a central cause and feature of this crisis.[1]

Since the failure of the 1979–80 attempts to regulate the Eurocurrency markets, the exchange rate roller coaster continues, exaggerating the already serious levels of current account deficits and surpluses of the leading states. The underlying trends identified in this study continue to plague the international financial and monetary systems.

The ability of financial markets to channel massive capital flows through the unregulated Euromarkets was a prerequisite for the build-up of much commercial bank lending to the Third World from the mid-1970s through 1982. With the collapse of Mexico's external financial situation in 1982, and the resultant near global financial panic, the global political economy entered a new phase, chiefly characterized by the vast reduction of capital inflows to Third World nations and the increase of capital flight from them.

During these years the United States has benefited from massive capital inflows to finance its record current account deficits. Yet, the volume of these capital flows could well be reduced significantly should the interest rate spread between the U.S. and other capital markets decrease, a fear Paul Volcker of the Federal Reserve Board has often expressed. The consequences of past bad loans to many Third World states and the continued threat of renewed higher interest rates (especially if the dollar falls too low, too fast) will remain for the foreseeable future, not withstanding the current treble blessings of a devalued dollar, lower oil prices and interest rates, and still high levels of U.S. imports from Third World non-oil exporting states.

While the liquidity creating function of the Euromarkets in the current relatively noninflationary period is muted, the growth of globalized financial markets continues apace. These markets have not only grown quantitatively larger but are in the process of undergoing qualitative and innovative institutional changes. As the traditional demarcations among financial institutions break down, new and, in some cases, radically different forms of financial instruments proliferate. These trends will pose fundamental challenges to government macroeconomic policy formation and implementation, whether by individual nation-states or through coordinated actions among the leading states. In the future, there is little doubt that we will again witness a variety of attempts by governments to control and re-regulate increasingly integrated international capital markets and institutions.

The internationalization of capital

In the post–World War II period a major shift occurred in the geographical distribution of U.S. direct investment—from the underdeveloped areas of the world to its industrial core states. This was a competitive response to European and Japanese expansion in the world and U.S. markets.[2] As U.S. transnational corporations* moved into Europe, U.S. commercial banks followed in their footsteps. For the first time in the history of world banking, there came into being a truly international chain of commercial and investment branch banks. European banking had been international since the thirteenth and fourteenth centuries, but until recent decades its mode of operation has been to deal through a network of correspondent banks in foreign areas. Today two important factors distinguish the international commercial banking. The first is the expansion of the commercial bank network itself, with attendant implications for banking practices and operations and for the effectiveness of state central-bank regulation. A second new element, related to the first, is the development of the Eurocurrency system, the first authentically international banking system beyond the jurisdiction of one or many states. The emergence of the TNC and the TNB as the organizational forms of the new internationalization has altered the role and form of both finance and commodity capital.

Through the 1960s and 1970s and into the 1980s, the growth sector of the largest U.S. international banks was in their overseas branches and assets,[3] as

*By transnational corporation (TNC), I mean the largest units of capital which operate in six or more countries, have a centralized headquarters in one country and a board of directors the majority of whom are of one nationality, and whose operations cross national boundaries integrating finance, marketing, and production. The same definition holds for transnational banks (TNBs).

indicated in Table 1. The capital control programs proposed by successive U.S. presidents during this period were attempts to minimize the destabilizing impact at home of this new global banking order, which had initially developed in response to the pull of U.S. TNCs in Europe. Yet their effect was far from stabilizing. U.S. TNBs established European branches in record numbers in the mid-1960s and in the case of the largest banks these branches came to conduct a larger proportion of business than did their head offices in the United States. State efforts to impose controls in fact stimulated financial innovation and contributed to the expansion of the new global financial network, whose growth was intimately related to the growth of TNCs. In periods when TNCs were rapidly investing abroad, but were restricted from exporting capital directly from the United States—by the 1965 capital controls, for instance—they borrowed heavily from Eurocurrency banks. In periods such as 1976–78, when TNCs had large amounts of surplus liquid cash, they themselves became mini-financial institutions operating through banks and in their own name. They directly influenced events in the international monetary system, primarily through the intermediation of the Eurocurrency system.[4]

In sum, production, finance, and trade were increasingly globally linked primarily by transnational organizations, rather than primarily through trade. Direct rather than portfolio investment has been characteristic of the TNC. Commercial banks have interpenetrated one another's territory and have operated in an authentically international commercial banking system—the Eurocurrency system. To one degree or another, these transnational enterprises have become divorced from primary dependence on their national territories.

Charles-Albert Michalet characterizes this relation between transnational capital and the state in terms of a "conflict–cooperation" dichotomy. Changes in international capital are transforming the sovereign nation-state into a globally dependent "national territory." As higher degrees of global economic interdependence are reached, the new relation between states and transnational capital undermines a state's macroeconomic steering capacities. International competition among TNCs and TNBs is, in Michalet's words, "scarcely compatible with neo-Keynesian planning."[5] More generally, it is not compatible with macroeconomic policy direction of any sort, whether monetarist, supply-side investment inducement, Keynesian demand management, or with national economic policy and planning programs. Alberto Martinelli concludes that the global power of the TNC and the necessity for a domestically powerful nation-state are fundamentally contradictory: "The TNC needs a strong state and a stable social order, but this is impeded by TNCs themselves which at a certain point undermine the state. From the point of view of the national state, governments are confronted with a dilemma."[6] This dilemma has at least two dimensions. The first concerns the impact of the new internationalization on state–capital relations, especially on the nature of interests. The second concerns the relation to and the role of the United States in the world system, given the dichotomy of conflict–cooperation between it and

Table 1

U.S. Overseas Banks, Branches, Overseas and Domestic Assets

	Banks	Branches	Overseas assets	Domestic assets
			($ billions)	
1960	8	131	3.5	225.7
1967	15	295	15.7	448.9
1970	79	583	77.4	546.5
1974	129	737	115.0	872.0
1979	130	800	364.0	1,335.4
1981	NA	NA	462.7	1,613.5

Sources: Andrew F. Brimmer and Frederick F. Dahl, "Growth of American Banking; Implications for Public Policy," *The Journal of Finance* (May 1975), p. 345. *Federal Reserve Bulletin*, 56:12 (December 1970), p. A.19; 65:12 (December 1979), p. A.16; *Ibid.*, 68:12 (December 1982), p. A.18, A.56. See also Franklin R. Dahl, "International Operations of U.S. Banks: Growth and Public Policy Implications," in Thomas G. Giles and Vincent Apilado, eds., *Banking Markets and Financial Institutions* (Homewood, Ill., 1971), pp. 61–62; and Stuart W. Robinson, Jr., *Multinational Banking* (London, 1972), pp. 276–90.

U.S. transnational capital. Both of these dimensions have been influenced by and have had impact on the role of the United States in the post–World War II international monetary system.

Dollar domination and the U.S. balance of payments, 1945–1971

In the post–World War II global political economy the United States was the economically hegemonic power *par excellence*. There had been only two previous cases of economic hegemony within the world capitalist system: Holland (1625–1675) and Great Britain (1815–1875). As defined by Immanuel Wallerstein, hegemony involves more than simply core status in the system. Hegemony obtains when "the products of a given core state are produced so efficiently that they are by and large competitive even in other core states, and therefore the given core state will be the primary beneficiary of a maximally free world market."[7] The hegemonic nation-state must possess the necessary political, military, and intellectual power to preserve this position. Yet, as Wallerstein points out, the problem with hegemony is that, by its nature, it is a passing phenomenon: "As soon as a state becomes truly hegemonic, it begins to decline; for a state ceases to be hegemonic not because it loses strength . . . but because others gain." There is only a brief historical moment when a core power can manifest "simultaneously productive, commercial, and financial superiority over all other core powers."[8]

It is not coincidental that it was at the height of U.S. economic hegemony in the early 1960s (indicated by the record U.S. commercial trade surplus in 1964) that the issue of capital controls arose and with it, growing hostility between U.S. transnational capital and the highest levels of the U.S. government. The capital controls signaled the emergence of the politics of U.S. hegemonic decline in the international system. The controls had dual strategic priorities: to place protection of the U.S. world power position ahead of private sector expansion abroad and to maintain domestic political coalitions constructed around a minimal welfare state program.

The controls attempted to maintain dollar stability, which was threatened by the fixed exchange-rate regime of the Bretton Woods system, while enabling the United States to preserve its hegemonic status. The original creation of the Bretton Woods system and the establishment of the International Monetary Fund (IMF) in 1944 had attempted to link free trade with the restimulation of the war-devastated world economy. The Bretton Woods system should be seen, and at its inception was seen by some, as the international complement to the U.S. Employment Act of 1946, serving as an export subsidy to prime the U.S. and thereby the world economy. Michael Hudson comments:

> Without the financial resources of the Bretton Woods institutions, the United States would find itself obliged to supply these exports to Europe as outright grants. "We want our exports to increase," testified Under Secretary of the Treasury Harry Dexter White, "But we want other countries to be in a position to pay."[9]

In the original IMF agreements, the movement of capital was not accorded the same treatment as that of goods and services. The agreements acknowledged the legitimacy of capital controls, and instructed member nations to aid other nations in enforcing those controls. The agreements did not foresee and were not intended to facilitate the free international movement of capital, nor did they officially recognize the dollar as an internationally accepted reserve and transaction currency. Still, only the dollar represented a national economy which would be able to support a key currency. The postwar reconstruction of Europe and Japan through the Marshall Plan and the rearmament of Europe further ensured the dollar's status as the reserve and transaction currency. David Calleo and Benjamin Rowland argue that:

> In the postwar era, America's role in the monetary system and America's role in the military alliance have been two sides of the same imperial coin. Nuclear hegemony in NATO has matched dollar hegemony in the IMF. . . . The design of a monetary system, underneath its technical drapery, naturally reflects the basic political pattern governing the overall relations of member states.[10]

Throughout the Bretton Woods era, the U.S. balance of payments remained in deficit. The deficit was the primary mechanism by which world liquidity increased through the U.S. outflow of gold and, more importantly, of dollars. The U.S. payments deficit, supplemented by foreign aid, the Marshall Plan, and foreign arms spending, enabled European and Japanese reconstruction to take place. The willingness of foreign central banks to hold dollars as a reserve and of foreign individuals and firms to transact their business in dollars ensured that the United States could run a continual payments deficit with little threat to the dollar's status or stability prior to 1958. These *de facto* loans by foreign governments, individuals, and firms transformed the United States into a *de facto* central bank able to create global liquidity, promote trade expansion, and simultaneously run a long-term payments deficit. This method of financing under the Bretton Woods system was nearly automatic. As will be discussed shortly, it also bestowed upon the United States a special financial privilege.[11]

Yet the system contained a major flaw. The dollar was stable largely because it was convertible on demand into gold. The rate of increase and level of global liquidity, however, depended on the U.S. payments deficit. In time, short-term U.S. debt grew to exceed U.S. gold reserves, causing serious speculation against the dollar in favor of stronger currencies and gold. The first manifestation of this trend was the dollar crisis of October 1960, a direct result of which were the proposed (but not legislated) capital control provisions of the 1962 Revenue Act. As foreigners, private and public, grew reluctant to hold dollars for fear that they could no longer be adequately backed by gold, the dollar's liquidity functions and, consequently, its transaction functions were threatened. This was pointed out by Robert Triffin at the time:

> Additions to international liquidity made possible by the system [of key currencies] are entirely dependent upon the willingness of the key currency countries to allow their own net reserve position to deteriorate, by letting their short term liabilities to foreigners grow persistently and indefinitely at a faster pace than their own gold assets.[12]

Ultimately, this led to the speculative attacks on the key currency as U.S. gold reserves were drawn, culminating in the dollar being cut loose from gold in 1971. The Bretton Woods collapse thus ended a regime of "economic liberalism without tears," to use Calleo and Rowland's apt phrase.[13]

The U.S. payments deficit itself came to undermine the reality and ideology of free trade internationalism. The deficit allowed the dollar to be the primary global reserve and transaction currency. The United States was able to finance its deficit and thereby transfer real economic wealth to the United States from both developed and less-developed countries. As dollar instability increased after 1960, this transfer became a significant political issue both among the advanced countries and between the U.S. government and U.S. international bankers. The bankers argued in opposition to the Interest Equalization Tax of 1963 that they should reap the benefits of the dollar's hegemony, while the government defined itself, rather than Wall Street, as the world's central banker.

A central aspect of the conflict between the U.S. government and U.S. TNBs and TNCs was the division of the economic benefits which accrued to the holders (and, in the state's case, the first issuers) of dollars: which sector was to play and benefit from the central banker's role in the dollar reserve system. The conflict was not simply an economic one; also at stake, alongside continued expansion of U.S. transnational capital, were the state's political and military apparatus of hegemony and the relation of private sector global expansion to state expenditures.

The United States was able to assume the role of world banker under the Bretton Woods system when the dollar became as good as gold. This is crucial for understanding the character of the U.S. balance of payments deficit and the global transfer of wealth. The dollar, in fact, was far superior to gold as a reserve asset, since it could earn interest, and its supply could increase more rapidly than gold's to provide needed global liquidity. Thus the U.S. payments deficit was entirely different in nature from the chronic deficits of most of the less-developed countries. The latter's deficits were a consequence of the terms of trade and capital flows between the core and the less-developed peripheries of the world economic system. The United States, by contrast, was in a way like a commercial banking system which lends long on the basis of its short-term deposits. The United States was able to profit from its long-term indebtedness while providing needed liquidity for various forms of spending and investment. Yet this analogy, made by many economists, only partially captures the consequences of the United States' role as world banker. [14]

The financing of the U.S. payments deficit enabled the U.S. government to maintain its apparatus of global empire, while the private sector was able to enjoy a long-run profit on its foreign capital investments. From the perspective of the balance of payments, the state sector was in deficit, the private sector was in surplus; both were mutually dependent. The deficit was financed on the basis of the reserve nature of the dollar. Thus the willingness of the advanced capitalist states and, after 1974, of the oil-producing countries to hold dollars as reserves—in fact, their inability to refuse dollars, as the United States increasingly produced and exported them throughout the 1960s—contributed to the instability of the international monetary system. The United States benefited from this system not only through the direct gains to the reserve issuer but from its hidden ability to finance the politico-military apparatus of hegemony. A strictly economic analysis overlooks this crucial strategic fact. The fact that direct benefits accrue to the first issuer of a global currency helps to explain European states' toleration, if not active encouragement, of the Eurocurrency system's rapid growth, beginning in the 1960s, as a means to break the dollar monopoly of U.S. banks and the U.S. government. To the degree that a Eurobank could issue dollar credits, the control of global liquidity by U.S. institutions could be limited. The forced holding of dollars abroad as a reserve asset and a means of transaction, which forced financing of U.S. foreign aid and foreign military programs, became an especially important issue after the 1965 escalation of the Vietnam war. Arguments by John Odell and others suggesting that U.S. attachment to the Bretton Woods system was primarily ideological, overlook this material benefit.[15]

Let us now consider in greater detail the direct benefits to the United States as the issuer of the transaction and reserve currency. Prior to the emergence of a massive Eurodollar market, the United States maintained a monopoly on the production of the majority of the world's reserve currency. From this position a form of what is called seigniorage accrues to the issuer of money. Traditionally, the term meant the difference between the circulation value of a coin and the cost of bullion and minting. In the contemporary context, it has been taken to mean, in Herbert Grubel's words, "the net value of resources accruing to the issuers of money. Only when institutions are able to obtain a monopoly in the production of money, which allows them to keep out of the market effective substitutes and to prevent the payment of interest to holders of the money, will there be seigniorage in the long run."[16] The seigniorage obtained by the U.S. enabled it to command free returns for "foreign goods and services to the extent that foreign governments hold dollars in reserve," according to Alexander Swoboda. He continues:

> The United States does not have to pay for this loan, or, at least, the interest it services on foreign official balances is lower than the rate of return on capital in the United States. That is, the ability to issue international reserves enables the United States to reap gains from seigniorage. This concept can be extended to those dollars holdings by private nonresidents which result from the vehicle-currency status of the dollar.[17]

"The issuer of a vehicle currency," Swoboda concludes, "can reap significant benefits from the external use of its currency."

Since the U.S. government held the monopoly on dollar production, it gained the surplus from the loans granted to it, after 1960 often involuntarily, by foreign states. It was able to appropriate the real resources, commodities, and services of various countries as a means of financing the chronic U.S. payments deficit. Specifically, this meant the financing of foreign aid and military-related outflow payments.[18] This is a fundamental point. The International Economic Policy Association's 1973 policy statement, *The United States Balance of Payments: From Crisis to Controversy*, provides an excellent description worth quoting at length:

> As the Europeans have often pointed out, the United States had given them "paper dollars" for real goods, services and assets. The fact that the excess dollars received and resources they gave us in exchange were on *governmental account* is of no material importance to them.
> Under this system, the United States benefited by receiving or controlling the flow (to less developed countries and for common military purposes) of more

actual goods, services and assets than it transferred abroad.

For a long period [before the 1958 dollar glut] our trading partners benefited as well: they accumulated liquid reserves of dollars and gold which increased their financial security and therefore allowed them to liberalize their trade restrictions and currency controls. Their export industries were stimulated . . . their domestic economies were invigorated . . . and their military defenses were strengthened by the U.S. military presence abroad.

The weakness of the system was that it depended on the willingness of foreign countries to accumulate liquid dollar assets . . . without an effective mechanism to control the growth of such liquidity. . . . The crisis [of the system] was the culmination of the dependency of this monetary and trade system upon U.S. deficits. Foreigners became restive at giving real goods and services in exchange for "paper," which depreciated in value as American inflation grew; meanwhile, the money flows from the United States abroad increased foreign inflationary pressures.[19]

The dollar–gold exchange standard was thus more than just an efficient international payments system. H. L. Robinson argues that "the U.S. had shifted onto other countries the real costs of U.S. spending for imperialist defense and expansion which are in excess of its surplus balance on goods, services and investment income."[20] In terms of economic resources, the U.S. deficit was being paid for by the countries which absorbed the net dollar outflow. The process by which this occurred was that a foreign government would buy up dollars "in order to prevent the country's currency from being forced up in relation to the dollar against the government's will. What is in reality also happening, but is hidden, is that the country's savings are being channeled by the government to defend and expand U.S. imperialism—including its expansion in the dollar-receiving countries themselves."[21]

The U.S. state's payments deficit and the U.S. private sector's payments surplus created a two-sided problem, at once economic and political. The state's deficit (the government account) was a result of its costly position as global hegemonic center. As the instability of the dollar and the international monetary system increased after 1960, the politics of financing the deficit became a major wedge between the state's overall economic and politico-military vision of the global order and the narrower profit-defined orientations of most TNCs and TNBs.

In sum, the U.S. payments deficit was necessary for the expansion, maintenance, and financing of the postwar U.S. economic and politico-military hegemony under the Bretton Woods system. But the system was contradictory. Without a significant restructuring of the global order, neither government nor private capital outflows could be reduced significantly in order to eliminate or substantially reduce the deficit. In the long run, the two components were mutually dependent. Given the developing crisis in the international monetary system after

1960, itself reflecting the decline in U.S. hegemony, government and TNC and TNB leaders came to disagree on immediate priorities. The state defended its own strategic and political role over the short-run imperatives of foreign investment, while the private sector argued its own case against state needs and policies.

The structural roots of the division between state and transnational capital find an analogy in what James O'Connor calls the fiscal crisis of the state.[22] O'Connor characterizes a domestic fiscal crisis as rooted in the state's subsidization of selected direct and indirect costs of capital accumulation and of society as a whole. Of these, O'Connor calls social capital expenditures those which directly and indirectly subsidize capital; social consumption expenditures those which directly and indirectly subsidize the reproduction of labor; and social expense those which neither directly nor indirectly subsidize the reproduction of capital or labor, but legitimate the social order. In O'Connor's analysis, domestic fiscal crisis occurs due to the tax-supported nature of state subsidization. The corporate sector (what he calls the monopoly sector) of capital and labor disproportionately benefit from state subsidization. The competitive sector disproportionately bears the tax burden. This inevitably leads to a revenue shortfall, to long-term structural fiscal crisis, and to conflict between and among the two sectors and the state. These categories have their analogs in the relation of the U.S. state to the international monetary system under a fixed-exchange-rate regime: an international balance of payments fiscal crisis. The hallmark of this crisis is that the state sector is in deficit while the U.S. private transnational sector remains in a surplus position, although the composition of the surplus changes. The U.S. state provided the international social capital and social expenses for a Pax Americana. These activities are nonremunerative for the state and must be tax-supported. Taxes, however, are raised domestically in dollars. The government as first issuer of dollars had essentially unlimited access to foreign exchange. Thus the dollar–gold exchange standard partially offset these costs of empire, but at the high long-term cost of a continual downward speculative pressure on the dollar in foreign exchange markets.

The politics of this international fiscal crisis were perceived differently by state managers responsible for overseeing the payments deficit and maintaining the U.S. global position and by private sector managers responsible for their firms' profits. The short-run pressure among TNC and TNB executives against using any form of capital export restraints, limitations, or controls as a means to offset the payments deficit was a consistent theme from 1961 through 1971. Further, state managers realized that the state itself had a stake in the smooth operation of the international monetary system despite the global fiscal crisis, since it benefited, particularly in military terms, from the surplus appropriated through its dollar monopoly before the mid-1960s and from its dominant position thereafter. Hence the politics of the global fiscal crisis were played out over the terms of the financing of deficit between the state and the transnational private sector. This structurally based conflict was played out first and foremost around the capital controls.

A word should be said about how the form of global fiscal crisis varied under the Bretton Woods fixed-exchange-rate system in the period 1971–73, and afterward, under the floating rate arrangements. Under the Bretton Woods system with the dollar–gold value at $35 per ounce, fiscal crisis manifested itself directly in the balance of payments accounts, especially in the government's account. While speculative pressures on the dollar influenced U.S. international monetary policy under the fixed-rate system, it did not affect the U.S. dollar–gold relation. Under floating rates, however, the manifestation of global fiscal crisis was more complex. Not only could fiscal crisis appear directly in payments accounting, but it could also appear as one cause of downward pressure on the real, trade-weighted value of the dollar. Conversely, even if the government deficit grew, under a flexible system other factors (e.g., the high U.S. interest rates of 1981–83) could increase the dollar's value and tend to decrease the government account deficit.

U.S. balance of payments strategies, 1960–1971

A trade surplus strategy underlay all U.S. balance of payments policies in the 1960s and early 1970s. The trade account, however, could not be influenced in the short term by government policies. Consequently, policy with more immediate impact on the deficit had to be developed. Three phases of payments strategies can be delineated in this period. The first, beginning with the dollar glut in 1958 and slowly trailing off from 1960 to 1963, was marked by official optimism that the deficit could be corrected by a readjustment of political, military, and economic relations with the Western European countries.[23] From 1958 to 1960, the first years of *phase one*, the Eisenhower administration attempted to deal with the deficit in this manner through a series of interrelated military and political initiatives. The most important concerned the division of military responsibilities among the NATO powers. The United States unsuccessfully attempted to negotiate payment by West Germany to the United States to offset the cost of U.S. troops. Related to the military issue were directly economic ones, the foremost being the U.S. attempt to prevent the European Economic Community (EEC) from becoming a truly European free trade area as the British had proposed. Simultaneously, the United States wanted to lower EEC tariff barriers to its own products, especially agricultural ones.[24] These attempts at adjustments all proved to be either unsuccessful (e.g., sharing military expenses) or temporary (e.g., German prepayments of war debts or current arms purchases).

During the second part of phase one, late 1960 to 1963, the Kennedy administration wavered in its estimate of the seriousness of the payments deficit. The trade surplus strategy was emphasized through the passage of the Trade Expansion Act and the initiation of the Kennedy Round of GATT (General Agreement on Tariffs and Trade) negotiations. To parallel the multilateral approach to trade, a military "multilateral force" was proposed. It would have provided a collective nuclear deterrent, with the United States retaining a veto on the use of nuclear weapons for which the European NATO countries would have carried a greater share of the cost. This proposal failed to win European support. The most important attempt by the Kennedy administration to link trade, domestic investment, and payments problems was embodied in the Revenue Act of 1962 as introduced in Congress in 1961, which resulted in the well-known 1964 Keynesian tax cuts. The original provision of the act attempted to induce U.S. capital to invest domestically and in developing countries rather than in the advanced economies of Western Europe. Thus, to a degree, payments considerations led the Kennedy administration to challenge transnational capital initially over how foreign income was to be taxed. The original version of the 1962 Revenue Act, which would have altered the foreign tax credit provisions for transnational corporations, was defeated in Congress.

In spite of the failure of these programs to eliminate the deficit, government attitudes remained optimistic. The most influential expression of this view was the Brookings Institution study *The United States Balance of Payments in 1968*, published in 1963. The study concluded that "Our best guess is that the basic deficit will be eliminated. . . . There is a definite possibility that a significant basic surplus will develop."[25] This would be due to a new increase in the export of goods, a rise in income receipts from private and service income investment, a decline in military expenditures, and a decline in the rate of private, long-term, mainly direct investment. Although 1963 would be a turning point for government attitudes on payments, the Brookings study had a major influence on all sectors of opinion at least through 1965. The study's assumptions were Keynesian and trade-based to the core. Direct investment was dismissed as relatively unimportant.[26]

The beginning of *phase two* coincided roughly with the Interest Equalization Act (IET) in mid-1963. This era was characterized by a voluntary payments strategy, although other voluntary policies agreed upon between business and government dated from 1961. During the period from 1963 to 1967, the idea and reality of a smoothly operating U.S.-dominated Atlantic partnership receded, de Gaulle vetoed British entry into the Common Market, the multilateral force idea was abandoned, and France produced its *force de frappe*. The expanded U.S. military presence in Southeast Asia turned U.S. foreign policy attention away from Europe, while greatly complicating the payments deficit after 1963.[27] Phase two also encompassed a debate within the administration over the role that the dollar should play within the world monetary system. Secretary of the Treasury C. Douglas Dillon (1961–65) argued that the dollar should maintain its reserve currency status. The problem of increasing global liquidity was the responsibility of the U.S. as world banker. The means by which liquidity would be expanded was the enlargement of the quotas of member countries in the International

Monetary Fund. Dillon resisted a more fundamental reorganization of the monetary system, specifically, a move for the creation of special drawing rights in the IMF. Under great international, especially European, pressure for monetary reform, Dillon and Treasury Under-Secretary for Monetary Affairs Robert Roosa left office in mid-1963. Shortly after, Henry Fowler replaced Dillon as Treasury Secretary and a world monetary conference was called to discuss a new reserve system. While little came of the conference, it represented a turning point in U.S. policy toward greater state intervention, which opened the way for the creation of Special Drawing Rights (SDRs) in 1967.[28]

The voluntary period of phase two was explicitly a holding operation, awaiting the effects of underlying forces which most liberals, and some conservatives, believed would salvage the dollar and permanently end the deficit. As this did not occur, the policy of voluntary restraint on dollar outflows gradually gave way to a radically new approach that led to a policy of benign neglect. The voluntary period came to a close with the U.S. support of the British pound in November 1967. The United States supplied gold to the London gold pool which had been set up previously to stabilize gold's free market price. Speculative pressure on the dollar increased as it came to the support of the pound, resulting in another large U.S. gold drain.[29]

With the dollar linked to the defense of sterling in late 1967, new measures were designed by the Johnson administration to reverse the gold losses and minimize speculation. This necessitated a general reorientation of U.S. strategy, paving the way for *phase three*. To regain the initiative in international monetary politics, mandatory capital controls were imposed in January 1968. These were the first element in the new strategy. Second, President Johnson announced a plan for a tariff surcharge on imports from Europe and Japan and corresponding rebates on U.S. exports. This attempt to force the Europeans and Japanese to expand their imports, aimed at increasing U.S. exports, was moderately successful. More importantly, the London gold pool agreement was abrogated by the United States in March 1968, thereby creating a two-tiered market for gold: the official rate of $35 an ounce, and a floating free market rate. In effect, this abolished the free convertibility of dollars to gold in violation of the Bretton Woods agreements and constituted a partial devaluation of the dollar.

This third element in the new strategy forced speculation against the dollar into official governmental channels by requiring speculators to sell dollars for other strong currencies. The resulting pressure on central banks in dollar-holding countries to maintain fixed exchange rates in the face of massive dollar build-ups spurred revaluations of other currencies against the dollar. The effect was partly to relieve immediate pressure on the dollar. The United States could "do nothing," hence the term "benign neglect."[30] The Johnson administration actually initiated the policy, which was carried out by the Nixon administration until devaluation in 1971. The policy implied the use of what Henry Aubrey has called the "dollar deterrent": the forced holding of unwanted dollars by foreign central banks to avoid an otherwise certain collapse of the world monetary system.[31]

Nixon continued this strategy, maintaining the mandatory capital controls intact by continuing a policy of benign neglect and taking a hard line in trade and monetary negotiations with the other advanced nations. Domestic economic considerations were given priority over easing the developing international dollar crisis. This too was a continuation of benign neglect. The administration's goal in the 1971 crisis (like Johnson's goal with the tariff surcharge threat in 1968) was to force an upward revaluation of the German mark and the Japanese yen in relation to the dollar. The closing of the U.S. gold window on August 15, 1971, forced the world onto a pure dollar standard, while also forcing the mark and yen to float upward.

In sum, U.S. official policy toward the payments deficit began as one of minor adjustments in the late 1950s. This was superseded by a more substantial, but still relatively minor, series of adjustments focusing on various accounts of the U.S. balance of payments deficit during phase two. Both were characterized by an optimistic faith that underlying forces would correct the deficit. When this assumption proved unrealistic, phase three developed, characterized by more aggressively nationalist attitudes toward European and Japanese competitors and by a benign neglect payments policy.[32]

Global monetary disorder 1971–1980

As the U.S. payments deficit haunted all foreign economic policy decisions during the 1960s and early 1970s, generalized global monetary disorder strongly influenced all policy in the 1970s. With the collapse of the Bretton Woods system in 1971 and the *de facto* acceptance in 1973 of floating exchange rates with state intervention into foreign exchange markets (ratified *de jure* at the 1976 IMF meetings in Jamaica), the U.S. balance of payments deficit receded in degree and importance as a prime indicator of monetary instability. The politics of managing the U.S. payments deficit, represented primarily by the capital controls, was succeeded by the politics of managing the global and domestic economy in an increasingly troubled sea of monetary disorders. The problem of managing the domination of the dollar remained, but the mechanisms for management were transformed by continual financial innovation, exemplified by the Eurosystem's rapid growth and the collapse of the fixed-exchange-rate system. The control of capital flows for payments reasons became less of a problem, while the control of increasing global and domestic instability became a primary object of policy. Monetary instability during the 1970s was characterized by extreme exchange rate fluctuations and the decreasing ability of national governments to control the growth rate of their own currencies given the internationalization of finance.[33] The lessened capacity of states to determine and implement their own monetary policies meant that one important instrument of macroeconomic policy became less effective. The divisions between U.S. state managers and transnational capital, manifested in the earlier capital controls efforts, resurfaced in the late 1970s over state-initiated efforts to insulate domestic monetary policy from the unstable Eurocurrency system by regulating the Eurocurrency markets.

In this regard, there are two important elements of global monetary developments in the 1970s: exchange rate instability and the explosion of international liquidity. These developments have reopened the controversy, to be discussed in a later chapter, about the merits of a fixed- versus a floating-rate system and the role of state policy under alternate forms of monetary regimes.

Foreign exchange rate instability has been endemic to the post-1973 monetary system. There is a floating-rate system which has often relied on interventions by national bank authorities,[34] in contrast to the fixed-exchange-rate system of Bretton Woods, or a gold standard with flexible exchange rates among various national currencies. National and multilateral central bank intervention has become a fixed feature of the post-1973 system.[35] Such interventions may have a number of motives: to balance payments, to resist market-determined adjustments, or to account for factors such as differential national rates of interest and inflation.

One important consequence of this system has been the institutionalization of currency speculation as a necessary component for TNC, TNBs, and other international actors to protect themselves against unknown fluctuations. In addition, regular and extreme exchange rate fluctuations provide a gambler's lure for a quick profit. The potential for substantial abuse, especially during economic contractions and near-panics, is evident in the history of the 1974 Herstatt bank failure and other failures of the 1980s.[36]

Another significant consequence of the managed float system has been its impact on global economic interdependence. With managed floating rates, the national macroeconomic policies of each state within the world system are less independent, although the degree of dependence varies. Harold van B. Cleveland and Ramachandra Bhagavatula suggest that foreign central banks respond more quickly to moves by the United States Federal Reserve under a managed floating system.

> The reason is the greatly increased sensitivity of financial markets [for foreign exchange] . . . to changes or anticipated changes in Federal Reserve policy. So on two occasions in 1980 . . . the dollar's swift rise on the exchanges (in anticipation of Federal Reserve tightening and thus higher United States interest rates) forced the German central bank to tighten domestic credit, thereby turning a mild business slowdown in Germany into what is likely to be a 1980–81 recession.[37]

Ralph Bryant concludes that ''Any extra room for maneuver in one nation's macroeconomic policies attributable to the openness of its economy [under a

Table 2

Inflationary Explosion of International Liquidity 1969–mid-1978 (In U.S. dollars, billions)*

	End 1969	End 1972	End 1977	Mid 1978	Mid-1978 as % of 1969
I. Foreign Dollar Claims	78	146	363	373	478%
A. On U.S. Government and Banks	49	85	210	221	451%
B. On Foreign Branches of U.S. Banks	29	61	153	153	524%
II. International Monetary Reserves	79	159	319	339	418%
A. Foreign Exchange	33	104	244	256	776%
1. Dollars and Eurodollars	20	81	197	na	985%
2. Other Currencies	7	15	27	na	386%
3. Other	7	8	22	na	314%
B. Other: World Monetary Gold, SDR Allocations and Investments	46	55	75	75	163%
III. Commercial Banks' Foreign Liabilities in:	121	217	658	700	579%
A. Dollars and Eurodollars	94	157	481	na	512%
B. Other Currencies	27	60	177	na	656%

*Data are not fully comparable due to differences in definition of foreign liabilities in U.S. and European reporting. Figures are rounded to nearest billion.

Source: Robert Triffin, "The International Role and Fate of the Dollar," *Foreign Affairs*, 57:2 (Winter 78/79), p. 270.

managed exchange-rate system] must come at the expense of policy flexibility for other nations. All countries cannot enjoy additional flexibility simultaneously.''[38]

The susceptibility of foreign exchange markets to fluctuations, necessitating central bank intervention, was heightened by the explosion in the amount of foreign exchange itself during the 1970s. While all major currencies have increased, the dollar's growth stands out. In spite of the dollar's relative devaluation between 1971 and 1980, it has remained the primary international currency both for official reserve and for private and official transaction purposes. The dollar, in the words of Rimmer de Vries, ''as a practical matter. . . has emerged from the turmoil as the sole international money.''[39] This naked dollar standard has had two important effects on international liquidity. First is its effect on reserve creation. As Richard Cooper characterizes it, there is a

> total lack of control over the volume of international liquidity, which arises from the absence of asset settlement, the unconstrained freedom to place reserves in Euromarkets, and possibly also from fluctuations in the value of gold reserves that may result from variations in the [free market] gold price.[40]

Second, with the growth of the Eurocurrency system, national governments are no longer the only source of issue of international reserves. Increasingly, private sector Eurobanks can also create international reserves, outside the direct influence of Federal Reserve policy. Between 1969 and 1975, for instance, there was a global trebling of international liquidity, measured in dollars—from $78 billion to about $225 billion.[41] The overwhelming source of this explosion was in foreign exchange, primarily in the Eurocurrency system. Table 2 indicates massive growth of foreign exchange markets. Especially noteworthy is the trend away from official monetary expansion (item IIB) and toward private sector expansion (items IB; IIA; and III).

In sum, with the breakdown of the Bretton Woods system emerged a set of unstable world monetary arrangements, largely as a result of the creation of uncontrolled world liquidity based in the internationalized private sector. The international monetary system of the 1970s came to be dominated by private banks operating primarily through the Eurocurrency system with the dollar remaining the primary currency. The system was and continues to be characterized by extreme exchange-rate instability necessitating repeated central bank intervention into foreign exchange markets. The United States attempt in 1979–80 to regulate the Eurocurrency system was a logical reaction to these extremely costly interventions. But it produced only limited and temporary results.[42]

2. The 1962 Revenue Act

The balance of payments problem

At the height of the 1960 presidential campaign, in October 1960, a gold crisis forced candidates Richard M. Nixon and John F. Kennedy to address the issue of the U.S. balance of payments deficit. Prior to the crisis, Kennedy had raised the alarm about the stagnation of the domestic economy and called for an easing of monetary policy in order to stimulate the economy. But before Inauguration Day had arrived, Kennedy, seeking to reassure jittery European bankers about his intentions, pledged to maintain the value of the dollar to gold at $35 an ounce and ceased speaking about his campaign pledge to achieve a 5 percent growth rate and easy money.[1]

The new Kennedy administration faced two major interrelated economic problems: domestic recession and the balance of payments deficit. The unemployment rate reached 8 percent in February 1961, the rate of new investment was low, and the gap between potential and actual GNP, reflecting the degree of unemployment of labor and capital, was $30 to $50 billion annually. Kennedy was pressed to develop a program to "get the nation moving again," as he had so memorably promised.[2] The dilemma was classic: the administration confronted a sagging domestic economy in need of traditional countercyclical policies of fiscal debt stimulation and monetary expansion, while the balance of payments deficit and the international economy generally appeared to demand exactly opposite policies—restriction of credit and money through high interest rates and a surplus in the federal budget.

During its first eighteen months the administration instituted a series of new, primarily technical measures to finance the payments deficit, which reduced it temporarily. A series of bilateral central bank swaps were arranged which served to minimize the impact of payments imbalances on gold and foreign exchange reserves among the major trading nations. The short-term credits provided through the swaps were used to intervene in the spot (current) and forward (future) world currency markets in order to restrain short-term money flows which arose either from speculation or from the interest-rate differential between the United States and Europe. Another innovation was the sale to foreign central banks by the U.S. Treasury of nonmarketable medium-term securities (fifteen months to two years), denominated in either foreign currencies or U.S. dollars. These Roosa Bonds, as they were called after Under-Secretary of the Treasury for Monetary Affairs Robert Roosa, whose brainchild they were, were guaranteed against a devaluation of the dollar and were immediately convertible at the option of the buyer. They refinanced the deficit by changing current liabilities into future ones.[3] Another measure instituted was the establishment of the London Gold Pool to insure stability against the speculative London gold market. The pool was a selling and purchasing arrangement among central banks, of which the U.S. share was 50 percent. The United States was committed to supply or purchase 50 percent of the net gold transfers needed to stabilize the price of gold on the free London market at or near the official U.S. price of $35 an ounce.[4]

In addition to these technical measures, the administration reduced duty-free tourist allowances from $500 to $100; paid a higher interest rate on dollars that foreign central banks held in New York as an inducement for nonconversion into gold; continued the Eisenhower "Buy America" program for military and state operations abroad; and continued to press West Germany to pay for a larger share of U.S. troops stationed there.[5] These actions won general support from all sectors of business.

In April 1961 the administration proposed a major reform of the Internal Revenue Code which would have increased the taxation of U.S. foreign investment abroad. This approach to the problems of domestic stagnation and international monetary instability had begun shortly after the election and came to an end by November 1961, when Kennedy shifted the administration's attention away from the controversial taxation of foreign income to the familiar tried-and-tested ground of trade expansion.[6] This first phase of the administration's balance of payments policies was based on the optimistic view that the payments deficit was temporary and could be corrected within a few years through a combined series of technical reforms, without sacrificing either the U.S. hegemonic apparatus abroad or the domestic living standard.

Central to this strategy were the tax recommendations of the 1962 Revenue Act presented to Congress on April 29, 1961. In order to stimulate the domestic economy, a Keynesian-style incentive for business investment was proposed; to aid in the elimination of the deficit, removal of the tax deferral on foreign business income was proposed. Kennedy stressed that the two should be considered "as a unit," since, in his view, balance of payments problems were directly related to the poor performance of the domestic economy. This approach contradicted the classical remedies for a chronic payments deficit—domestic deflation and credit restriction—with a "new economics." Kennedy saw the softness of the economy and the softness of the dollar as one problem, not two. A dynamic export-oriented economy producing competitively priced goods would maintain the strength of the dollar.[7] The productivity of U.S. industry and labor was the basis for the country's "high standard of living" and "leadership in world markets," which in turn was the basis for a strong and stable dollar. A strategy based on domestic expansion would correct the payments imbalance through a greater trade surplus.[8]

The Kennedy strategy assumed that the surplus in the trade account could be increased in order to make up for the deficit in the other accounts. The existing trade surplus, while large, was not large enough to "cover our expenditures for U.S. military establishments abroad, for capital invested abroad, . . . for government economic assistance and loan programs."[9]

The 1961 version of the export surplus strategy was the opposite of the immediate postwar trade surplus strategy. The central problem in 1961 was not overbuilt industries in relation to effective demand as in 1945 through 1947; it was a problem of the relative decline of the competitive status of U.S. exports and the consequent burden on the trade account to correct for all other deficits.[10]

The administration saw correction of the balance of payments deficit as crucial not only to pull the country out of recession, but also because the United States was the "principal banker of the free world." World trade and with it the political stability of the "free world" depended "on the dollar to finance a substantial portion of . . . free world trade." More than any time in the past the United States had to "take its balance of payments into account when formulating its economic policies and conducting its economic life."

Kennedy elaborated four guiding principles for his administration: (1) the price of gold would be maintained at $35 an ounce, there would be no exchange controls, and the government would continue all national security and economic assistance programs; (2) "maximum emphasis" would be placed on "expanding exports"; (3) there would be no return to protectionism; and (4) the "flow of resources" from industrialized to developing countries would have to increase.[11]

Keynesianism and direct investment

The tax recommendations of the 1962 Revenue Act included two measures designed to stimulate investment in the U.S. economy. Tax credits against a firm's tax liabilities were to be granted on investments in assets with a life of six years or more. The objective was to provide the "largest possible inducement to new investment which would not otherwise be undertaken."[12] The second proposed measure was removal of the tax deferral on foreign business income from direct investment in other advanced industrial countries. The tax law allowed foreign-based U.S. subsidiaries to defer payment on earnings until they were repatriated to the United States as dividends to the parent corporation. Under the proposed legislation, the deferral would be eliminated and annual undistributed profits of the foreign corporations would be deemed distributed as dividends to American shareholders whether or not these profits actually were received by the U.S. parent corporation. The administration argued that this revision would eliminate a tax inducement for investment abroad at the expense of domestic investment. In his tax message, Kennedy stated:

> Recently more and more enterprises organized abroad by American firms have arranged their corporate structures—aided by artificial arrangements between parent and subsidiary regarding inter-company pricing, the transfer of patent licensing rights, the shifting of management fees, and similar practices which maximize the accumulation of profits in the tax havens—so as to exploit the multiplicity of foreign tax systems and international agreements in order to reduce sharply or eliminate completely their tax liabilities at home and abroad.[13]

Underlying this view was the assumption that because of the deferrals, U.S. firms were investing abroad for tax reasons beyond what the market found "efficient." If this margin of "inefficient" investment could be shifted to domestic investment, it would improve the U.S. competitive position in the world market and simultaneously ease the payments imbalance.

This tax program was developed in the month after the election by a tax task force which included Harvard law professor Stanley Surrey, a former member of Truman's tax staff and an advocate of tougher tax treatment for corporate income.[14] Kennedy's Republican Secretary of the Treasury, Douglas Dillon, played a central policy role in the early 1960s as he had in the last year of the Eisenhower administration as Under-Secretary of State. The former Chairman of the investment banking house Dillon, Read and Co., Inc. had, with Secretary of the Treasury Anderson, formulated the Eisenhower administration's program to deal with the payments deficit. Described by *Fortune* as a "conservative-liberal," Dillon was perhaps the most important cabinet member in the new administration. Commerce Secretary Luther Hodges, who opposed the program to end deferral, was not permitted a public role during the legislative activity. The Commerce Department, whose clientele included major transnational corporations, was silenced by the more powerful Treasury Department.[15]

Dillon's 1961 program consisted of a campaign to persuade the Western European countries and the Japanese to ease their discrimination against U.S. goods; to increase exports by improving techniques for short-term credits to exporters; to revise tax laws affecting U.S. corporations operating abroad; and to redistribute the U.S. burden of military and aid programs to the Western Europeans and the Japanese. Foremost in Dillon's mind was that "the U.S. should continue as the banker for the world." His policies reflected a prime concern to defend the preeminent role of the dollar in the international monetary system, even at the expense of short-term capital investment.[16] It appears that President Kennedy himself pressured for a faster, more far-reaching solution to the payments imbalances by suggesting a more direct restriction of the export of capital. Dillon and the Treasury Department successfully resisted these pressures.[17]

The House Ways and Means Committee held hearings on the tax recommendations during May and June 1961. In his testimony before the committee, Dillon argued that the United States had recently fallen behind Europe and Japan in its rate of growth. In the era of international competition in which "our friends are once again our vigorous competitors," U.S. leadership depended on a faster rate of growth. The differential growth rate between the United States on the one hand, and the Europeans and the Japanese on the other was in part attributable to postwar catch-up—the advantage of backwardness. But increasingly, Dillon argued, it was also due to the role the European and Japanese governments had played in relation to tax incentives for domestic investment: accelerated depreciation, initial allowances, and investment credits. Dillon stressed that U.S. plant modernization and technology lagged behind its competitors, noting that the U.S. government did not play an interventionist role as did the European and the Japanese states. The role of the federal government should be to pursue policies that would create incentives for capital to invest domestically and, to a certain extent, direct capital to the most productive forms of investment as viewed from an overall, primarily a balance of payments, standpoint. Summing up, he said: "The investment credit is needed this year to stimulate modernization . . . so that we can secure a higher rate of growth, create jobs, and stabilize the dollar both at home and abroad. There is not a moment to lose."[18]

The proposed legislation came on the heels of the 1960 gold crisis, a reflection of declining confidence in the dollar. The administration viewed the situation as requiring immediate response. Dillon argued for the elimination of the deferral with the dollar foremost in his mind: "Today the situation is such that we must look first of all to the more immediate balance of payments results . . . rather than to long-run income from foreign investment." The costs of compromising this priority, he warned, would be to "jeopardize the economic health of the entire free world."[19]

The main economic assumption behind the proposed tax reform on foreign income was that to the extent that funds " . . . flow out from the United States, they are withdrawn from use in the United States and there is a competition [with foreign capital]. . . . Therefore, they are not used here. . . . They do not provide work here and profits which are part of our economy."[20] This is a dubious assumption, as many corporate witnesses during the legislative hearings pointed out, since decisions to invest are not dependent only on the amount of capital available, especially at the comparatively low interest rates then prevailing in the United States. Investment decisions are also based on a calculation of a market's capacity to absorb new products. The problem was one of profit realization and hence of effective demand, not of abstract investment opportunities.[21]

The administration's trade surplus strategy assumed that the late 1950s trend toward increasing direct investments in the advanced capitalist countries could and should be slowed or perhaps even rolled back. In Dillon's words: "During the postwar period, the promotion of private foreign investment in both advanced and less developed countries was in the public interest. Times have changed, and

Table 1

U.S. Direct Investment in Subsidiaries in Two Developed Areas[22] (millions of $)

		Dividends remitted	U.S. capital outflows	Remitted dividends minus capital outflow
W. Europe	1957	245	281	−36
	1958	302	161	+140
	1959	392	447	−55
	1960	390	860*	−470
Canada	1957	257	473	−216
	1958	269	316	−47
	1959	284	299	−15
	1960	284	240	+44

*$370 million was in a single stock purchase by the Ford Motor Company in England.

the need to stimulate investment in advanced countries no longer exists.''[23] The administration made it clear that it viewed the ''deferral privilege'' as in effect a subsidy of foreign investment. The proposed legislation would not have cut off future direct investment in the advanced countries but would have made it more expensive by increasing the need for foreign financing, thus slowing the rapid rate of TNC expansion into the advanced capitalist countries.

Toward the conclusion of the committee hearings, Dillon, rebutting business witnesses, grew somewhat more circumspect in his description of the administrations's intent. ''The Treasury does not oppose foreign operations. It does not seek to prevent additional foreign investment, even in the developed countries, unless that investment is taxed induced.'' The ending of deferral was based on data that indicated ''that deferral is harmful to the balance of payments in the short run, so that its removal at this time would be consonant with other steps being taken to strengthen the U.S. dollar.''[24] The Treasury estimated that eliminating the deferral would improve the payments balance by about $390 million annually as a result of increased tax payments on foreign income and repatriated dividends, and a slower rate of new capital outflow. To support the Treasury position data was presented which showed that the outflow of U.S. direct investment capital to both Canada and Western Europe was greater each year (with one exception) than the dividends remitted. These data are summarized in Table 1.

It should be noted that Table 1 does not include invisible income—from management fees, royalties, patent right income, and the like—which would, in some cases, show a positive income inflow to the United States. This omission in

Table 2

U.S. Income from "Private Miscellaneous" Services 1959–1960[25] (millions of $)

	1959	1960	Income on direct investment only	
			1959	1960
Total: world	1,199	1,218	2,235	2,395
W. Europe	551	557	4.5	435
Canada	135	139	378	345
Latin America	239	240	593	673

the Treasury data was pointed out by industry representatives during the hearings, but the Treasury responded that it was irrelevant, because this form of income was not subject to the proposed tax on dividend income. This is true. Nevertheless, direct investment restrictions would still undoubtedly have some indirect, long-run effect on invisible income, although it has been argued that invisible income could be maintained or perhaps even increased without direct investment—through licensing, patent, and rental agreements. The flow of U.S. invisible income (unfortunately available in aggregate form only) is presented in Table 2 for the years 1959 and 1960.

Dillon argued that the favorable balance in U.S. total direct investment income annually was not a result of investment in the advanced countries, but rather was due to extremely profitable investments in the "less developed" countries. Between 1957 and 1960 total global income remitted to the United States was $9 billion, while total capital outflow was $6.6 billion. The aggregate data, if divided into investment in subsidiaries and investment in branch operations, indicate that in branch operations there was a total outflow in the same period of $2.4 billion and a total inflow of $5.1 billion, while in subsidiary operations there was a total outflow of $4.2 and a total income remittance of $3.9 billion.[26] The dominant form of foreign investment in the advanced countries was in subsidiaries (by about 15:1), while the majority form of investment in the Third World countries was in branches (by about 7:5). Most branch operations were concentrated in the extractive industries, especially mining and petroleum. Most manufacturing operations (including petroleum refining and distribution) were concentrated in subsidiaries, in both advanced and Third World countries. The difference between a branch and a subsidiary is that the former cannot reinvest its earnings and must remit its income to the parent corporation annually, while subsidiaries do not have to do so. A tax preference favors branch operations in the extractive industries. The administration's tax reforms aimed at only subsidiary income in the advanced countries.[27] The extra profits of branch plant operations thus covered the deficit in capital transactions with Canada and Western Europe.[28]

It is noteworthy that in its attempt to restrain the growth of direct investment in the advanced capitalist economies, the Kennedy administration neither fully understood nor accurately estimated the growing economic importance of direct investment in the advanced states. Kennedy's vision was a trade-centered view of the economic relations between the United States and its allies, with a development-investment vision of United States-Third World relations. Thus, he initially set his administration against the then rapidly expanding forces of direct investment. Kennedy perceived that qualitative expansion of direct investment in Europe would weaken the U.S. trade surplus in the long run. In this sense, he adopted the traditional, neo-nationalist analysis of the advantages of trade over investment: trade stimulates domestic growth and development, while direct investment may discourage development. For this reason Kennedy's tax recommendations received the enthusiastic support of organized labor, in spite of his "jaw boning" to keep wage increases in line with productivity increases.

Nevertheless, given the importance of direct investment among advanced capitalist countries, the Kennedy program was an ineffective way to deal with the growing reality of the internationalization of capital. It would not have solved the problem of the most dynamic areas of U.S. industry: how to get exports over the common tariff wall of the Common Market. The administration's method of dealing with the trade problem was through what became the Kennedy round of the GATT (General Agreement on Tariffs and Trade) talks. Yet GATT could not undercut the *raison d'être* of the Common Market without a major political realignment between the United States and the Europeans. Thus, the logic of Kennedy's strategy implied increasing U.S. economic nationalism and growing hostility to a European economic unification. It also implied a role for the U.S. state in directing reluctant capital toward domestic rather than direct investment, fundamentally transforming the relations between the state and U.S. business. On neither of these points was Kennedy, least of all his advisors, willing to push. This explains the rapid retreat in the autumn of 1961 from the initial tax reform proposals, especially the elimination of the tax deferral on foreign income.[29]

Corporate reaction to the tax recommendations

The 1961 tax proposals held out the carrot of domestic tax incentives to large capital while wielding the stick of potential foreign tax restructuring. The strategy did not work. Domestic tax incentives held little real gains for major corporations and, at the same time, encountered the opposition of small- and medium-sized business, which felt they would not adequately gain from accelerated depreciation and other tax cuts. Intense corporate opposition to foreign tax restructuring, in the face of minimal mobilized political support for such restructuring, spelled defeat for the administration.

Business arguments against the proposal to eliminate the tax deferral are difficult to summarize neatly, in part because sectors of business pleaded their own specific interests while ignoring larger issues and in part because the administration proposals were justified by reference to the payments deficit, about which few business representatives had developed positions. The Treasury Department's defense involved a macroview of the interactions of the economy and geopolitical relations. On the whole, representatives of large corporations responded with an individual orientation, although some corporate policy organizations were important exceptions. While there had been an extensive discussion of the balance of payments issue in the business press for two or three years prior to the congressional hearings, corporate representatives proposed few policy alternatives. What is striking about the substance of corporate capital's response to the legislation is neither its opposition, nor its intensity, but the lack of clarity about the relation of the administrations's proposal to the balance of payments and international monetary policy issues. There was division of opinion, lack of agreed-upon programs which could be opposed to the Kennedy legislation, and a single-minded, firm-oriented opposition to the ending of the deferral.

The divisions among TNCs and TNBs themselves, between various TNBs and TNCs and what are usually taken to be "their" representative organizations (such as the Committee for Economic Development), and between capital as a whole and state policy makers, reveal the complexity of both the interest intermediation and interest formation processes. The debates over the 1962 Revenue Act suggest that corporate and bank managers viewed the ability of their own firms to prosper in relation to the international monetary system from different perspectives, viewed the system itself, the importance of the dollar and gold in that system, the degree of dependency of the U.S. military on that system, and the significance, if any, of the U.S. payments deficit in a variety of complex and muddled ways. The situation was one which Theodore Lowi has characterized as promoting maximum freedom of choice for state action. Substantially less complex and muddled, however, were the immediate corporate benefits threatened with elimination by the proposal to end foreign tax deferral.

When the House Ways and Means Committee held hearings on the foreign income sections of the tax recommendations in June 1961, and when the Senate Finance Committee held similar hearings almost a year later, both committees were deluged by hostile witnesses representing corporations and business organizations, large and small. Senator Javits of New York commented that he had "never encountered a tax bill which has exercised the financial and business community of New York more than this one. . . . I have been subjected . . . to extended conferences on this bill by the most distinguished leaders in the business and financial fields, who express their gravest disquiet as to its consequences."[30]

In defense of eliminating the tax deferral Secretary Dillon argued that it was a "privilege" not allowed domestic producers, and thus was unfair competition. Business representatives responded that deferral was not a privilege but represented a long-standing practice necessary to make U.S. corporations competitive with European and Japanese ones. Its elimination would mean that U.S. subsidiaries would be at a disadvantage relative to their overseas competitors and would threaten a long-term reduction in U.S. income from investment. Business spokesmen argued that since income earned in a foreign country was taxed at the rate established for all businesses in that country, the end of deferral would, in effect, be a double taxation. It would slow the growth rate of the foreign subsidiary in relation to the foreign competing firm. Summarizing opposition to the argument that ending deferral was justified on the basis of "unfair domestic competition," the U.S. Council of the International Chamber of Commerce stated: "What the privilege of deferral has done is to permit U.S. subsidiaries to operate under conditions more nearly equal to their rivals in the Western European countries by permitting them to finance a larger part of their investment out of retained earnings."[31]

Behind the administration's tax equity argument was the assumption that if capital could be induced to stay home or to be invested in Third World countries rather than in Europe, it would be possible to achieve a faster rate of economic, domestic, and Third World growth. This would aid in the balance of payments, since dollars invested in manufacturing subsidiaries in "developing" countries tended to flow back into the United States in balance of payment terms. It was assumed that the main reason that a corporation invested abroad was for a higher profit rate, which would, of course, be tax-influenced. The administration made it explicit that a higher profit rate abroad was desirable, but not if it was "tax induced."

The Machinery and Allied Products Institute, a policy study group composed of representatives of large- and medium-sized capital producers, argued in response to the government position:

> The Administration implies in its argument that, with deferral, U.S. capital is induced to invest abroad where it would otherwise invest in the United States. It is our contention that business usually has no such alternative. In most instances its alternative is rather to invest abroad or not to invest at all simply because it cannot hold or penetrate markets abroad by manufacturing in the United States in the face of import restrictions, regional market developments, etc.[32]

The dual program of the domestic tax incentives and the elimination of deferral was designed primarily to strengthen the competitive edge of the domestic U.S. economy. In this sense, ending deferral was an important divergence from the postwar U.S. foreign economy policy of business internationalism based on free trade and the free movement of capital. Faced with a dollar crisis and an unstable world political and military situation, U.S. state managers faced one set of institutional imperatives while the managers of TNCs and TNBs faced another. These imperatives are reflected in the overall ideological views of each group.

The central difference between them was not a disagreement over the competitiveness of the domestic economy relative to the challenge from the other advanced capitalist countries, but over the policies that should be implemented to correct the gap. The top national administration policy makers (with the exception of the unorthodox Dillon who often differed with other investment bankers) were men from the academic world and central banks. Their world view tended to be that of the economist rather than the corporate executive. For the economist, capital was a unit of wealth only to the extent that it could be invested with a reasonable expectation on overall return. That there was a need for domestic investment did not mean that it was profitable to make such an investment. Government policy makers believed the directive role of the state could induce such long-term profitability. What corporate executives saw was an expanding market in Europe, and a sagging one domestically.

This ideological difference was apparent in the ensuing debates about the reasons that corporations undertake foreign direct investment in the advanced countries. The administration's position was made clear in President Kennedy's statement and in Dillon's support testimony during the hearings. Corporate response was direct: the government cannot undertake to redirect capital from European and Canadian to U.S. investment, nor can it effectively redirect it from developed to underdeveloped countries. Emile Collado, Director of Standard Oil of New Jersey and an important CED member, stated, "There is no reason to believe that foreign investment denied outlet in Europe will seek outlet in the developing countries. . . . The location of the bulk of foreign investment is determined by basic considerations of markets, costs, and sources of supply and will not be affected by marginal incentives."[33] The reasons for the rapidly increased investment in Europe were much deeper than simply a higher profit margin. The National Foreign Trade Council, which often represented the most aggressive positions of TNCs, argued that the formation of the Common Market created a "new pattern of trade and investment," and thus stepped up the rate of U.S. investment in response to a changed structure of trade and investment. The role of the state should be to "assist and not penalize" U.S. business abroad in "making whatever adjustments are available to it to pressure and increase the sale of its products and services within the now large and increasingly mass producing and mass consuming European market. This has been the compelling reason for the expansion in recent years of U.S. direct investment in Europe, and American business has had no effective alternative."[34]

The administration argued that there was a low level of domestic investment due to an underutilization of capacity in certain basic industries and an outmoded capital stock in many of the same industries. It would seemingly be easy to redirect capital from foreign investment to domestic by adjusting the tax mechanism. But this logic was that of an abstract economic model which assumed a certain degree of effective isolation of the domestic from the world economy. Kennedy summarized this position in late 1961: "Are we going to export our goods and our crops, or are we going to export our capital? That is the question we are now facing.''[35] What appeared as a capital shortage from the administration's view (low rates of new domestic investment and a slow growth rate) was from the corporate view not a shortage of capital at all, but rather a problem of low aggregate demand. The Chairman of Proctor and Gamble Co. argued: ''Our problem is not access to capital, and I believe this is true of most American companies. . . . Our problem is the development of management and the development of ideas that will justify the investment of capital.''[36]

The debate over whether a dollar exported as capital was a dollar transferable for domestic investment reflected the larger issue of the health of the U.S. domestic market. The initial Kennedy program was a position halfway between the few liberals in Congress who wanted to stimulate demand through a consumer subsidy via individual income tax reductions, and the large corporations which preferred faster depreciation allowances to stimulate a faster rate of investment.[37] This interchange between the Kennedy administration and business underscores one aspect of the complexity of capital's interests. Faced with sagging domestic aggregate demand and a slow rate of domestic economic growth relative to overseas markets, business looked to government for assistance on both fronts. Yet business opinion tended to favor higher domestic interest rates and consequently slower growth as a solution to the payments deficit problem. This seems paradoxical in light of businesses' expressed concern about slow sales.

The dominant economic vision of the early Kennedy period was not of a mature creditor nation increasingly dependent on foreign dividend returns and invisible income; it was a vision of the United States as a major competitive center of technological innovation exporting goods and services. This export vision clashed with emerging TNC growth. Corporate representatives argued that the Treasury Department data, cited previously, was based on a limited, unrepresentative time period, 1957–60, a period of response to the newly formed Common Market. It was true, they conceded, that in this period there was an ''initial surge'' of investment, ''to maintain or penetrate markets which cannot be served from the United States,'' but it was expected that these high levels of investment would level out, and the traditional income inflow would be greater than the capital outflow.[38] They argued further that even if the pace of capital outflow were to slow down as the administration desired, this would not really have an important balance of payments impact, since about four-fifths of capital invested in Europe and Canada was composed of retained earnings reinvested or of capital raised abroad. This last argument missed the essence of the administration program which was not so much to restrict the outflow of capital directly—as controls would do after 1965—as to raise the inflow of dividends through the use of a tax mechanism and thus slow the growth rate of TNC subsidiaries. This would slow the rate of new foreign investment, regardless of the source of new capital. The payments effect would have slowed the outflow of capital and raised the inflow of dividends.[39]

The debate over direct investment versus export

One of the central issues raised during the House and Senate hearings was the relation of direct investment in the advanced countries to the export of goods and services from the United States. Was direct investment a substitute for exporting, and, if so, to what extent; was it short-term or long-term? Or was direct investment a supplement to exporting? This debate was significant because it underscored the state's interest mediating role in two ways. First, the state's commitment to economic growth necessitated the stimulation of domestic economic growth and investment. Its global hegemonic position required it to minimize or wipe out the balance of payments deficit, as long as it was committed to the Bretton Woods par value system. Consequently a marginal restriction of the rate of direct investment growth was perceived as a minimal price to pay for growth and stability. A trade-centered vision informed this thinking. It assumed a growing domestic economy would improve U.S. trade competitiveness while slowing direct investment. Long-run global hegemonic stability with rapid domestic economic growth was the strategic goal of the Kennedy administration. Transnational capital's immediate competitive expansion would have to be mediated by domestic economic growth and by politico-strategic global stability.

The second aspect of the debate concerned capital's interests. TNCs and TNBs argued in their opposition to the proposed removal of deferral that it would "kill the goose that laid the golden egg." However, beyond unanimity about profits and freedom of capital movements, there was little business consensus regarding general macroeconomic policy or the strategic issues of global hegemony. In this sense, although Kennedy retreated from his initial strong defense of the tax deferral proposal, he had substantial room to maneuver regarding the economic implications of politico-strategic issues. The debate over the export effects of direct investments was, in effect, a debate about the role of the state in domestic economic policy.[40]

One side in the debate assumed that if there were no other ways to penetrate a closed market, such as the Common Market, then exports of a certain classification would decline; consequently, direct investment was a supplement, not a substitute. The alternate assumption suggested that if exports could penetrate directly, or indirectly through other means such as licensing arrangements, then the actual decline of exports could be viewed as a result of direct investment. The principal difficulty is that it is impossible to know what would happen if firms did not make any indirect investment abroad. Related to this primary issue are two others. The first is whether foreign direct investment reduces the volume of domestic investment, as the tax recommendations argued, or leaves it unchanged; and the second is whether investment abroad tends to increase foreign demand for U.S. products or whether such demand should be taken as given and fixed. A 1972 Commerce Department staff study dealing with the policy aspects of foreign investment argued that all the evidence, arguments, and especially the conclusions drawn on both sides of the debate in the preceding decade needed to be viewed with "some skepticism": "In the present state of knowledge, it is therefore impossible to determine with certainty the quantitative effects of foreign direct investment, or even at times the direction of the effects."[41]

The principal issue was whether it should be assumed that there is a "single-injection" (that is, a one-time) capital investment over a period of time, in which case the returns from dividends, interest, royalties, and fees will, over a given period of time, surpass the original capital investment. This is the model that most corporate representatives used during the hearings. If, on the other hand, it is assumed that there is a "continuous stream" of investment (that is, each year), calculated on either a constant or a compound rate basis over the same time period, the balance of payments effect (as compared to the yearly profitability effect) will be negative in the short run, if not forever. This was the assumption of the Treasury in presenting its case.

A 1963 survey of leading TNCs for the Conference Board suggested that the main motive for direct investment was not an incremental addition to earning power, but rather that "maintaining competitive position required continuing investment." The study concluded that since the most dynamic factor is international investment, not international trade, "the movement of capital to activate production is evidently the key to higher levels of output at home and abroad. The state of the balance of payments can be adequately evaluated only in this context."[42]

The study illustrates the limitation of business thinking about the balance of payments. The study defined the most significant measure of the payments deficit as the basic balance, which nets out short-term capital inflows and outflows from the more regular, long-term "basic" flow of receipts and expenditures. The basic balance is useful in measuring underlying movements, but not useful for measuring the status of a currency's reaction to short-term factors. Short-term influences are, however, most important for the dollar as a reserve and transaction currency. Consequently, the basic balance cannot indicate the impact of interest rate differentials and speculation against the dollar. The Conference Board study tends to be limited by one-sided concern about production versus trade while ignoring the financial aspects of the relation between production and the monetary system. An example of this relation is that the postwar rate of foreign investment in Europe especially would not have occurred if the dollar had not been overvalued in relation to European currencies. Yet overvaluation, seen by many to be the Achilles heel of the dollar, was related to the hegemonic components of the payments deficit—military expenditures abroad, foreign aid, and capital exports. According to Seymour Harris: "This overvaluation . . . is real only because the United States needs to export about $5 billion more than it imports in order to cover military and aid expenditures abroad and large capital movements. Treatment of these items could quickly end overvaluation; that is to say, without our serious obligations abroad there might well be an undervalued rather than an overvalued dollar.''[43] The rate of capital export was linked with the exchange value of the dollar as the key currency; its key currency status recipro-cally depended on the strength of the U.S. economy.

The direct investment versus export debate, which originated during the 1961–62 hearings and continues to the present, has reflected both structural and ideological differences between the state and representatives of TNCs and major corporate policy organizations. The Kennedy administration's proposal for tax law revision reflected its dual priority of eliminating the payments deficit and improving the domestic competitive position of U.S. industry. Ideologically, the position flowed from an export-centered concept of U.S. strength, emphasizing the link between the U.S. payments position and dollar hegemony under the Bretton Woods system. Implicit was that the liquidity balance was the key indica-tor of the stability of the dollar, and with it the political, economic, and military position of the United States in the world system. The defense of an export-centered economy and of dollar domination was linked to the structure of the balance of payments. The concern of the state was not only the profitability of corporate investment, but the stability of the system as a whole. In this case, balance of payments was the measure not only of stability, but of the ability to manage hegemony. If what was seen as marginal overseas corporate competitive advantage had to be sacrificed for the balance of the whole, then this was to be justified in the short run.

From the onset of the 1960 gold crisis, Kennedy and his advisors accorded the payments problem high priority. In contrast to most sectors of the business world, including the CED, the administration felt that the payments crisis, while not long term, was critical. As one Kennedy advisor recalled, ''few subjects occu-pied more of Kennedy's time in the White House or were the subject of more secret high-level meetings.''[44]

Corporate opposition to the tax recommendations lacked alternative programs to reduce the payments deficit. In the first place, the business press and corporate policy institutions, as well as government officials and advisors and many aca-demic economists, were of at least two minds on the seriousness and duration of the deficit. Some individuals in corporate and banking circles as well as some academic economists shared the administration's optimistic approach. The divi-sion between optimists and pessimists, however, was not the only basis for the divisions over the tax recommendations. The optimists themselves were divided between those who thought the deficit was temporary and would rapidly right itself without government attention and those who believed that even if the deficit were temporary, if not attended to immediately, it would cause serious damage to the dollar.

The divisions and confusion within the business world made a sharp contrast with the administrations's clear priorities. Different points of view were reflected in the business press and in statements by influential corporate and banking leaders. While the views of the business press should not be taken *ipso facto* to be the views of "business," in this case the variety of views in the press and among business leaders coincided to a great degree. *The Wall Street Journal*, for instance, tended toward the pessimistic side, arguing that the cause of the deficit was the government's own "undisciplined spending at home and abroad over many years," which generated domestic inflation and thus aided in making the United States less competitive. It called for a cut in foreign aid and action to get the allies to "assume a fair share of the cost of defending their own countries. . . ." The *Journal*, reflecting a position to the right of the dominant corporate policy institutions, identified expansionary monetary policy in both "good and bad times" as an important cause of the deficit and in one editorial placed the entire blame for the deficit on monetary policy. The *Journal* argued that the payments problem had a simple solution: "there is absolutely nothing wrong with the U.S. dollar that a little (government) prudence won't quickly cure."[45]

The *Journal*, echoing the business and government consensus, advocated further measures to increase the U.S. trade surplus. Similarly, the Machinery and Allied Products Institute (MAPI) argued that there had been too much attention paid to the issue of the payments imbalance to the exclusion of the fundamental issue of the competitiveness of the U.S. economy: "If we cannot maintain our overall position of world leadership, which depends basically upon a strong and financially sound domestic economy, consideration of other, secondary objectives is academic. . . . Therefore, the government must look primarily to economic policies . . . which will make the economy more competitive." It suggested that the balance of payments was simply "a measure of our economic strength and international competitiveness" which should not assume priority over alternative economic policies. MAPI questioned the administration's short-run need to improve the payments balance in one year, to the detriment of the balance of payments in three or four years, which MAPI calculated was the full payback period on worldwide direct manufacturing investment.[46] Typical of most corporate representatives, MAPI tended to minimize or ignore monetary policy issues, specifically the impact of gold outflow and currency speculation on the stability of the dollar. It concluded that since the government was committed to foreign aid, and overseas military programs could not be cut substantially, the only alternative strategy was to increase the trade surplus. Both MAPI and the *Journal* suggested that the government's overseas expenditures, especially foreign aid, whose necessity they challenged, were the fundamental cause of the deficit, and they were pessimistic about the government's willingness or ability to change its foreign economic assistance programs. MAPI and the *Journal* did not represent large corporate capital as a whole, but did speak for a significant minority position.[47]

Arguing the pessimist case from a more sophisticated perspective, a 1960 article in the journal *The Financial Analyst* stressed the structural nature of deficit given the political commitment to full employment policies and consequently an inflationary countercyclical federal budget deficit. The "crunch" would come when the Federal Reserve had to choose between lower interest rates to stimulate the domestic economy and higher ones to restrict domestic inflation and minimize short-term capital outflow.[48]

In contrast to these business pessimists, Malcolm Forbes took a more optimistic view in a lead editorial in *Forbes*, suggesting that the gold outflow would subside, U.S. exports to Europe would continue to increase, and the trade surplus would be enlarged. He criticized "misguided people" who hit the panic button to demand either depreciation of the dollar, a new round of restrictionism, or the strangling of foreign aid. Forbes felt that the deficit could be rectified through government programs to aid competition at home and abroad.[49]

Stating the position of many large corporations and international banks was the International Economic Policy Association (IEPA), and the CED. These policy organizations, like most of the representatives of large corporations who testified at the congressional hearings, assumed that overseas military and economic expenditures were a necessary and justified response given the world political and military situation. The IEPA argued that the problem of the deficit was a long-term one, since it was a reflection of the "prospect of honoring commitments for military expenditures abroad . . . and of increasing the amount of . . . outlays for economic aid . . . in addition to . . . securing from abroad larger and larger quantities of necessary imports, particularly raw material." The IEPA did not present alternative balance of payments policies, except to encourage actions promoting a larger trade surplus.[50]

David Rockefeller, President of the Chase-Manhattan Bank, took a broader and more somber view of the problem than most. He defended the political rationale for foreign aid, stating that "on the balance sheet of history" there was no economic gain that would outweigh the loss its suspension would cost the "free world" of recipient countries. He noted that everyone in the business community agreed that export expansion was the key but that the deficit was a critical issue. "There is a logical limit," he commented, beyond which the surplus cannot be expanded and will call forth "vigorous counter-reactions by competitors in the world market." Even if increases could occur in the trade surplus, in tourism to the United States, and in foreign capital investment, these measures could not solve the deficit problem. Rockefeller thus moved beyond the position of most corporate and banking spokesmen and periodicals. Capital control should be "avoided to the end, if possible. . . . And yet, I don't suppose anyone would hesitate to place controls on private capital, if the only alternative were to weaken seriously the national security of our country."[51] Rockefeller did not make explicit what he meant by security reasons but added immediately that it was of central importance that the dollar be maintained as the key currency. He concluded that there should be a "conservative economic life": high interest rates and no countercyclical policies. In the end, he provided no specific program for correcting the deficit but was one of the few in corporate, banking, or government circles to emphasize that the trade surplus expansion strategy had limits and therefore that it could not be the long-term solution. He hoped for a long-run reform of the international monetary system which would remove the squeeze on the dollar and the British pound, but he made no specific proposals.[52] What is significant about Rockefeller's position was his willingness to accept capital controls if they were linked to conservative domestic economic policies. Slow or no domestic economic growth (high unemployment and high interest rates) would stabilize the dollar. In this view, capital controls would not become a necessary corollary to an expansive Keynesian domestic policy; rather, they would substitute for such a policy.

Typical of the corporate optimist view was that of I.T.T.'s Harold Geneen. He argued that in the "long-term trend" (1951–61) there was an inflow of funds greater than the outflow, although he did not identify the nature of these funds. The exceptions to this trend were due to the restoration of full currency convertibility in Europe in 1958, which had created a "bubble of investment" funds built up by U.S. investors. This was not seen as long term since the deficit was a temporary result of convertibility.[53] In a similar vein, the representative of the U.S. Chamber of International Commerce argued that the temporary emergency of the gold outflow of 1960 and the continuing deficit could hardly justify a permanent structural change in the tax system. The postwar problem, on the whole, had not been the dollar glut, but the dollar gap. He expressed confidence that the "glut" was an exception to this long-term trend.[54]

The corporate optimists and the government optimists had different bases for their views. The former simply did not understand the implications of European currency convertibility and its relation to the dollar standard. The government understood this well but assumed that the deficit could be eliminated by correcting one or two components in the payments accounts.

The CED's position fell between the optimists and the pessimists. In May 1961 it called for an increase in earnings from abroad through a larger trade surplus, while stressing the importance of maintaining military and foreign aid levels necessary to meet "realistic" political and military contingents.[55] The export surplus strategy had broad and longstanding support from most sectors of business. The CED argued in early 1960 that the aim of eliminating the deficit must be the improvement of the U.S. competitive position in the world market, and that all restrictive solutions should be avoided. The CED summarized seven points of national postwar policy which it was critical to maintain: the United States should take a leading position in organizing the common defense of the Western world and bear the largest share of its costs; the United States should continue the major outside contribution to the "growth of the underdeveloped world"; the economic health of Japan and Western Europe should continue to be a main consideration of all policies; there should be a less restrictive international trade and payments system; there should be no national obstacles to the export of private capital; none of these goals should be allowed to conflict with the maintenance of high domestic employment; and finally, the primary objective should be the growth of domestic productivity.[56]

The foundation of this seven-point policy was the ability to sustain a large export surplus as "the only way in which we can make payments over any sustained period." The CED warned that there was no longer an assured U.S. export surplus. The policies of economic assistance, private capital export, and military assistance "must be harmonized with our ability to export." To better the U.S. competitive position, three components were needed for greater domestic growth and an increase in productivity: a domestic anti-inflationary policy, an increase in productivity, and a "self-controlled" business and labor policy on wages and prices.[57]

The CED program called for increased productivity and increased development of new and improved technological products; a "new attitude" from American business and labor so that productivity gains were not "swallowed up in higher money rates"; a higher short-term interest rate to slow the outflow of short-term capital from the United States to Europe, along with maintained or reduced long-term rates; a general tariff reduction and elimination of non-tariff barriers to international trade; and a more equitable distribution of the "defense burden" among the allies.[58] To one degree or another these policies coincided with the Kennedy administration's. For the CED and the administration, the key was U.S. ability to obtain cooperation from the Europeans in trade, monetary, and military policies. If this failed, then the CED saw four possible options: a sharp restriction of U.S. imports, foreign investment, and travel abroad; curtailment of U.S. foreign defense expenditures and economic assistance; the repatriation of U.S.-owned assets abroad; and/or suspension of gold payments.[59] The CED, like David Rockefeller, acknowledged that it might be necessary at some point in the future to restrict capital outflows. It argued strongly, however, that the events of 1958–61 did not justify such drastic measures.

The CED viewed the payments deficit as partially a structural problem: the United States had to maintain its overseas military and aid expenditures regardless of cost. CED policy statements, however, made no mention of the structural aspects of foreign investment. Short of gains made through cooperation with the European allies, the CED emphasized a strong anti-inflationary policy for the United States and the need to raise productivity in order to correct the payments imbalance. Deflation as the traditional payments imbalance policy was ruled out for political reasons, since "it would result in declining output and employment."[60]

The CED, primarily through its staff and exceptionally active corporate members, articulated positions and analyses which often differed markedly from its membership's views. In this sense, CED statements and positions did not "represent" corporate opinion, but mediated and attempted to shape and form what was often and typically a less coherent and less sophisticated corporate opinion. CED policy statements were consistently to the internationalist center when contrasted with individual corporate representatives or other corporate policy organizations, which were consistently to the nationalist right.

In this regard, the CED was substantially closer to the Kennedy administration than to the corporate community as a whole. The CED view of the payments deficit was more directly political than economic, stressing the inherently inter-linked nature of foreign investment, global stability, and the security of the dollar. Yet in other ways the CED was far from the administration. The CED proposed that anti-inflationary policy should not result in lower domestic prices as a result of productivity gains; nor should productivity gains be passed on as higher wages. Rather, they should raise the international competitive position of U.S. producers: "Such a development would require a considerable change in the collective bargaining and pricing policies of labor and management. . . . [This] would be appropriate to the altered position of the United States in the world economy."[61]

Thus, CED's Keynesianism was hesitant, its focus primarily global rather than domestic. It was limited to the opposition of those in the business community who had called for deflation and recession as the domestic solution to the payments deficit. The CED's position differed from the Kennedy administration's, which proposed the abolition of deferral along with domestic economic expansion, wage increases linked to productivity increases, and low unemployment policy. The CED proposed an expansionary economic policy but with the benefits linked to productivity policy. To the nationalist right of the CED and the administration were individual representatives of TNCs, speaking in their own names and the names of their corporations.

It was because there was little agreement within the corporate business community about the nature of the balance of payments problem that most corporate executives did not respond to the administration's proposal to end deferral with counterproposals. While the administration's program was neither long-term nor clearly directed, it did recognize the immediacy of the deficit problem, which most corporate representatives and policy groups did not.

Defeat of the proposal to end tax deferral

At the conclusion of the House committee hearings, in June 1961, the odds were against passage of the proposal to tax foreign income. A member of the committee commented that the administration "didn't check business very closely or they'd have known this was coming. . . ."[62] Toward the end of July, the committee decided to postpone until 1962 treatment of those sections of the tax proposals related to ending the deferral and imposing restrictions on tax havens. During the next five months, the Treasury substantially redirected its program by dropping the proposed tax deferral in the form in which it had been presented during the Ways and Means Committee hearings. In early 1962 the Treasury presented a new proposal which would have taxed only the foreign annual income of nonman-ufacturing subsidiaries of U.S. corporations which operated in tax havens for the purpose of avoiding immediate taxation in the U.S., provided that more than one-half of the voting stock of the subsidiary was held by U.S. citizens or corporations. The plan to end tax deferral for all TNC subsidiaries in advanced capitalist countries was thus entirely dropped from the new proposal to the committee.[63]

The Ways and Means Committee initially rejected the Treasury's new plan with regard to foreign investment as too sweeping a reform. Instead it substituted a plan that would have taxed the earnings of foreign subsidiaries only if they were accumulated abroad without being reinvested in the parent corporation's overseas operations. The committee's plan would have prohibited deferral if the overseas corporation invested its earnings in a non–U.S.-controlled company, that is, in a tax haven. Committee Chairman Wilbur Mills strengthened these new proposals, with Treasury approval, by adding that income from royalties, licensing, and copyright fees were to be taxed as annual income. Thus, taken as a package, the ending of deferral was no longer to affect direct investment subsidiaries, but only so-called tax haven corporations, whether located in advanced countries (e.g., Switzerland or Luxembourg) or in underdeveloped countries (e.g., the Bahamas or Panama).[64]

In an abrupt turnaround, Mills then formally dropped this plan and substituted a plan similar to but more flexible than the Treasury's original recommendations made in 1961. This move appeared to have neither the support nor the foreknowledge of the administration. The new Mills plan would have taxed the annual earnings of (that is, ended deferral on) overseas manufacturing subsidiaries of U.S. corporations unless those earnings were reinvested in the subsidiary or in an underdeveloped country within three months of the close of the tax year. The earnings of nonmanufacturing subsidiaries were to be taxed if used to finance an industrial project in an advanced country; in addition, earnings from royalties, rents, patents, and copyrights were to be taxed in all situations. The committee passed the new Mills version, voting along party lines. The House approved the committee's bill with minimal debate, 219 to 196.[65] The Mills proposals, embodied in House bill H.R. 10650, encountered renewed opposition from all sectors of business, prompting a repetition of arguments for and against the measure. Although the administration had moved to drop the tax deferral section of the legislation between mid-1961 and early 1962, it was nevertheless forced into weak support of its original proposal during the Senate hearings.

The changes in the administration's position were made possible by the fact that in 1962 the United States had greater international maneuvering space. West Germany had revalued the mark upwards by 5 percent; the intensity of speculation against the dollar had subsided, and with it gold outflow had decreased significantly; Germany, France, and Italy had agreed to prepay war debts; and Germany had agreed to large amounts of prepaid military purchases from the United States. In addition, due to the 1961–62 recession, U.S. exports to Europe were temporarily higher, increasing the trade surplus. Under-Secretary of State

George Ball reflected the administration's optimism when he stated at a congressional hearing that during the eighteen months between early 1961 and mid-1962 the U.S. trade surplus had nearly doubled while the deficit had been cut almost in half. He reasserted the trade surplus strategy as the main long-term program of the administration.[66] Robert Roosa also voiced the optimistic view, stating that the deficit was part of the "normal swings in our payments patterns" over the long run. He predicted that the balance of payments would be "back in order" by the end of 1963.[67]

These international factors, along with the intense opposition from business to ending the deferral, caused Kennedy to shift his strategic focus from attacking the structure of taxation to reemphasizing the trade surplus strategy. The administration made a major push to pass the Trade Expansion Act of 1962, the centerpiece of the administration's legislative efforts in that year. In line with this new strategy, the administration backed both the House and Senate versions of the tax bills (although they differed considerably over the taxation of foreign income) in order to facilitate congressional passage of the 7 percent tax credit.[68]

In July 1962 the Senate Finance Committee voted to soften the House version with regard to the taxation on foreign income of U.S. corporations. With Treasury backing, a compromise plan was proposed which would have subjected to immediate U.S. taxation the earnings of only those U.S.-controlled foreign subsidiaries which the Treasury considered "tax haven" operations. The proposal was passed by the committee 12 to 1. In an attempt at further compromise with liberal Democrats who favored the original tax recommendations, another section was added which would have changed the basis of calculating foreign income slightly to the disfavor of foreign subsidiaries.[69]

During the Senate debates on the bill a three-way conflict ensued. A minority of liberal Democrats wanted to amend the Finance Committee's version with the original 1961 proposal to end deferral. The middle ground, held by the majority of the Democrats and tacitly supported by the administration, favored the Finance Committee's version. The Republican position, supported by all sections of business, wanted to defeat the sections of the Finance Committee's bill which related to any change in the taxation of foreign income. In this first-round struggle over the imposition of capital controls in the postwar period, large corporations, supported by all other sectors of business, succeeded in eliminating the central feature of the administration's proposal and forced the administration into retreat. The final elimination occurred in the closed sessions of the Finance Committee. During the Senate debates Senator Kerr assured his listeners that "the Committee carefully screened out [from] the House provisions, those features which would have interfered with legitimate foreign operations."[70] The Finance Committee's version passed the Senate 59 to 24. In a joint House-Senate conference the House version was altered to fit the main features of the Senate bill.[71]

Conclusion

Why was the Kennedy administration's proposal to end deferral defeated by the intense lobbying and publicity efforts of transnational capital? Three factors are apparent. First, the easing of the dollar crisis after mid-1961 lent substantial credence to an optimistic analysis of the payments deficit, so that both business and many in the administration thought that altering the Internal Revenue Code was too extreme a move given the significant pressures against such an action. Second, within the administration itself there was not unanimous agreement on proper policy either toward the payments deficit or toward the larger question of the impact of direct investment on the growth of the domestic economy. This lack of clarity and unity impaired the effectiveness of the administration's programs. Finally, there was no significant support from below for the tax reform proposals. The AFL-CIO was the only constituency-based organization to support the administration, and their support did not involve the attempted mass mobilization of labor's rank and file. Nor did the administration attempt to create broad political support for its proposals in the name of renewed economic growth.

When the state attempts to restructure the direction of private sector investment decisions, it needs the support of large sectors of the population who perceive their interests as being at stake—in this case, as threatened by direct investment overseas. It also requires an alternative model of economic development, whether through the inducement of private investment or through a form of socialized investment such as a redevelopment bank or outright public ownership. Because it put the principle of foreign direct investment directly at issue, the debate over capital controls became in some respects a shadow debate over private investment as such. Corporate capital perceived better than did the administration that just such a shadow debate was in fact taking place. The Kennedy administration's view of the interests of transnational capital stressed a trade-centered U.S. economy with direct investment important only in the "underdeveloped" world. The tax powers of the state were to be used to manipulate capital's interests to conform to this vision. Widespread direct investment in the economically advanced states of Western Europe and Canada was a significant form of market innovation. Kennedy and many of his advisors perceived this but were unable or politically unwilling to articulate alternative models of economic growth. The ideological division between the administration and all sectors of transnational capital and its "representative" organizations encompass three areas: the national economic growth model of Keynesianism; a trade-centered vision of economic relations with the advanced states; and viewing direct investment in the Third World as an extension of the foreign policy priorities.

A number of theoretically significant points stand out in this history. The administration's concept of capital's interests was firmly rooted in Keynes's original vision of a trade-centered, export-oriented U.S. corporate economy. Direct investment was to be officially encouraged only if it were for purposes of development in the Third World. This vision was firmly committed to using state resources for the promotion and protection of TNCs in less developed areas, but was opposed to the rapid growth of direct investment in Western Europe in particular. Consequently, by means of tax restructuring the interests of TNCs were to be reformed toward increased domestic investment in order to more directly compete with the export-oriented economies of Japan and Western Europe. Tax legislation was used as an instrument to promote national investment. The confidence of the business community necessary to this end was to be gained through significant domestic tax incentives accompanied by the elimination of previous tax subsidization of foreign direct investment.

This strategy is a good illustration of the use of state power to structure the interest of capital by means of the tax system. The trade-centered vision of capital's interests was initially emphasized by Kennedy and his advisors, only to meet with the intense opposition of TNCs and TNBs. The ensuing debates between transnational capital and the administration concerned the nature of capital's profit-defined global interests in relation to the growth of the domestic economy and to the payments deficit. Both interest formation and the mediation tendencies are revealed in these controversies.

Another important point concerns the state's response to market innovation by capital, specifically the rapid growth of direct investment outflows to Western Europe in the late 1950s. These increased capital flows limited the state's ability to manage the payments deficits, which in turn intensified pressure on NATO over military and economic issues. Direct investment played little role in the Keynesian ideology which motivated Kennedy and his economic advisors. Large shifts in global investment were perceived in terms of their immediate impact on state capacities, especially since the then received wisdom of the "new economics" discounted their long-run importance.

The third, final factor of importance in this episode is that the debate between the administration and global business was really about profit: how important foreign profits of the largest corporations were to be for the national economy and what were to be the linkages between foreign profits and domestic economic growth. This was a theme which was to haunt all the capital control programs through 1974. It was aptly called by business leaders the problem of killing the goose that laid the golden egg. If the state restricted free foreign investment, it limited the ability of U.S. transnational capital to compete in and for foreign markets. It threatened business confidence. If capital controls were imposed, or once imposed were maintained for too long, the goose would slowly die, profits would decline, and the foreign and domestic business climate would contract. This business metaphor was as much prophecy as threat, for it was a commentary on the state of business confidence and on the willingness and ability of an administration to promote a pro-business climate. The problem of the goose that laid the golden egg embodies a major inherent tension between state and capital— how to reconcile capital's unimpeded expansion with continual state intervention to maintain an international system and to promote and manage domestic economic growth and stability.

The history of the Revenue Act is important, for it illustrates that, given the rapid growth of direct investment, the state, in order to effectively oppose capital's expansion, has to be politically and programmatically prepared to do more than merely reform tax structures as a means of slowing capital outflow. It would have to begin to restructure the basis of and means by which all investment decisions are made. It would not merely have to have some sort of national planning apparatus and perspective, but also be willing to be the investor of last resort if it proved impossible to effectively induce private sector capital to invest domestically through the means of tax incentives. Thus, the failure of the foreign tax provisions of the Revenue Act of 1962 indicates a critical weakness of the U.S. state. The logic of state-directed investment planning points to state investment in and control of the newest, most dynamic, and therefore most profitable industrial sectors as well as of all capital markets. Yet the U.S. state has neither been willing, nor is presently structured, to do this. The result has been the guaranteed failure of even the modest reforms, such as those in the 1962 Act.

The direct approach to channel capital movements, which had characterized the first ten months of the administration's balance of payments program, was defeated by the intense opposition of all sectors of business, although business itself was seriously divided. By the end of 1962, after more than eighteen months of debate, there was no long-term program to deal with the payments deficit, and, officially, the administration remained optimistic about its piecemeal solutions while enjoying the breathing space granted between mid-1961 and mid-1962 by international monetary events. However, beginning in early 1963, it became increasingly clear that a new problem had arisen in the outflow of capital to Europe, Canada, and Japan. While direct investment capital continued to be exported in increasingly large amounts, there was also a rapidly growing movement of short-term capital from the U.S. and a rapid increase of long-term U.S. portfolio investment abroad. In response to this new problem, the administration developed a fundamentally different approach to capital controls by imposing the Interest Equalization Tax in mid-1963.

3. The Interest Equalization Tax, 1963-1971

On July 18, 1963, the Kennedy administration brought to Congress the Interest Equalization Tax (IET), the first peacetime capital control program. The IET was not intended to restrict direct investment. Rather, it placed a tax on all new issues of foreign equities (common and preferred stock) and on all foreign bonds sold in the United States. Foreign bonds and equities were purchased primarily by U.S. investment banks and secondarily by U.S. commercial banks. The dollars paid out for these bonds were a net drain on the U.S. payments balance. A tax placed on these transactions would stem the rate of portfolio capital outflow, which had increased from $573 million in 1960 to $1.1 billion in 1962 and by the end of the first quarter of 1963 threatened to rise to about $2 billion annually. This chapter traces the history of the IET, stressing the administration's strategy in proposing it, the reaction of the New York investment and commercial banks, the impact of the IET on the U.S. balance of payments, and its role as a precursor to the voluntary program which was instituted less than two years later.

The payments problem

By early 1963 the Federal government had exhausted its temporary policies to stem the outflow of U.S. dollars. The proposal to end the foreign tax deferral had died by the end of 1962, and the various temporary intergovernmental arrangements with foreign governments to minimize their U.S. dollar holdings had ended. In the first half of 1963 the seasonally adjusted annual rate of private capital outflow reached $5.8 billion; new U.S. issues of foreign securities rose at an unprecedented rate to over $1 billion during 1962 (double the figure for 1961) and reached $1 billion again in the first six months of 1963, when the IET was imposed. Administration officials were aware that several hundred million dollars of additional floatations were planned in the near future.[1]

The 1963 capital outflow was part of the continued trend toward a large rate of overseas investment, but ironically, it was also spurred by the earlier government countercyclical policies designed to end the recession of 1961-62. Personal savings rose from $21.7 billion to $27.5 billion in 1963, while corporate savings

increased from $47.6 billion to $58.5 billion. High profit rates on direct investment and higher interest rates on foreign stock and bond issues had attracted a
percentage of domestic savings which, while marginal as a capital outflow from
the United States, was important for the balance of payments.

The administration faced four alternatives in dealing with the immediate
dollar drain. It could restrict long- and short-term credit, pushing the country
further back into recession, with unemployment already at 5.7 percent. This
classical payments policy was rejected as politically unfeasible and economically
undesirable, as it had been since the end of World War II. Second, the administration could formally propose some form of direct capital controls, as some administration members suggested. Third, the administration could abandon the fixed
rate system in favor of some form of floating rates, but this radical policy change
was ruled out by all policy makers as politically extreme and too disruptive. Its
advocates were a relatively small—but later influential—group of academic
economists. The fourth alternative, and the policy pursued with the IET, was
indirect capital control.[2]

The IET was proposed as a temporary measure, not to apply to securities or
loans of maturity of less than three years. The intention was to create a two-tier
market in long-term investment by separating the U.S. portfolio capital market
into a national and an international component, each able to operate insulated
from the other. It was hoped that the tax would not affect domestic long-term
interest rates and thereby slow economic growth. The IET represented an important break with the U.S. postwar policy of developing free capital markets with
minimal governmental restraint. The purpose of separating capital markets was
to minimize New York's role as the center of world portfolio finance, a necessary
cost of reducing the payments deficit. In order to make the tax immediately
operational and to discourage speculation and maintain confidence in the U.S.
financial markets, the administration proposed that it be made effective from the
date of the President's message to Congress on the balance of payments (July 18,
1963).[3] As proposed by the administration, the IET was not to include commercial bank loans abroad; nor was it to apply to the sale of securities of firms
operating in less-developed countries. However, the final version of the legislation gave the President discretionary power to tax commercial bank loans if he
determined that they caused a serious dollar leakage as a substitute channel for
securities purchases. This power was invoked in 1964. The President was also
given the power to exempt a foreign country's new securities issue to avoid
disrupting the international financial system.[4]

The IET levied a tax of 15 percent on foreign equities. The tax on foreign
bonds was graduated according to their maturity, from a minimum of 2.75
percent on a three-year bond to a maximum of 15 percent on a 28½ year bond. A
borrower who chose to float a bond in the United States would pay about 1 percent
above the prevailing U.S. domestic interest rate—to approximately equal average
interest rates in Europe. By attempting to equalize interest rates between the

United States and Europe, the administration hoped that long-term portfolio capital would be induced to stay at home. The IET thus acted as a tariff, influencing the supply and demand of capital indirectly through the marketplace.[5]

The IET was not well-planned policy. In the original IET announcement Kennedy did not make a distinction between the countries of Western Europe and Canada and Japan. The latter two were historically heavily dependent on U.S. long-term portfolio capital: Canada depended on U.S. markets for about 20 percent of its total portfolio capital needs. Shortly after the IET was announced, Canada was exempted from the tax, while Japan managed to obtain partial exemption for periods of time throughout the tax's duration.[6] In the immediate period before the IET was proposed, Europe did not yet account for the largest amount of U.S. outflow of portfolio capital, although its share was growing most rapidly. In 1960, European countries accounted for only $13 million, while Canada absorbed $180 million and Japan $115 million; in 1961 Europe accounted for $46 million, Canada $164 million, and Japan $60 million; in 1962, Europe absorbed $178 million, Canada $361 million, and Japan $97 million. In 1963 (using first quarter figures annually adjusted) Europe accounted for $228 million, Canada $1.3 billion, and Japan $188 million.[7] Given the Canadian exemption, a significant amount of leakage could be expected via Canada into Europe. This leak was not plugged by Canadian authorities until 1968, after considerable pressure from the United States. This lack of planning prior to the issuance of the IET was also evident in the absence of Treasury Department mechanisms through which the New York stock market could report the tax; this forced suspension of all foreign securities sales for the day following the announcement of the tax. The Treasury then granted the market a thirty-day grace period.

The administration's long-term strategy

Although the IET may not have been well planned, the strategy underlying it was clear: central was the desire of the administration to shift a significant component of world portfolio and short-term borrowing from New York to Europe. Since the end of World War II, New York had served the needs of a capital-hungry world as the major lender of portfolio capital and short-term money. New York, functioning as the world's financial center, was more than simply a provider of savings to countries in need of funds. It had developed into an international clearing-house in a market relatively free from regulations limiting size of issues, interest rates, and length of maturities.[8] New York had been able to play this central financial role, much as London had in the nineteenth century, due to the position and strength of the dollar as the major reserve currency of the world. Yet by the early 1960s, the growing U.S. payments deficit and the surplus position of some Western European countries were intensifying the pressure to curtail certain capital outflows.

The administration's approach to correcting the payments deficit had been stated a year earlier, in May 1962, by Treasury Secretary Dillon in a speech to European bankers in Rome. He urged them to improve and expand their capital markets in order to reduce their reliance on the U.S. market, relieving the pressure on the U.S. payments position.[9] The U.S. government's encouragement of a larger European capital market directly challenged U.S. finance—the broker-age and investment banking houses of Wall Street. Dillon argued for the passage of the IET by stating that "A substantial portion of rising demands [for capital] must be directed to markets in other nations [with strong reserve positions] . . . if the stability of the international finance system as a whole is to be protected."[10] Given a choice between a threat to the international monetary system and the dollar's hegemony and the immediate profitability of U.S. banking operations, the Kennedy administration opted to limit the flow of portfolio capital and restrain the outflow of short-term credits. It took this course of action knowing it would contribute to raising international interest rates, since European capital would be that much more in demand.

Dillon argued that the major motivation for the issuance of new securities and long-term bonds in the New York market by foreign companies and governments had been "the ready availability of funds at a relatively low rate of interest, rather than a pressing need for capital from outside the borrowers' own country." There had been an increased demand for funds by European firms, although these comprised a minority of the total new issues. Since 1960 European firms had been under increased financial pressure; growth could no longer be financed from retained earnings to the degree it had been. The local and provincial foreign government agencies which were large borrowers in the New York market had experienced similar pressures. This increased demand for public and private sector capital was met by the rise in domestic U.S. savings, given, in Dillon's words, "the relative shortage of profitable domestic investment outlets and the ability to earn a higher return on foreign issues."[11] This shortage of profitable domestic investment was attributed both to relatively high U.S. wages and low profitability in older industries. Foreign portfolio and direct investment was typically made in those sectors of industry where the United States had slower overall growth and lower profitability relative to European growth rates. Al-though by the early 1960s European corporate profits were declining relative to the 1950s, they were still higher than those in the U.S., hence attracting surplus U.S. capital.

The administration viewed the IET as a tax that would lower the amount of sales of foreign securities in the U.S. without preventing their issuance. Accord-ing to Dillon, it was a structuring of the free market: "The IET serves domestic and international needs in a way that supports the essential freedom of our trading and financial markets, and fulfills our special responsibility at the center of the financial system of the free world."[12] Dillon rejected the argument that in the long run the returns on portfolio investment made a positive contribution to the U.S. payments balance. He argued that future earnings "cannot substitute for the urgent need to protect the dollar by bringing the current portfolio capital outflow within the limits of our immediate capacity to lend.''[13]

In this analysis the plight of the dollar was partially a result of the very success of New York as the global financial capital. Consequently, administration strategy desired to restructure the direction of world portfolio borrowing and lending through the IET as well as in other important ways. In a 1963 position paper the Treasury Department argued that the trend of the 1950s toward a higher degree of European corporate self-financing from retained annual earnings was slowing. In 1955, for example, European corporate self-financing peaked at about 70 percent and declined thereafter. In the United States, by contrast, self-financing reached 99 percent in 1962 and would not begin to decline until 1965.[14] In addition, European local and provincial governments were also turning to the expanding U.S. capital markets to float bonds and raise funds. While this outflow of capital was profitable for the U.S. financial market—and in the long run a positive contribution to the payments deficit—in the short run it presented a threat to the payments balance and, with it, to the stability of the dollar.

In spite of declining retained earnings by European firms, the U.S. Treasury report saw the potential for overall European savings as substantial, given the general economic expansion and the surplus balance of payments of most European countries, but that the potential was dispersed within each country and savings were broken down into smaller pools of resources. In 1962 total Common Market and European Free Trade Association new foreign issues were only $444 million, indicating that a European-wide capital market was negligible. One indicator of the relative size of the U.S. and European (including British) capital markets is outstanding long-term obligations: at the end of 1962 total U.S. outstanding bonds, stocks, and state and local government obligations amounted to $699,900 million; for Europe, $109,320 million.[15] The Treasury analysis also acknowledged the significance of European state restriction on the free movement of capital across borders in stimulating the long-term outflow of U.S. capital:

> . . . where the legal and institutional restrictions limit the amount of capital funds in a particular market below that which would be available if the market operated with full freedom and efficiency, or where markets are compartmentalized in such a way that interest rates rise to inordinately high levels in a particular sector, the normal market place allocation of international capital will be disrupted and the actual directions of flows can be disequilibrating [to payments imbalances].[16]

The Treasury analysis pointed out that among the important institutional differences between patterns in European and U.S. savings were: European governments played a comparatively larger role in gathering and allocating savings to alternative uses; a smaller proportion of European savings was channeled through nonbank financial intermediaries (especially insurance institutions and pension funds); a smaller proportion of total savings originated in the household sector in Europe; Europeans tended toward greater liquidity preference (thus limiting long-term nonliquid financing); and, finally, European financing included a larger proportion of direct credits such as banking credits and a smaller proportion of new securities issued. The Treasury's long-term goal was to stimulate new forms of intra-European long-term lending to compensate for the contraction of the U.S. market which would immediately result from the announcement of the IET.[17]

What is most significant about the Treasury's study is an omission: nowhere does it discuss the then rapidly growing Eurodollar and Eurobond markets as possible new forms for centralizing international capital. Whether this was an oversight or policy decision is not clear, although I have not found any public reference to Euromarket developments by administration officials prior to 1968. Most importantly, administration officials assumed that surplus dollars in private and official European hands were unrelated to the development of a European capital market. They tended to see the expansion of a European capital market in traditional terms: it would consist of securities and bonds denominated in European currencies. If such a market could be developed, it would relieve the long- and short-term pressure on dollar outflows.[18]

To develop European capital markets in this period the formation of an integrated Europe-wide market uniting the Common Market countries was necessary. Yet such a market, which had been called for by the 1958 Treaty of Rome, did not develop for political reasons. First, European governments had combated the inflationary factors of public and private borrowing and wage rate increases (beyond proportional productivity increases) in large measure through monetary rather than fiscal policy. Monetary policy, being more opaque, was politically less threatening; altering tax and government spending patterns would be both more cumbersome and more controversial. European central bank action was relied upon to raise interest rates and tighten liquidity. This policy, seemingly able to attract long-term investment through high interest rates, in fact encouraged shorter-term, highly liquid investments. Capital markets charged a higher interest rate, which discouraged savers from purchasing long-term fixed interest obligations as the higher yields were always anticipated. This ratcheting effect meant that investors were fearful of locking themselves into what could have been lower current rates at the expense of higher future rates.[19]

The second force working against the integration of the European capital markets was the fear by governments, especially in France, that such a liberalization would neutralize national monetary and fiscal policies concerning balance of payments, inflation control, and national planning. The integration of capital markets necessarily implied the lessening of national government control. Before 1963 New York performed this integrating function well, but to the detriment of the U.S. payments balance. (After 1963 London began to assume this role, but only through the floatation of securities denominated in dollars rather than pounds; the British economy did not generate enough domestic savings to come close to replacing the dollar with the pound. [20]) A policy of capital market integration, as called for by the original Common Market documents and post-1962 U.S. policy, implied the relaxing of controls by various European governments over the issuance of foreign securities in their domestic securities markets and permitting a free flow of long- and short-term funds among capital markets. This would result in the relative loss of national control over interest rate structures and the weakening of monetary action as a tool of economic policy.

Thus, the U.S. Treasury Department's strategy had two components. First, it desired to reduce the dominance of New York in the global bond and equity markets for European issues. Second, as this would stimulate the European and especially Common Market capital markets, the policy would buttress those European domestic political forces supporting the Common Market while weakening the nationalist, anti–Common Market forces by limiting the effectiveness of traditional monetary policy. The IET continued the logic of the Marshall Plan and of the Atlanticist and internationalist orientations of postwar administrations, which in this case sacrificed the immediate economic interests of investment for stabilization of the global monetary and geopolitical order. The interests of the state in minimizing the payments deficit coincided with the interests of supporting European economic development and growth, and specifically, the stimulation of what administration officials hoped would be revitalized nationally based European capital markets. The state, responsible for the protection of the dollar's hegemony, clashed with one main sector of capital, itself benefiting from and dependent on the dollar standard. Noting that this legislation was being presented by a renowned former investment banker [Dillon], conservative Republican Congressman Durounian of New York observed to the Investment Bankers' Association: "Yesterday, I suggested that Mr. Dillon was wearing the Treasury hat, and if he had testified today he might be wearing your hat. As I stated, he is a good soldier in the cause where they don't tolerate much disagreement." [21]

The Treasury Department's strategy assumed that an efficient capital market in the New York style would be necessary to provide long-term capital for direct and portfolio investment. What was efficient in the U.S. market, and in the interests of U.S. TNCs and TNBs, might not, however, be the most efficient for European countries. For example, if a truly Europe-wide integrated capital market had developed, interest rates would have tended to equalize, penalizing countries with traditionally lower rates, such as Switzerland and the Netherlands. Those with generally lower rates would have been forced to raise them in order to secure internally generated lending funds. Traditionally high West German and Italian rates would have been lowered, but proportionally less than rates in other countries would have risen. Borrowers in low-rate countries and lenders in high-rate ones both objected—for opposite reasons—to any change. European capital market integration would have limited the effectiveness of indicative economic planning, especially in France and the Scandinavian countries. It would have undermined the planning structure by eliminating restrictions on nonresident borrowing in domestic capital markets without government permission for each separate issue, as was required within each national capital market.[22] Given the lack of a Europe-wide economic planning apparatus, national governments were reluctant to undertake a full-fledged integration of capital markets, although some relaxation of national controls did occur throughout the 1960s. Ironically, the effects which many feared would result from a conscious policy to integrate capital markets occurred anyway, in spite of policy, in the wake of the subsequent massive growth of the Eurocurrency system. The system's growth, precisely due to enduring national controls, is a significant instance of financial innovation.[23]

This new system was not, however, a national system of capital export as the Treasury envisioned. It was a system in which the dollar continued to play a central role, and the majority of new bond issues remained dollar denominated. The Eurobond market was thus born out of the U.S. controls on the export of portfolio capital. What had distinguished the New York capital market prior to 1963 from the various European national ones and as well from London was the absolute size of its market and, consequently, the number of participants and the rate of buying and selling—the average turnover per year. In New York new issues were routinely between $50 and 100 million; in London $30–40 million; in the continental markets issues of over $30 million usually required special arrangements and on the average floatations were much smaller, between $5 and 15 million. Thus, the attractions of the New York market for both lenders and borrowers lay in its absolute size and in the related lower transaction costs. As this market was restricted, beginning with the IET in 1963 and later with the Voluntary Foreign Credit Restraint Program, the European and London markets began to perform the role New York had earlier.[24]

Capital's response

The strategy behind the IET of the Kennedy, Johnson, and Nixon administrations was to structure the means by which U.S. TNBs could expand abroad while protecting the dollar and state concerns. At first, this was to conform to the Department of Treasury's vision for nationally based European capital markets in which U.S. banks could play a role. But as these markets failed to develop, a *de facto* Treasury Department strategy emerged. It quietly approved of the emergence of the Eurocurrency market and actively supported the rapid growth of U.S. branch Eurobanking and off-shore bank markets in general. The conflict between the three administrations and the Federal Reserve Board on one side and U.S. TNBs and investment banking houses on the other revolved around the exact latitude that financial institutions were to have in the evolving financial system.

By levying a tax on U.S. issues, the IET did not directly intervene in the market, but structured it, forcing the process of financial innovation. The tax approach and the fact that the IET was at first directed only toward portfolio and equity issues by New York investment banks, rather than at commercial banks as well, eased initial corporate and bank opposition to the IET. Having learned from the legislative failure of its earlier attempt to channel direct investment by means of the deferral provisions of the 1962 Revenue Act, the administration also made a point of arguing that the IET would not affect the export position of the United States. The IET aimed specifically at Wall Street and not at TNCs in general. This had the effect of dividing a formerly united business opposition, as will be detailed below.[25] In the 1963 congressional hearings only those firms directly affected by the IET opposed it. Representatives of TNCs were neutral on the specifics of the IET while expressing long-term reservations over any capital control precedent. When the hard core of the deficit proved intractable, the IET, initially portrayed as a temporary measure to aid in the short-term reduction of the payments deficit, was extended and its scope expanded in 1965, 1967, and finally in 1969. Opposition to IET was articulated in each case by banks, and in each case opposition was defeated by Democratic and Republican administrations on the basis of the imperatives of the "short-term" payments deficit.

The TNBs, TNCs, and various policy organizations of capital responded politically as interest groups; there was no capital-wide reaction. Significant policy organizations (the Committee for Economic Development, the International Economic Policy Association, the U.S. and International Chambers of Commerce) and other sectors of industry and finance had dissimilar responses to the IET announcement. The IET itself was a compromise between those in the Kennedy administration who wanted more extensive and direct capital controls, and those who wanted to prevent direct control until all other means had been tried and failed. This latter group was led by Dillon and Roosa who wanted first to try the IET approach—indirect control through structuring of the free market—to aid in reducing the deficit. In response to many bankers' claims that the IET was a thinly disguised form of exchange control, Roosa responded that it was in fact a move to prevent direct controls. "Two months from now [August 1963] the bankers will see this tax as a move to prevent controls. I knew they would have this presumption, and I knew we would have to live through it."[26] In the year prior to the IET proclamation, the Treasury Department and the Federal Reserve Board had attempted moral suasion to convince New York investment bankers to sell a larger percentage of new foreign issues to foreigners rather than to U.S. residents. In response the bankers had complied on paper, but within days after the initial sale, issues were resold to U.S. residents.[27] The failure of the suasion policy convinced the administration that legislation was required. The threat of more drastic controls proved a convincing argument for some members of Congress initially resistant to the IET. In closed testimony before the House Ways and Means Committee, Dillon warned that direct controls over U.S. investment in foreign securities would be necessary if the IET were not passed.[28]

When the administration announced the imposition of IET, it provoked a storm of controversy among financial institutions and central bankers throughout the world and at home. Abroad, most central bankers welcomed the IET, not for any of its specific attributes but because it represented a commitment by the U.S. government to "do something" about the payments deficit. Nevertheless, many central bankers feared that the IET might be a forerunner of direct controls which would disrupt the international monetary system. At home the IET met with immediate opposition from financial interest groups, and with responses ranging from neutral to mildly negative from corporate representatives.[29]

The Wall Street Journal was quick to label the IET as a "reckless" move designed more to attack Wall Street than to correct the payments imbalance. It attacked Roosa's and Dillon's strategy of developing European capital markets as a form of "international capital isolationism" which would undercut the whole basis of the postwar growth of the U.S. capital market. It offered its traditional alternative for payments imbalances: tighten monetary and fiscal policies and reduce foreign aid.[30]

More indicative of the split between the financial and corporate institutions was the ambivalent attitude of important business policy and lobbying organizations. In August 1963 the U.S. Council of the International Chamber of Commerce, representing the largest U.S. TNCs, stated that it neither supported nor opposed the IET. However, by July 1964 it had reversed its position and called for abolition of the IET. The National Association of Manufacturers (NAM) neither supported nor opposed the Act throughout its duration. The U.S. Chamber of Commerce, also representing small- and medium-sized businesses, supported the IET. The Machinery and Allied Products Institute (MAPI) initially took a view of "guarded opposition" to the IET. A year later it had reversed its position and did "not oppose" the IET, but wished only to "raise questions" about it.[31] The reactions of these important business organizations were in marked contrast to their united opposition to the ending of tax deferral two years previously. The divisions indicated that the business organizations representing most sections of large- and medium-sized capital had no consistent and united opinion about indirect tax-based capital controls for U.S.-issued foreign bonds and equities.

It appears that those organizations representing primarily domestically based industries (including those with important exporting interests)—NAM, the U.S. Chamber of Commerce, and significant sectors of MAPI—could support or at least not oppose the IET because of its attempt to separate domestic from global capital markets. The Kennedy administration strategy on interest rates buttressed this division. "Operation Twist" attempted to keep short-term interest rates high to protect the dollar, while keeping long-term rates low, thereby maintaining high domestic investment and growth rates. Thus, those industrial sectors with most to gain from low U.S. rates—domestic industry—did not at first oppose the IET, while those with significant foreign interests felt potentially threatened, since the IET was correctly perceived initially as a forerunner of extended capital controls.

Consistent opposition to the IET came from banking institutions and stock brokers. The Investment Bankers Association (IBA), composed of the largest and most important U.S. investment banking houses, argued that the IET would not aid in easing the payments deficit and, in the long run, would undermine the U.S. balance of payments by curtailing return profits on portfolio investment.[32] The IBA maintained that the IET's very announcement had disrupted international monetary and financial markets, alienated Canada and Japan, both dependent on U.S. capital markets, and threatened to displace New York as the world's capital center. The IET would cure only symptoms of the deficit, not its cause, which the IBA believed lay in large governmental expenditures for overseas aid and for the military. The IET did nothing to improve the competitive position of the U.S. in exports or attracting foreign investment. The IBA argued that the IET would damage U.S. capital markets, "a precious national asset which should not be dissipated without convincing reasons of national interest. Because of this position, the United States has, in effect, become the banker of the free world and has attracted a large volume not only of domestic U.S. capital, but also of foreign capital." The IBA suggested that prior to the IET the uncontrolled free market had provided confidence to foreign borrowers and lenders. If the U.S. government began to structure the market, the confidence of future investors and borrowers would decline. They would attempt to second-guess what future government policy would be and how it would affect the market, thus undercutting the market's strength and stability.[33]

What is significant about the IBA's position is its narrow definition of the U.S. role as world banker, identifying that role solely with the lending status of Wall Street, ignoring the central role of the dollar as the major global reserve and vehicle currency. By disregarding the dollar's global role, the IBA negated the major source of U.S. global and monetary power, stressing instead the secondary and derivative role of dollar-based New York capital markets. In effect, the IBA argued that the only item in the balance of payments that established the United States as the world banker was its capital outflow account. The government's position, in contrast to the IBA's narrowly conceived interest, illustrates the complexity of the role of the dollar hegemony and U.S. global military power. The IET was justified not in terms of military necessities, but in terms of the overall balance of payments. But since the military outflow comprised a large part of the payments deficit, transnational capital often criticized U.S. military expenditures abroad, although usually without specific proposals for reform aside from "efficiency cuts." The IBA wished to protect the long-term position of the United States as the central world capital market. It feared that the IET would effectively close down the U.S. market and end New York's role as world portfolio center even after IET's expected expiration in 1965.

As an alternative to the IET approach, banking and financial interests proposed a voluntary capital issue committee to be composed of members of the various banking and financial groupings, working in cooperation with the Treasury Department. This committee would impose self-policing limits on the amount of issues in a particular year.[34] The proposal was formalized by Senator

Jacob Javits from New York, a moderate Republican and a consistent voice of New York financial capital, and introduced during the Senate debate on the IET. It failed to pass. Javits opposed the IET and favored a capital issues committee, saying "I represent, in part, the leading financial community in the United States, which understands only too well what is afoot here. . . ." He agreed with the IBA's position that reducing any form of capital outflow held "dangerous implications" for the U.S. position as the financial leader of the world. Concerned about the rising competition in Western Europe, he added, "we should not lose our present preeminence to Paris, London, Zurich or any other financial center."[35] The administration opposed the formation of a capital issues committee on the grounds that, ultimately, the government would bear the responsibility for whatever decisions and limitations the committee informally made. This would, said Dillon, "inject the government squarely into the process of individual decision making . . . in the free market." Dillon particularly feared that an informal capital issue committee would logically develop into a formalized one, inadvertently aiding those in the administration desiring more direct capital controls.[36]

During the congressional hearings on the IET, the IBA and other representatives of financial institutions identified three "fundamental causes" of the payments deficit: overseas military expenditures, the lagging export position of the United States, and inadequate domestic economic growth to attract foreign investment. To correct these three problems simultaneously, while at the same time minimizing or stabilizing capital and other balance of payments outflows, seemed impossible. Increased domestic growth—to the degree that macrofiscal and monetary policies could influence it—could occur only at the cost of greater capital outflow due to lower U.S. interest rates. It would be unlikely that increased capital inflows could offset this current. A redivision of the defense burden with the European allies had been explicitly raised, not for the first time, during the extensive balance of payment debates in 1961 and 1962 with little success. The logic of the position was that U.S. interests lay in pressuring the Europeans substantially to increase their share of defense costs. The U.S. military in Europe would be increasingly subsidized by European states which would thereby eliminate the deficit. This stance was considerably to the nationalist right of the Atlanticist-internationalist position which characterized postwar U.S. foreign policy.[37]

The implications of the IBA's position were developed most consistently by the International Economic Policy Association (IEPA) and its director, N. R. Danielian. Although the IEPA is less well known than other corporate policy organizations such as the Committee for Economic Development or the Council of Foreign Relations, its board of directors represents a significant, although less diversified, cross-section of the largest U.S. TNCs. IEPA membership overlaps with that of the CED: I.T.T., Goodyear, Proctor and Gamble, Minnesota Mining and Manufacturing, Owens-Illinois, Alcoa, American Cyanamid, Eaton, Owens-

Corning Fiberglass, and Hanna Mining are members of both organizations and their representatives serve on the board of directors of the IEPA. The average corporate assets of these firms in the 1970s was about $2.2 billion, approximately equal to the thirty-seventh largest corporation ranked by assets in *Fortune*'s listing of the top 500 corporations. The other five directors of the IEPA represent a bank (thirty-seventh largest), the largest privately held corporation (Cargill), a large corporate accounting firm, and a major corporate law firm. What is striking about the representatives on the IEPA board of directors is that, with two exceptions, they are not corporate presidents or chairmen. Rather they are vice chairman (one case), vice-presidents (eight cases), and a managing director of a corporation's international division (one case). The IEPA's 1968 Balance of Payments Committee was self-described as being "composed of some of the most knowledgeable financial officers of member companies." In short, the IEPA is a meeting ground and lobbying organization for some of the top experts of the largest U.S. TNCs in the areas of international finance, trade, and investment. The positions of the IEPA should, therefore, be taken as a major, sometimes dominant, segment of thought of the most powerful sector of U.S. TNCs.[38]

Testifying before Congress for the IEPA on the IET, Danielian argued that the payments imbalance was not rooted in any specific or technical economic problem, but in the nature of U.S. political and military relations with Europe. Since it was politically and militarily unfeasible to eliminate foreign aid and military expenditures, it was necessary to isolate the cause of the payments imbalance, which lay in the "large transfers of wealth from the United States to other countries for military and political reasons and that [therefore] we must not expect the ordinary international pricing mechanism and existing exchange rates to carry the burden of this huge unilateral transfer problem." The only solution was a political one: sharing of the budgetary burden among the developed countries. Failure to convince the allies of this would possibly result in recession in the United States or inflation and depression in the European countries.[39] The inability of the United States to convince the allies to support the aims as well as the costs of foreign policy had led, in Danielian's words, to the U.S. "guaranteeing, practically unilaterally, the security of Western Europe"; moreover, the U.S. had "undertaken singly the enormous and fearful obligation to contain the expansion of 700 million Communist Chinese."[40] Danielian was, of course, referring to the growing U.S. commitment to expanding the Vietnam war. He concluded: "until there is collective assumption of responsibility for the defense of the free world against Chinese expansion as well as Soviet expansion in Europe, I don't believe we are going to be able to solve this balance of payments problem."[41]

For the IEPA the implication was clear: the guns and butter policy of the Johnson administration was not economically viable. Yet even a guns only policy would not work. The dollar-dominated fixed-exchange rate system conflicted with U.S. foreign policy imperatives and the policy of free movement of international and especially U.S. capital. Politically, however, the implication of the corporate nationalist position was not achievable within the framework of the Atlantic alliance, which protected the Europeans from complete subordination to the United States. The Johnson administration, trying to gain a modicum of support from the European allies for the Vietnam war, moved cautiously to apply pressure for defense sharing. As in the past, this produced few results.

The IEPA concluded that, while the IET itself would not affect its members' interests directly, it would not in any case be an effective means to halt the outflow of capital. Danielian suggested that if complete direct controls were to be adopted in the future—if the IET proved to be a forerunner of those controls— then it was not a desirable development, since the root cause of the deficit problem was political, not economic.[42]

Danielian's logic was correct, although partial. The transfer of U.S. state resources abroad for military purposes and political aid comprised both social capital and social expense items. The most obvious social capital item was foreign aid, which under Public Law 480 was tied to U.S. purchases and so increased U.S. exports. About 80 percent of all U.S. foreign aid in this period was tied to U.S. purchases, assisting the balance of trade account and linking the trade balance to congressional foreign aid appropriations. Yet the payments deficit itself was not simply a matter of government spending, as it might first appear. The political and economic essence of the pre-1971 dollar standard was its ability to shift a proportion of the real costs of U.S. hegemony (military costs, political aid, and capital export) to other countries. This transfer of real costs occurred because the U.S. payments deficit was financed to a great degree by the countries that absorbed the net dollar outflow, as they had to do in order to maintain adequate reserves. The U.S. deficit was a central banker's deficit, and while it had dangerous destabilizing potentials—borrowing short to lend long has limits— its nature was different from a traditional payments deficit. For example, Great Britain's deficit reflected a real outflow of wealth, as sterling was less and less accepted as a reserve asset.[43] Thus, taking the U.S. payments deficit as a whole, a real transfer of wealth to U.S.-based institutions occurred not only due to profitable investment and trade (while the trade account was in surplus through 1968), but also due to the very nature of the domination of the dollar as the global reserve and vehicle currency.

Yet the result of this system in terms of balance of payments was an international fiscal crisis for the U.S. state because the net flow of wealth into the United States accrued to TNCs and TNBs. The state provided the social capital and social expense which underpinned this inflow but could not compete with the private sector in the direct appropriation of profitable investment. As in the domestic fiscal crisis, the state's revenue relies overwhelmingly on either taxation or the inflationary creation of paper wealth. Insofar as balance of payments are concerned, taxation can be directly on profits or in some form of capital restriction or control. The state can also continue to produce additional world liquidity on which it would have the profits of seigniorage, as first issuer of a currency unit.[44]

Danielian's and the IEPA's correct apprehension of the political character of the U.S. payments deficit failed to consider the transfer of wealth that was accruing to U.S. transnational capital. Consequently, Danielian proposed to raise the costs to Europe for U.S. military and political hegemony—for which they had already been paying, although in a hidden form. The IEPA viewed the IET and other capital control programs as compensatory rather than corrective policies to buy time during which the government "hoped the situation [would] not get worse." The capital restraint programs were not aimed at the causes of the problems. When asked by a congressman to present an alternative program, Danielian was vague, suggesting only that "our commitments" abroad be "reconsidered" and that the government should "scale our expenses down."[45]

The IET was originally formulated as a temporary measure, but was in fact renewed approximately every two years through 1973. It was renewed in 1965 over the protests of the major banking and financial institutions: they argued as they had two years previously, but emphasized that the IET, in addition to shifting portfolio capital from New York to London, stimulated a large increase in the export of short- and medium-term capital abroad via the commercial banking systems. Actually this banking system leakage had been halted in 1964 under the terms of IET, and the amount exported was insufficient to prevent the rise of European interest rates due to greater demand for capital. This intensified the problem of keeping other forms of U.S. capital at home, since the Federal Reserve Board regulated the interests on all time deposits through the use of Regulation Q. Given higher European interest rates and the Eurodollar market, short- and medium-term U.S. capital found other legal and extralegal means of reaching Europe for a greater return. (The voluntary capital restraint program initiated in 1965 would further block U.S. capital from reaching Europe. However, it would also stimulate the borrowing of European-raised funds by U.S. TNCs and push global interest rates even higher.) In short, the original aim of the IET to equalize interest rates through a tariff proved to be elusive, as money is fungible and financial institutions are innovative.[46]

In 1965 the IBA renewed its proposal to make the IET and the new voluntary program more flexible, urging the government to formulate and coordinate a comprehensive capital export policy to replace the then emerging piecemeal measures. The IBA concluded: "If the tax is permitted to continue for two additional years in its present form, the damage to the investment and commercial banking community, to the U.S. capital market, and thus to the standing of U.S. leadership in the world will be seriously increased."[47] IBA opposition to the IET was somewhat more tempered in private surroundings than in congressional debates. In late 1964 Nathaniel Samuels, Chairman of the IBA's Foreign Investment Committee, admitted that, contrary to the position of *The Wall Street Journal* and others, the IET was a retreat from an internationalist position, was merely a "circumscription" of international capital flows while the government experimented with *ad hoc* measures. Although this did fundamentally change the nature of international capital markets, government policy ultimately would not displace New York financial institutions as the center of the world capital market. But it did force those institutions to adopt innovative practices to expand abroad by enlarging their European operations in order to meet the demands of the new capital market structures. Thus Samuels began to recognize that Dillon's "structuring of the free market" might indeed have long-term benefits: it necessitated financial innovation.[48]

Consequences and conclusions

By 1967 most financial institutions had come to see what Samuels had seen in late 1964 and Dillon and Roosa in 1963. The IET did not remove Wall Street institutions from the center of world financial power. Rather, it provided an incentive for restructuring the mechanism through which that power was exercised. Nevertheless, this restructuring could not have been achieved by the institutions of Wall Street acting alone. Self-regulation would not have worked, as there was no immediate business reason to induce such a venture. Voluntary restructuring of capital export involved a risk to the individual firm. Further, there was no agreement among Wall Street institutions about how important such a restructuring was to the payments balance and, more generally, no agreement as to how important the payments deficit was.

The IET controversy reveals initial policy incoherence among corporations and banks. Most commercial bank representatives who spoke on the IET were more nationalist than either the administration or the Committee for Economic Development which "represented" those banks. The divisions within capital and between capital and the administration concerned the geopolitical system, its global financing, and the role of the United States in that system, specifically with reference to division of the military burden with the European allies; the role of the United States in stimulating the European private sector; and the nature and responsibilities of the United States as central banker. In short, the divisions among banks and corporations and between them and the Kennedy and Johnson administrations focused on the politics of global fiscal crisis under the fixed-exchange rate system. This illustrates the inherently contradictory interests of TNBs and the interaction of these contradictory interests with the problems of financing the payments deficit. In the IET case transnational capital as a whole was unable to formulate its own interests, and this left the state greater room for autonomous action. One result of state action was the restructuring of financial capital's global interests.

In defense of this restructuring the new Treasury Secretary Henry Fowler argued in 1965 that the IET, during its first two years, had effectively reduced private portfolio capital outflow without adversely affecting domestic economic growth or the international position of the dollar. The IET had fulfilled the secondary objective, aiding in the development of the European capital market.

Fowler's defense of the European capital market reflected an internationalist spirit reminiscent of the Marshall Plan in the 1940s. "In the long run," he stated, "having larger and more competent and effective capital markets in Western Europe is going to be for the benefit of the capitalist system . . . in the entire western world."[49] This implied that a proportion of the profits and privileges of New York's former monopoly on the world capital market had to be forfeited in order to meet the requirements for long-run stabilization of the dollar and the U.S. payments balance. A similar orientation was evident in Fowler's support for the slow creation of a global dollar substitute (later to be called the Special Drawing Right or SDR) in his 1965 call for the first international monetary conference to be held since Bretton Woods to reform world liquidity mechanisms. The long-term interests of U.S. business, Fowler argued, would be met by the development of European capital markets: "We think over the long pull American business will profit in the long-run from the development of industrialized societies in other parts of the world. . . . We helped to create the competitors, but in the process of creating some competitors, we also created markets, and we undoubtedly, from a political standpoint, strengthened the political fiber and fabric of the countries with which we are associated."[50]

In 1967 the Johnson administration proposed to extend the IET for two years and to raise the effective interest rate equalization from 1 percent to 2 percent, to reflect the interest rate war in progress between the United States and Europe. This was overwhelmingly passed by both houses of Congress after being amended to give the President discretionary power to raise or lower the interest rate equalization from zero to 1½ percent rather than the proposed 2 percent. Major banking and financial interests moderated their opposition to what they saw was a foregone renewal of the IET, attempting in vain to limit the renewal period to one year rather than two. They also opposed the rise of the equalization rate to 2 percent.[51]

In 1969 the Nixon administration proposed further extension of the IET to run twenty months (until March 31, 1971) and that the President be given the power to authorize lower rates on new and outstanding issues. Arguing for the renewal of the IET, the Under-Secretary of the Treasury for Monetary Affairs stated that, while it was the policy of the Nixon administration to dismantle all capital control programs, including the IET "as soon as possible," this could be accomplished only with "prudent concern for the realities of our balance of payments situation." "Permitting the IET to lapse . . . would hurt our position on capital [account] at a time of deterioration in our current account. This could clearly result in increased pressure on our reserves." He concluded that the IET had "substantially supported our payments situation since its inception."[52] Indicative of the lack of Wall Street opposition to the IET was that Senator Javits did not oppose renewal, but argued unsuccessfully for only a one year renewal. The full renewal of the IET passed both houses on a voice vote.[53] The opposition of financial interests to the IET, strenuous in 1963 and 1965, was thus muted in

1967. By 1969, there was no audible voice against the IET extension.

The impact of the IET on U.S. financial institutions and on the world financial system was complex. The growth of the Eurocurrency markets in part directly resulted from the IET and subsequent capital control programs. The Eurocurrency system would have developed in any case, but how quickly or to what extent is difficult to estimate. U.S. commercial banks dominated the Eurocurrency markets from the middle 1960s and their volume of business was in large part initially due to the capital control programs. It is not possible to estimate what volume of business was lost due to the IET and what volume was merely transferred to London and to U.S. commercial banks' overseas branches. The IET stimulated the initial rapid growth of the Eurocurrency system in 1963, promoting the internationalization of finance. In so doing the IET aided in denationalizing the Eurocurrency system by placing it beyond the effective control of national governments and international agencies, ultimately creating a financial structure which was instrumental in the downfall of the dollar in 1971.

The IET's tactical success in slowing a particular form of capital outflow was achieved at the relatively short-term cost of increasing the outflow of commercial banking capital. But this, in turn, necessitated further capital controls. The logic of capital controls is further controls. The effectiveness of the IET here must therefore be seen in terms of the capital controls taken as a whole.

The government's attempt to restructure world capital markets through the IET is an example of state interest formation. The power of taxation enabled the government to induce foreign expansion of investment and commercial banks, substantially altering their global operations and consequently aspects of their interests. The impact of the IET, in line with the Treasury Department's larger strategy of developing European capital markets, forced financial innovation upon otherwise unwilling financial institutions. Yet the immediate impetus for the IET was neither financial innovation nor the development of European capital markets, but rather the perceived need for an immediate response to the balance of payments deficit in order to maintain the real and symbolic strength of the dollar. The response of financial institutions was to innovate, thereby rapidly developing the Eurocurrency markets, and in the long run this undercut the government's own monetary stabilization efforts. The resultant long-term decline of U.S. state capacity to directly influence global markets, or to influence them without continually escalating costs and unwanted side effects, diminished the state's ability to protect capital from itself.

4. The Voluntary Capital Control Programs, 1965–1967

In his 1965 balance of payments message to Congress, President Lyndon B. Johnson issued a series of "voluntary" capital control guidelines for U.S. transnational banks and the largest U.S. transnational corporations. The intention was to restrict the overseas loans of the banks and to raise the individual balance of payments surpluses of the corporations through greater repatriation of overseas earnings.

The administration had remained concerned about the deteriorating payments situation after the IET was approved retroactively by Congress in 1964. In spite of the IET, the outflow of portfolio capital continued. In place of large quantities of equities and bonds sold to U.S. residents, U.S. commercial bank loans to non-U.S. residents rose markedly. In addition, throughout 1964 direct investment outflows increased steadily. The overall payments deficit in 1964 was $2.8 billion, $1.3 of this in the fourth quarter alone. The fourth quarter's rapid increase provided impetus for the administration to propose the voluntary program. The new outflow of private U.S. capital in 1964 was $6.4 billion, an increase of $2.1 billion over 1963. Direct investment abroad in 1964 exceeded the 1963 level by $400 million. Most of the increase went to Common Market countries. These outflows were concentrated in the manufacturing sector and the petroleum industry. The transfers were overwhelmingly between TNC subsidiaries and the U.S. parent. Little funding was for new acquisitions.[1] Short- and long-term lending by banks amounted to about $1.5 billion in 1963, increasing to $2.5 billion in 1964. Reported short-term loans (less than one year) accounted for a major proportion of the year's and fourth quarter's outflow, rising from $734 million in 1963 to $2.1 billion in 1964.[2] The Department of Commerce commented: "Directly or indirectly, such capital outflows also substituted for sales of securities that were shut off by the interest equalization tax."[3] The impact of capital outflow deficits was partially offset by a small reduction in the government account deficit and, more importantly, by a near-record surplus in the trade account. In 1964 U.S. exports expanded by 15 percent over 1963 to a net export surplus of $6.6 billion. From the government's vantage, the overall liquidity defined deficit of $2.8 billion reflected the sharp increase of capital outflows in the third and fourth quarters. Evidently, the IET had merely channeled U.S.

capital into other forms of export, mainly to commercial bank loans. The voluntary program was formulated to reduce the deficit dramatically enough to bolster the faltering dollar. The program's political advantages were that it could produce quick results with a minimum dislocation of U.S. foreign policy and that it would be operational without congressional action.

Administration strategy and concerns

On February 10, 1965, in his annual Balance of Payments Message to Congress, President Johnson noted the "progress" in the reduction of payments deficit, from $3.6 billion in 1962 to $3.0 billion in 1964. "But," he said, "our progress is too slow." He declared that the dollar and the U.S. economy were strong, but added "we cannot—and do not—assume that the world's willingness to hold dollars is unlimited." He proposed a ten-point program to "deal with our payments deficit and protect the dollar in a way fully consistent with our obligations . . . to sustain prosperity at home; to supply private and public funds to less developed countries, to build both their strength and their freedom; to avoid "beggar thy neighbor" restrictions on trade . . . [and] to work with our trading partners toward a more flexible world monetary system."[4] The program was a "do-everything" policy informed by a Keynesian world view; its strategy relied almost exclusively on restricting U.S. capital exports. The administration proposed that the IET be extended and its scope increased. The Federal Reserve Board, along with the Secretary of the Treasury, were to be in charge of limiting the "further outflow of banks loans" and to "enroll the banking community in a major effort to limit their lending abroad." (This cooperation among bankers was specifically to be exempt from antitrust action through proposed legislation.) Point six of the program called for the reduction of "business capital" outflow abroad. The secretaries of Commerce and the Treasury were to "enlist the leaders of American business in a national campaign to limit their direct investments abroad, their deposits in foreign banks, and their holding of foreign financial assets until their efforts and those of all Americans have restored balance in the country's international accounts." Secretary of Commerce John Connor, speaking to the Economic Club of New York, emphasized the seriousness of the payments deficit: "We cannot permit a deepening deficit to develop or the present gold drain to continue . . . the deficit has become an urgent problem."

In spite of the felt urgency, the program was based on a long-run optimistic assessment of the causes of the deficit.[5] Hence, like the IET, the voluntary program was conceived as a temporary expedient. The administration viewed the payments deficit as a passing, although potentially critical, problem which would be self-correcting in time. Connor stated that "the voluntary program is a temporary device to serve until more basic measures can take effect. We are confident of a deep underlying strength in our international payments situation." This underlying faith was supported by relative U.S. price stability which, given the higher rates of inflation in Europe and Japan, increased competitiveness for U.S.

exports. The administration's optimism was also based on increased income from foreign direct investment earnings as well as its efforts to minimize the dollar outflow from government outlays for foreign aid programs.[6] From the outset, Connor and several others in the administration saw the program as a temporary expedient and when asked whether business would support the voluntary program, Connor replied: "I do not think it would be supported indefinitely . . . because too many puzzling problems would be raised for each company."[7]

The temporary, *ad hoc* nature of the IET and the voluntary programs reflected the prevailing optimistic views of Presidents Kennedy and Johnson and their economic advisors. The assumptions underlying these policies were as political in origin and purpose as they were economic. Connor stated it succinctly: "Our policy should not be directed toward shrinking either foreign or domestic business. Economic problems are usually much more easily solved under conditions of expanding economic activity than in an environment of contraction."[8] *The Economic Report of the President* explicitly rejected laissez-faire market solutions based on the gold standard because they could only function by "subordinating domestic welfare to the requirements of external balance." Consequently, payments problems could be solved only at the "expense of economic growth, high employment and price stability."[9] Political reasons ruled out solutions to the payments problems at the expense of domestic and international economic growth. An official Treasury Department publication made this explicit.

> Depressing the American economy is as unacceptable to most other nations of the world as it is to the United States. The United States occupies a unique role in the world economy. It is by far the largest exporting and importing country. It is the principal source of international capital. It is the largest donor of aid. Military forces stationed abroad are indispensible to the security of many countries. For all these reasons the entire world is affected by the U.S. economy and the U.S. balance of payments. . . . The United States must seek a solution to the payments imbalance through the expansion of the world economy rather than the contraction of its own, and consequently the world economy.[10]

By 1965 this optimistic view became tempered by the growing influence of the idea, associated with Robert Triffin, that a reserve currency system was inherently unstable. Many policy makers came to perceive this instability as causing speculative pressure on the dollar. With Henry Fowler appointed as Treasury Secretary in 1965, it was possible to overcome the prior objections of Robert Roosa and C. Douglas Dillon to an international monetary conference which would consider establishing a nondollar reserve asset. Fowler and others maintained an underlying faith in the Bretton Woods system and in continued domestic expansionary policies, but on condition that a nondollar reserve asset supplement the dollar itself. These reforms provide the larger context in which the voluntary capital controls were seen as a temporary expedient.[11]

The approach of combining domestic economic expansion with reform of the liquidity mechanisms of the Bretton Woods system (including capital controls) contrasted with the traditional conservatism of some members of the Federal Reserve Board. Although there was general agreement on the long-run goal of expansion, there were sharp differences on the necessary preconditions. This difference in strategic emphasis is visible in two related issues: how long "temporary" was to be and whether an optimistic or pessimistic view of the underlying causes of the payments deficit was held. In general, those who pessimistically felt that the underlying causes of the deficit were structural and permanent tended to want a more fundamental corrective than temporary restraints on capital exports and reform of Bretton Woods. Those who held the more optimistic view that the deficit was transient, although a critical problem in the short run, tended to opt for temporary *ad hoc* policies. This latter position characterized the administration's thinking in early 1965. However, after 1964, the increase of military and other expenses incurred by escalation of the Vietnam war began to affect the payments deficit. These, too, were seen at this time by the administration as temporary factors, given the perennial light at the end of the tunnel. Former Secretary of the Treasury Douglas Dillon made it clear in any case that the administration rejected *a priori* any reduction of the military budget. The impact of military-related dollar outflows could be minimized, he argued, but not significantly reduced without a major military redeployment. This "would have a major effect on our political and strategic interests in the world." Therefore, until 1968, military strategy was to be exempt from balance-of-payments considerations.[12] Treasury Secretary Fowler emphasized this in a major policy statement to a CED symposium on "The International Position of the Dollar" in June 1965. He stated: "the international stability and standing of the dollar directly affects our national security and our capacity for effective diplomatic, political and military action. A strong currency is essential to our success in meeting our world-wide responsibilities."[13]

The administration's goal was to encourage economic expansion in order to decrease unemployment, relying on the domestic wage-price guidelines and the voluntary programs to correct the payments deficit. This explicitly shunned the use of higher interest rates to reduce inflation and minimize the payments deficit for fear of initiating a recession. Henry Fowler informed the CED in June 1965:

> I am not here to argue whether this program is right or wrong. I happen to believe that it is right. I am here to tell you that this time the program *must* work. The possibility of failure is too dismal to contemplate.
>
> What is at stake in this program?
>
> The protection of the dollar in ways fully consistent with sustaining prosperity at home, maintaining our defenses abroad when our allies are threatened, supplying private and public funds to less developed countries, avoiding renewed restriction on trade, and the achievement of a more flexible world monetary system that will permit continued free world trade and development.[14]

Fowler, an optimist in the long run, sounded grim warnings in the short run: "There is no magical arrangement which will automatically do away with the present imbalance, or which will make possible [the] continued large outflow [of capital] without endangering the position of the dollar . . . we cannot wait for the long run to eliminate our payments deficit," he argued. "The time is too short and the risks are too great to take chances."[15]

Administration representatives consistently refused to specify how temporary the voluntary program would be, or what actions would be taken should the program prove successful. The Federal Reserve Board, however, made clear its view that the program as originally announced in February 1965, would not produce the necessary results. Chairman William McChesney Martin argued before a congressional committee that the program "has been regarded as a temporary measure. It buys time pending more basic adjustments." The original guidelines for banks were general, merely setting global dollar targets. In the future, "much more specific guidelines may become necessary."[16] J. L. Robertson, Federal Reserve Board member in charge of overseeing the voluntary program for financial institutions, stated: "You are going to have great difficulty making a voluntary program of this nature work smoothly for more than a period extending through 1966, and I would hope it wouldn't have to go that long."[17] Martin argued that the top priority had to be the elimination of the payments deficit and defense of the dollar, at the expense of domestic expansion if necessary.[18] In short, the Federal Reserve viewed the program with reserve, arguing that it was an inadequate *ad hoc* response to a fundamental problem; it would have to be either eliminated within a year or two or strengthened, made less flexible, and perhaps mandatory. The better alternative, Martin emphasized, would be a restrictive monetary policy—a policy he would institute by late 1965 over President Johnson's strenuous objections.[19]

An informal corporate state

The unique feature of the first year of the voluntary program (February–December 1965) was President Johnson's call for "businessmen and bankers to enter a constructive partnership with their Government" in order to reduce the dollar outflow. This implied the development of an informal neocorporatist state apparatus through which leading corporate executives and top government officials would regularly consult on foreign investment decisions and (after the first year) on foreign investment guidelines as well. This incorporated the suggestions made by leading TNB spokespersons during the IET hearings for the formation of a business-government capital issues committee. Previously rejected by the Kennedy administration, on the grounds that it would promote government intervention in day-to-day business decisions and encroach on the free market, the idea was favored by Johnson, who argued that the free marketplace, in fact, depended on business and government cooperation. *"We seek to preserve the freedom of the marketplace.* But we cannot succeed without the full cooperation of the business and financial community."[20] The voluntary programs for corporations placed special responsibility on the Commerce Secretary, who was to "remain in close contact with the responsible corporate officials" to implement the voluntary program and "request periodic reports as the basis for appraising their contributions to . . . [the government's] balance of payments targets."[21] Corporate presidents and chairpersons, rather than financial officers, were asked to be responsible for the detailed monitoring and control of their companies' foreign investments as the latter would be more interested in maximizing the return on investment than on implementing policies in the "national interest."[22] Within a few weeks of the voluntary program's announcement, Secretary of Commerce Connor established a nine-member Balance of Payments Advisory Committee, with Albert L. Nickerson, Chairman of the Board of Directors of Socony Mobil Oil Co., as chair and Carter L. Burgess, Chairman of the Board of Directors of the American Machine and Foundry Company, as vice-chair. The other seven members of the committee represented five of the largest TNCs, and two large TNBs.[23]

At its first meetings with Secretary Connor, the committee urged that the voluntary program "be set up on as informal and personal basis as possible, with a minimum of formal reporting requirements and other 'red tape.' " The committee favored "a flexible approach that enables each company head to work out his own [balance of payments program], based on the operating facts of his own business, rather than limit the means of meeting each company's objective by having the government prescribe some formula of general application." During the first year Connor's role in the program was central. He supported business suggestions for informality: "This makes sense to me, and the form of the program we had been planning has been modified along the lines suggested."[24] In 1966 Nickerson elaborated: "The advantage of the voluntary system is that it keeps decision-making in private hands. While the government is taking a very strong role in trying to indicate those areas where industry and the banks can be most helpful, the administration has nevertheless sought our advice and left decision-making in our hands. The program is quite unbureaucratic."[25]

During its first year the voluntary program relied on informal "jawboning" of the largest 600 TNCs by the Advisory Committee and government officials to improve their individual corporate "balance of payments accounts" by at least 15 percent to 20 percent over the previous year. No specific guidelines were set, no means of enforcement instituted, no publication of the results of a particular company made. Connor asked the 600 target corporations to develop a company balance of payments "ledger" for 1964 based on a worksheet prepared by the Commerce Department. Using the 1964 results (which were expected to be in overall surplus due to repatriation of overseas profits), the corporations were asked to propose how improvements could be made in 1965 and 1966.

The Department of Commerce and Balance of Payments Advisory Committee formulated the voluntary program for corporations based on President Johnson's original balance of payments message to Congress. The program called for the expansion of exports and the development of new export markets. Corporate executives expressed pessimism about achieving these aims, since they felt that export penetration in the rapidly growing Japanese and European markets had peaked. The program called for investment income from the developed nations to be repatriated more rapidly than in the past. In practice this meant that short-term, liquid or near-liquid funds were repatriated during the second and third quarters of 1965, declining thereafter. So-called marginal investment projects were to be avoided or postponed, and restraint was to be exercised for nonmarginal new direct investment projects financed with funds from the foreign markets. Thus the program encouraged foreign borrowing for direct investment purposes. The initial strategy permitted each corporation to apply a mix of these options in order to raise its payments surplus. For example, if a firm wanted to continue direct investment projects at its former rate, it could do so if it also exported proportionately more goods, or financed the investments overseas, or repatriated short-term funds.[26]

Behind the logic of restricting direct investment was the relation of corporate overseas earnings to investment in the advanced capitalist countries as compared with the less developed countries. As indicated in Table 1, since 1960 net capital outflow to Western European countries had consistently exceeded the income derived from them, while the rate of investment increase was substantially greater than that of income received. The pattern was directly the opposite for all other geographic areas, notably for the less developed countries. In addition, the government viewed the strength of the export sector as dependent on the increase of exports to Western Europe and Canada. The logic of restricting European direct investment was bolstered by the concurrent increase in the merchandise export account.

The voluntary phase of the controls applied only to corporations and not to financial institutions. From early 1965, banks' cooperation with the voluntary capital control program and its specific standards for compliance were overseen by the Federal Reserve Board, on whose economic life banks depended. For example, in the late 1960s, Federal Reserve Governor Andrew Brimmer's shadow hung over all banks; he served as overseer of the voluntary and later mandatory programs and was also responsible for approving all bank applications for overseas branches and subsidiaries. While he never explicitly made use of this unspoken but understood power, bankers knew that in order to obtain his cooperation for their foreign expansion plans they needed to remain within the capital control guidelines.[27]

The task of organizing the voluntary system among the 600 TNCs was complex: it involved a variety of forms of investments, short- and long-term assets, and there was to be no government overseeing mechanism to assure individual compliance. The task of organizing the program among banks was comparatively

Table 1

Capital Outflow and Income Received on Foreign Direct Investments, by Area, 1960–64 (millions of $)[28]

	1960	1961	1962	1963	1964
All areas:					
net capital outflow (−)	−1,674	−1,599	−1,656	−1,888	−2,207
income received	2,355	2,767	3,050	3,059	3,557
Canada					
net capital outflow (−)	−451	−302	−314	−339	−224
income received	361	464	476	441	558
Western Europe					
net capital outflow (−)	−962	−725	−869	−893	−1,212
income received	397	486	526	507	596
Less developed countries					
net capital outflow	−220	−453	−290	−476	−570
income received	1,511	1,698	1,916	1,988	2,271
Other developed countries					
net capital outflow	−41	−119	−181	−180	−201
income received	86	119	132	123	132

simple, as it involved only a few large banks and only one type of financial outflow, with the regulatory mechanisms of the Federal Reserve in place. During 1964, about one-third of the total U.S. capital outflow of $6 billion consisted of bank credits to foreign institutions, including branches of U.S. banks operating abroad. This was a dramatic increase in bank loans, and a direct result of the IET, which permitted a variety of legal loopholes for alternate forms of portfolio capital export. The IET, while effectively reducing the purchase of foreign stocks and bonds in the United States, did not reduce the demand for U.S. capital abroad, especially in Japan, Canada, and Western Europe. Short- and long-term bank loans increased between mid-July 1963 and 1964. Short-term loans would often be rolled over at the year's end into long-term ones.[29]

The guidelines drawn up by the Federal Reserve Board were to apply to banks and other nonbank financial institutions involved in overseas lending. The formulation of specific guidelines insured that the Federal Reserve's program would be more successful than the more flexible program developed by the Commerce Department. Banks were not requested to balance their own books or increase their balance of payments surpluses as were corporations. They were simply and directly asked to reduce loans. The guidelines stated that "banks, in undertaking a voluntary role in the program, are being relied upon to make sacrifices. . . . They will be forgoing some of the gains that would otherwise have accrued to them. . . . [Banks'] decisions must be made primarily with an eye to the national interest rather than profits." In short, "it is expected that nonexport credit to the other advanced countries will be cut back to the extent needed to achieve the goal

Table 2

Foreign Claims of U.S. Banks by Size Group: December 1964[30]

Banks ranked by size of foreign claims	$ amount of claims (billions)		% of total claims (cumulative)
	group total	cumulative total	
5 largest	5.0	5.0	53
6–10	2.1	7.1	75
11–15	.6	7.7	81
16–20	.25	8.05	85
21–25	.25	8.3	87
Total (156)*	9.5	9.5	100

*Total claims totaling $1.2 billion

of the President's program." The program for banks was also designed to encourage the lending activities of the foreign branches of U.S. banks, "insofar as the funds utilized are derived from foreign sources and do not add to the dollar outflow."[31]

From the onset, Federal Reserve officials believed that the bank program had a good chance of success since they possessed a variety of means to influence the few large TNBs lending abroad, unlike the Commerce Department, which lacked means to influence the largest TNCs. Table 2 indicates the number of banks involved in the program and the concentration of U.S. banks' overseas investment assets. (The voluntary program's impact on the approximately 15,000 smaller banks which made no foreign loans tended to be to increase overall U.S. bank concentration, since under point six of the Federal Reserve's *Guidelines* they were specifically prohibited from undertaking new non-export related loans.)

Aside from the differences between the Department of Commerce's flexible corporate program and the Federal Reserve's specific guidelines, the advantage of the voluntary program over the IET approach was that it could be operationalized faster than statutory regulations or tax revisions. It could be altered by administrative decision without congressional action and was consequently more flexible and provided the government greater latitude in fiscal and monetary policies to influence the domestic economy. Martin was optimistic that the program's impact on bank lending abroad would be successful. He was less sure, however, about other forms of capital escape. Of all important government officials, he alone warned of the possible problems with voluntary cooperation. If the programs were to fail for lack of cooperation, "we must all be prepared to take whatever additional measures are needed."[32] Martin was particularly concerned that capital controls, especially when implemented piecemeal, tend to work in the short run until firms innovate around them. Thus, controls tend to breed further and more stringent controls in the face of capital's innovation.

The tightening of the 1966 and 1967 voluntary programs spurred financial innovation. The administration viewed the initial, limited successes of the 1965 program as evidence to support strengthening it in 1966 to achieve payments equilibrium. If limited restraint achieved limited gains, greater restraint could be expected to achieve greater gains. Informed by this perspective, on December 10, 1965, the administration announced its intention to renew a tightened voluntary program. The nominal approaches of the 1965 and 1966 programs were similar: the promotion of foreign tourism and investment in the United States, and the minimization of the payments effects of government transactions, most importantly the Vietnam war. Once again these proved elusive. Thus, the Council of Economic Advisers concluded that the principal focus of the 1966 program had to be on the further containment of direct investment outflows.

The 1966 program for banks remained essentially the same.[33] Most significantly, specific guidelines were developed for nonfinancial corporations. The guideline approach removed flexibility for individual corporations, replacing it with a voluntary, yet specific ceiling for maximum annual outflows of direct investment capital. The number of corporations subject to the guidelines was expanded from the original 600 to 900. These corporations were requested to hold their combined 1965 and 1966 direct investment outflows (plus retained earnings abroad) in the advanced capitalist and certain mineral exporting nations to no more than 90 percent of the total of these items for the base years 1962–1964. Thus, under the program, direct investment would be lower in 1966 than in 1965, but could remain at a historically high level.[34]

From cooperation to opposition, 1965–67

The response of TNCs and TNBs to the capital control program moved from initial relief at avoiding more stringent guidelines to opposition to the renewed (and more restrictive) voluntary programs by late 1965. At the program's initial announcement, there seemed to be more business support than either the government or the business community itself would have predicted, including active cooperation with the newly created Balance of Payments Advisory Board. Yet many executives commented off the record that the program set a poor precedent: given its unlikely long-run effectiveness, it could provide the administration with a future justification for a less flexible program. After mid-1965 opposition increased; by 1967 no corporate or bank leader or business organization supported the voluntary programs, and many actively opposed them. After mid-1966 government officials no longer bothered to "jawbone" business leaders. As the programs became less flexible, more TNCs and TNBs turned against them.

Business opposition to the voluntary program centered on three significant divisions with the administration. The first division was on monetary and fiscal policy. As noted previously, until late 1967 the administration opposed an orchestrated contraction of the economy to balance payments. Increasingly, business, supported by the Federal Reserve, favored traditional conservative economic policies—the tightening of monetary policy and substantial reduction of the federal domestic budget deficit. Behind this conflict lay differing political and economic assumptions. The administration, acutely conscious of the escalating and unpopular Vietnam war, believed that it could not politically afford to reduce domestic social programs. Conservative economist Harry O. Johnson put the issue succinctly in 1966: "Within the concept of the present balance of payments program, then, the issue is between tighter guidelines and tighter monetary policy; this is also, not surprisingly, the issue in domestic economic policy."[35]

The second strategic division centered around foreign civilian and military aid programs. In the late 1950s and early 1960s only conservative politicians and small businesses had criticized these programs, but by the middle 1960s such views found increasing support from international capital. This was related to the third area of division between the state and international business: the greater economic nationalism among the large majority of articulated international business opinion. This debate focused on the maintenance of U.S. troops in West Germany, and the general Atlanticist orientation of the administration. These three areas of division became the basis for opposition to the voluntary payments program and for the different interpretation of the program by the administration and by TNCs and TNBs.

Transnational capital reacted to the initial announcement and implementation of the voluntary program by pledging cooperation. The program represented a new departure for the U.S. state in the postwar period: it set informal guidelines for investment decisions. This was recognized by leading corporate and banking representatives and journals. Labeling the program "an unusual experiment," the First National City Bank of New York commented that the voluntary program "breaks new ground" in that it relied on business–government cooperation. "Against the background of trial balloons about stiff controls that had been coming from Washington for some weeks before, the program has been received with some measure of relief. The administration deserves credit for avoiding imposition of direct controls."[36] According to Federal Reserve Board member J. L. Robertson, most business leaders "responded to the program with spontaneity and unanimity that has not only astonished our foreign critics, but even some of us here at home."[37]

During the six weeks between the voluntary program's announcement and the issuance of specific guidelines, business leaders expressed both guarded support and mixed feelings. Economist Fritz Machlup articulated the negative, although at this point, minority consensus during a congressional hearing: "Not since the NRA in 1933 has this country attempted in peacetime to transform the managements of private business into lengthened arms of the Government. We have taken an enormous step away from our system of free enterprise."[38] *Business Week* reported that while members of the Business Council representing about one hundred top corporate executives supported the program, many other executives did not. The general consensus was that other balance of payments remedies should have been attempted first, especially tightening domestic credit and reducing military and foreign aid spending abroad. On the other hand, "There is also the realization that if the voluntary approach fails, the next step could be direct exchange controls," commented *Business Week*, quoting a spokesman for a major electronics company as saying: "We shudder to think what would happen if voluntary controls don't work."[39] The concern of most corporate spokesmen was that a voluntary program would work until market competitive pressures clashed with voluntary restraints. Summarizing what appears to have been the general feeling, *Business Week* wrote: "bankers and businessmen aren't sure how well it will succeed over the long haul," but businessmen were cooperating for the moment. The mood of one company was "moderately ill-will acquiescence." "How long this sweetness and light [between government and business] will last is something else."[40]

Illustrative of initial weak business support was the Committee for Economic Development's stress during the program's first months on the necessity for early "successes," a perspective that differed from the administration's long-term interpretation. In March 1965, Emilio G. Collado, vice-chairman of the CED's influential Research and Policy Committee and vice president of Standard Oil of New Jersey, told a congressional committee of his "confidence that U.S. investors will respond generously to the President's request for added assistance to his program." The basis for cooperation was that the losses for investment possibilities, or their increased costs, "will be more than offset by advantages to be achieved in stability for the dollar and in avoiding the disruption and chaos which would accompany any attempt to introduce direct exchange controls into the U.S. economy." He emphasized, however, that the long-run solution did not lie with capital. It would, he said, "be more constructive . . . if we look for further possible cut-backs in some areas of government grants and loans abroad."[41] Collado shared the administration's optimistic assessment of the overall payments situation and the view that the controls were to be temporary. He stated: "there may well be reason to suspect . . . that there are structural factors working toward a longer-term adjustment in our basic balance of payments position." If the administration, in addition to the voluntary program, would raise the short-term interest rate, slowing the domestic economy and providing capital an interest rate incentive to remain in the United States rather than seeking higher rates abroad, "the immediate and (I believe) substantial, impact of the voluntary program should provide time for these forces to work, and make possible the early return to the free use of the dollar in international transactions."[42]

Collado's acceptance of the program in March had, by June, been transformed into guarded opposition. He called for a "gradual dismantling" of the restrictions. The first three months of the program, he argued, had produced "impressive gains."

> I have no doubt that it was necessary, at the time these programs were launched, to achieve an immediate and dramatic reversal of the massive dollar outflows of the last months of 1964 and early 1965. However, we must bear in mind that these short-run measures, while effective in counteracting a current deficit, do not really deal with the underlying causes of the chronic deficit which lay in the government account.

While Secretary of the Treasury Fowler called for maintaining and strengthening the program, Collado called for its phasing out: "We must plan the return to an open capital market. Unless we are able—selectively and gradually—to dismantle these temporary voluntary restrictions on capital outflow, we shall be storing up serious problems for the future, especially in the area of direct business investment abroad."[43] The CED's definition of "temporary" was in terms of months, the administration's in years.

A similar position was expressed by the American Bankers Association (ABA). Speaking for the Association in 1965, Charles E. Walker, formerly Assistant to the Secretary of the Treasury (1959–61), agreed with the administration's assessment of the payments crisis, stating that it represented "the greatest threat to economic stability, here and abroad, in the past thirty years." The nation's banks, he said, would cooperate. Yet he emphasized that the program, "valuable as it is at the moment . . . cannot be regarded as a permanent or continuing solution to this nation's payments difficulties. . . . [The] voluntary program does not provide a long-run answer to our payments problems," he said, because corporations would be less willing to forgo investment abroad, nor he added, "should they be expected for very long to refrain."

> To expect a voluntary credit restraint program to produce sustainable results is to ask American corporations and foreign credit users not only to subordinate profit and competition motives, but actually to make daily operating decisions which are contrary to their own interests and those of the stockholders.[44]

The ABA developed its alternative more specifically than did the CED, reflecting the ABA's clearly defined set of political priorities which differed from the administration's. Walker called for a wage-price stabilization program of undefined scope; a tightening of credit; and reduction in the outflow of U.S. dollars resulting from foreign aid and military programs. Like many representatives of large capital, Walker was vague on exactly where the cuts in military-related outflows should be, save for a diminished military presence itself.[45]

The ABA's position was similar to those of other representatives of large banks. George Champion, Chairman of the Board of the Chase Manhattan Bank, suggested that the government account was responsible for the payments problems. The IET and the voluntary program were merely "expedients"; basic changes were called for. First, tighter credit should be introduced immediately, since credit inflation was leading to price inflation, hurting the payments situation by making U.S. products less competitive and indirectly encouraging imports. Second, the government should have a "responsible fiscal policy," a balanced federal budget. This conservative interpretation of Keynesian policy stressed that during periods of full employment a budget surplus should be the goal of federal policy.[46] Third, Champion reiterated the ABA's and the CED's call for a reduction in foreign and military expenditures. Champion, however, went further and was more specific: the NATO allies were not "living up to" their commitments. "I believe we must drastically reduce military expenditures in Europe."[47]

Dr. Roy L. Reirerson, Senior Vice-President and Chief Economist for the Banker's Trust Company of New York, agreed, arguing that while the President's Balance of Payments Message ranged over a broad area, its specific proposals exclusively concerned capital. He argued that given the program's existence, it was essential that the credit policy of the administration be tightened.

> Credit policy is now working at cross purposes by making funds readily available and thus stimulating the search for profitable outlets. The same applies to Government spending abroad; it will not be easy to keep enthusiasm for voluntary restraint alive in the banking and business community . . . if the administration is not convincingly energetic in curbing the dollar outflow created by its own operations.[48]

John R. Petty, vice-president of the International Department of the Chase Manhattan Bank of New York, wrote similarly that the "agonizing problem" for TNCs and TNBs in the second half of the 1960s "will be how to adjust to national priorities and economic necessities . . .":

> We are trapped between actions that invite discrimination (on the part of foreign governments), for by doing all that the U.S. government wants we intensify the fears of the foreign countries that our interests in their countries are secondary. . . .

If the voluntary program was to be extended (or, "worse," made mandatory) then a fundamental dilemma would exist:

> If 1966 finds the United States faced with the requirement of an even more stringent payments program, the choice for sacrifices must be in the governmental, military and foreign aid fields.

In Petty's analysis, the preconditions which "have made possible the overseas military and economic aid commitments of our Government," have been the activities of private industry. Petty concluded:

> If it ever comes to a choice, we must select the continued overseas activities of the U.S. corporations, as theirs is truly a lasting and vital contribution to a freer society. The Government must decide that the risk of having a much smaller "trip wire" or military commitment overseas is less than the long-term risk of curtailed foreign investments.[49]

This line of analysis was even more clearly developed by the International Economic Policy Association. In the IEPA's view, the most serious consequence of the voluntary program and the payments deficit was that "our [geopolitical] independence of action as a nation is being reduced"; specifically, that the United States refrained from using its potential power to extract concessions from the Common Market during agricultural tariff and terms-of-trade negotiations in 1965. The IEPA proposed that the Common Market should be put on notice that the United States would take steps to reduce

> its military expenses and tourist expenses in the balance of payments surplus countries by at least $1 billion unless they make an offer to purchase, additionally, from us at least that amount of incremental products by reducing their protectionist devices against U.S. agricultural products for which they have need.[50]

Alternatively, they "should be offered sharing in the costs of Western defense." The political implication was made clear:

> You must be prepared to take action which would not be too pleasing to them [the Europeans], in order to bring them to the bargaining table on that issue. . . . If, after we take that strong position they still maintain they do not wish to participate in the cost of the defense of Europe, then we should be prepared to reassess the need for many of our installations there.

The IEPA opposed the controls both because they would undercut U.S. business abroad and because they would not work.[51]

The view that the roots of the U.S. payments deficit lay primarily in the government sector was also articulated by important academic advisors to corporate organizations and policy groups. Jack N. Behrman of the University of North Carolina stated the issue succinctly:

> The problem stems essentially from the assumption by the United States of the defense of the free world. . . . The expense of supporting [it] cause(s) a continued outflow of funds, ending up in European coffers. These are really the

"abnormal" and "excessive" outflows in the balance—at least they should be so considered both in economic and political terms, unless we should assume that the United States will be normally and habitually committed to foreign wars and defense efforts during the rest of the twentieth century.[52]

The significance of this thinking is that as a conflict developed between corporate and government global positions, the majority of articulate TNC and TNB opinion proposed various forms of global geopolitical retreat. The justification was purely economic: business felt it was being asked to shoulder the burden of the government payments deficit. Behrman was willing to have the U.S. government opt for a greater sharing of the defense burden with the Europeans, with the implied threat of partial disengagement if they should renege.[53] The government, however, placed geopolitical concerns over the global role of TNCs and TNBs: if necessary, it would sacrifice "short-term" corporate and financial profits and markets in order to maintain overall foreign and domestic policies. These divergent analyses of the global order became more focused after 1965. The lack of a unified approach by TNCs and TNBs to the 1965 program was due to the program's flexibility and apparently temporary duration. With its 1966 extension and strengthening, concerted opposition developed.

How temporary is "temporary"?
Growing opposition, 1965–66

In early October 1965 it became known that the voluntary program would be extended and made more restrictive of corporate investment, adopting the guideline approach already in force for banks. The announcement was greeted by corporate executives with a "mixture of resignation and dismay." It was acknowledged by Secretary Connor that there were "widespread feelings" among businessmen for an early end to the program.[54] The National Foreign Trade Council meeting in November 1965 noted that both business and government agreed that the voluntary curbs were a "necessary evil," but disagreed with the administration over the implementation of the curbs.

An informal survey of business opinion published in September 1965 found that most "are convinced that Americans will have to live with the program for a long, long time to come." The survey indicated the majority accepted the general direction of the President's balance of payments program—its attempt to increase exports and to raise overseas borrowing—and that there was widespread agreement that the government had to cut its expenditures to achieve fundamental correction of the payments deficit:

> Over and over it is suggested either implicitly or outright that industry is already pulling its weight, and that all will not be well until the government prunes and modifies its own overseas spending. . . . It will be necessary to consider fundamentals rather than palliatives. Foreign aid and military spending will have to be reduced to levels that do not result in a major drain on our funds.[55]

This strategic division between top corporate executives and the administration over the kind and importance of military expansion and various forms of economic aid became more important with the escalation of the war in Southeast Asia, the partly related continuing payments deficit, the growth of domestic inflation, and the resultant weakening of the dollar.

The main area of conflict was on the program's restriction of direct investment decisions, the survey found: "It is in the touchy area of reduction or postponement of direct dollar investment overseas that the panelists [the top 300 executives] are most at odds with the Administration." The critical issue was: "Is it in the national interest for American industry to be required to reduce its investment in developed countries?" *Business Abroad*, reporting on the National Foreign Trade Council Convention in 1965, noted:

> To the men attending the conference whose corporations not only do the bulk of U.S. investing abroad, but also account for the major share of $26 billion of merchandise shipped abroad annually, the answer was a resounding "no." The administration, in effect, says "yes."[56]

It was reported prophetically that some business leaders "say it is the straw that will break the back of Johnson's program of voluntary restrictions."[57] Michael Haider, chairman of Standard Oil of New Jersey, summed up the new business consensus:

> I see no real evidence that the government is facing up to the task of devising those basic domestic economic policies needed to make us fully competitive internationally; nor is the government revising its own international transactions in a way that would lead to a viable payments positions without controls, restraints or gimmicks. And unless government does tackle these basic issues, we face continuation of controls.[58]

In the pages of leading business journals transnational capital expressed its discontent over the length of the "temporary" program. "Businessmen are uneasy because they wonder now temporary it will be," commented *Business Abroad*. "They are not sure the government will resist the temptation to rely on this successful expedient as a substitute for more difficult measures."[59] Rudolph Peterson, president of the Bank of America, commented to the same effect:

> There is little doubt that, given our balance of payments problem, guidelines are needed as a temporary expedient. However, we should stress "temporary." We continue to believe that the best long term strategy is the expansion, not the restriction, of funds and investments overseas.[60]

The longer the "temporary" program existed, business feared, the less competitive U.S. capital would be with foreign capital. The debate over the length of the investment "payback" or recoupment period, which had dominated the 1962 Revenue Act hearings, arose again.

The concern of the Treasury Department under Fowler's leadership appeared to be similar to Dillon's concern five years earlier: direct foreign investment flows had to be moderated. Addressing the U.S. Chamber of Commerce in mid-1966, Fowler suggested that:

> Investment outflows have been growing too fast in relation to the inflows they generated in the short term period. We cannot sit and wait for the return flows to mount, for in the meantime there would grow abroad an ever rising tide of short term liquid claims . . . that could seriously endanger the dollar.[61]

Business feared that these views would decide the future of the temporary program as the Vietnam war-induced inflationary boom cut into the U.S. trade surplus. The Department of Commerce emphasized President Johnson's original plea to increase the export surplus, in contrast to the Treasury Department's position, which increasingly stressed the more basic problem of direct investment flows and turnover periods. The logic of the situation was to give the Treasury's position more weight since a successful export surplus strategy in 1966–67 would require domestic inflation in order to reduce foreign imports. This difference of emphasis between the Treasury and Commerce departments posed a difficult dilemma for business leaders. Commented *Business Abroad*:

> The Department of Commerce's preoccupation with exports as the best way to cut the deficit contrasts with the business leaders' repeated assertions that investment overseas has become the best way to bring earnings home.[62]

The division between the administration and business became increasingly sharp. "What business leaders do not want to do," declared a leading business journal, "is weaken their corporations through their uncomplaining acceptance of government's strategy which many feel is misguided and likely to be self-defeating."[63] The National Foreign Trade Council in November 1966 urged that the government remove existing capital restraints programs as rapidly as possible and "refrain from any extension or intensification of the existing restraints on capital movements."[64] The U.S. Council of the International Chamber of Commerce issued a statement calling on the government to reconsider the voluntary program. The Council's chairman, Arthur K. Watson, President of IBM, argued that the program's original intent was to "minimize the impact of the outflow of funds" for direct investment overseas. Under government pressure this had been transformed to mean restraint of investments themselves. Only in recognizing the positive role of direct investment, argued Watson, could the government correct the deficit. The Council's alternative was twofold. First, in order to achieve greater access by U.S. firms to foreign markets (through export sales or direct investment) outflows of capital might be required. Second, monetary and fiscal policy should be aimed at holding costs and prices stable to encourage exports, regardless of the domestic economic consequences. In addition, the Council supported a foreign policy which would ensure that "no nation in NATO should gain or lose gold or foreign exchange reserve because of its contribution to common defense programs." This, it appears, was meant to include Vietnam war-related expenditures and apparently called for increased European subsidization of U.S. Vietnam-related activity.[65]

In December 1966 the Council for Economic Development, which during the first two years of the voluntary program had taken no formal position, recommended its elimination at the earliest possible date. In language far milder than that of many a corporate executive, the CED pointed out:

> Curtailment of private capital outflow rarely if ever yields dollar-for-dollar benefits to the United States balance of payments. Failure to make additional investment means losses of future income and of export volume. Restrictions on United States capital outflow may have improved our balance of payments temporarily, but only at significant costs to prospective income.[66]

The CED reemphasized its support for freedom for worldwide capital movement; for a reduction of aggregate domestic demand through tight monetary policy; and for a surplus in the federal budget through restricting outlays, in spite of the increasing costs of the Vietnam war. While moderate in tone, the 1966 CED position reflected the views expressed by corporate executives and policy groups: all wanted a reassessment of military costs and agreements in Europe, as well as some reduction of aid programs. A significant area of difference between the CED and individual executives and policy groups lay in the area of U.S. relations with European governments. The CED called for pressing the allies for a multinational defense payments system which would not let any partner suffer or profit in regard to balance of payments from any NATO expenditures. It opposed any attempts or threats to reduce U.S. forces in Europe. Diverging from other policy groups and individuals, the CED felt that "we must assure our allies of our continuing support for European defense" rather than threaten eliminating military aid or troops.[67]

In sum, although transnational capital initially cooperated with and supported the program, its vision of how long temporary was to be, and its interpretation of the role of voluntary capital restraint in the overall balance of payments programs, differed radically from the administration's. The ultimate failure of the voluntary programs, in spite of tightened guidelines between 1965 and 1967, lay in the ability of business to pursue its perceived interest through innovational activity, undermining and eventually destroying the program.

Results and conclusions

In 1965 during the first year of the voluntary capital control program, of the 600 subject corporations requested to submit quarterly reports, 475 did so. In 1964 these 475 TNCs accounted for $2.5 billion of the total $2.7 billion in direct U.S. foreign investment and for $2.4 billion of the $2.9 billion earned on all direct investment. In 1964, prior to the program, these 475 TNCs had increased their holdings of foreign short-term financial assets, especially in the developed countries. During this calendar year, total short-term foreign holdings by the 475 companies had increased by 49 percent (from $926 million to $1.4 billion). In addition to these funds held directly and through U.S. banks, the 475 reporting firms' foreign affiliates' short-term assets increased 19 percent in the developed countries (from $1.1 billion to $2.0 billion), while they decreased in Canada by 9 percent (from $789 million to $718 million). Thus the government believed that if there could be a return flow of short-term foreign funds (in addition to faster repatriation of overseas income and a restraint on new long-term direct investment) a substantial immediate improvement could be made in the balance of payments capital account. Yet, it was obvious to all that repatriation of short-term funds could be only a one-time affair.[68]

The initial impact of the voluntary program did reduce the net outflow of capital from $6.5 billion in 1964 ($8.9 billion at an annual rate for the 4th quarter of 1964) to an annual rate of $3.6 billion for the first three quarters of 1965. This one-time gain was due primarily to short-term capital repatriation by financial and nonfinancial firms during the first two quarters of 1965. From a net short-term capital outflow of $2.1 billion in 1964, the first three quarters of 1965 witnessed an annual rate of new inflow of $1.0 billion. The *Report* of the President's Council of Economic Advisers commented: "The success of the voluntary program in shifting the movement of short-term funds was reinforced by the intensified demand for funds in the domestic market, as a result both of sharply rising [economic] activity and some tightening of monetary policy."[69] The initial goal for the voluntary corporate program set by the Department of Commerce was an improvement in individual firm payments ledgers of between 15 percent and 20 percent for 1965. This was not achieved. The improvement averaged about 11 percent, including one-time repatriations of short-term funds. By mid-1965, the return flow of short-term capital for banks and financial institutions had declined to the level of late 1963. But thereafter substantial gains in rates of inflow proved elusive, especially for long-term capital flows. For financial institutions, the net outflow of capital in the first quarter of 1965 of $435 million was transformed into a net inflow of $370 million during the second quarter. Much of this gain, however, resulted from increased demand for domestic credit, as suggested by the fact that banks and financial institutions did not lend abroad to the maximum ceilings permitted under the Federal Reserve's guidelines.[70]

The critical category of direct investment outflow remained at a high level. In the second quarter of 1965 the seasonally adjusted rate of direct investment outflow was $880 million—below the $1.2 billion of the first quarter, but nevertheless a near-record high. The direct investment outflow in the first half of 1965 was about $2 billion, only slightly less than the total outflow for 1964 ($2.4 billion). Thus the voluntary program in its first five months did not have a significant impact on direct investment outflows. One factor responsible for this was that while the participating 600 corporations may have restricted some of their direct investment outflows, nonparticipating companies accounted for an additional outflow of about $800 million in 1965.[71] However, in spite of this, an increase in the trade surplus during the second quarter reduced the overall U.S. deficit.[72]

The trend of the first two quarters was reversed in any case during the third quarter of 1965, resulting in a deficit on liquidity basis of $485 million. This was accounted for by a seasonally adjusted net outflow of U.S. capital of $450 million. The liquidations of short-term banking and corporate assets in the first two quarters had ceased. Short-term claims by banks remained stable, while long-term loans increased in order to meet obligations made prior to the voluntary program's initiation. The results of the third quarter became known in November: the once-and-for-all benefits of short-term repatriation had ended.

Direct investments did decline from the second to the third quarter of 1965 from $375 million to $515 million. The decline resulted from corporate efforts to finance their overseas investments locally and curtail marginal investments. Over $300 million of the third-quarter decline occurred in the industrialized countries, principally Western Europe.[73] Yet, evaluating the results of the program in 1965, the Council of Economic Advisers concluded that in the area of direct investment restriction little progress was being made. Despite the 1965 decline, "there was disquieting evidence that plans for direct investment in 1966 remained at a high level. . . . [Thus] direct investment became the primary area of concern."[74]

Throughout 1965 the administration remained guarded in its estimate of the initial successes of the program. In August, Secretary Connor acknowledged that the positive results of the second quarter were due mainly to "one-shot" developments. Yet to be addressed were the long-term problems: most importantly, increasing the export surplus, decreasing direct investment outflows, and increasing the rate of return on direct investments.[75] Similarly, Secretary Fowler in his address to the CED in June 1965 warned:

Let me caution you vigorously against interpreting these results [of the past three months improvement in the payments position] as indicating that the battle has been won. We must, at all costs, avoid undue optimism. We cannot afford any premature relaxation of our determination or our efforts. . . . The elimination of the deficit is at once the most serious and the most difficult economic task facing the United States today.[76]

Table 3

U.S. Private Capital, Net and Direct Investment Outflows 1961–67 (billions of $)[78]

	1961	1962	1963	1964	1965	1966	1967
U.S. private capital, net	−4.2	−3.4	−4.5	−6.5	−3.7	−4.2	−5.4
Direct investment	−1.6	−1.7	−2.0	−2.4	−3.4	−3.5	−3.0

The 1965 fourth quarter's data indicated what the administration suspected. Overall outflows of private capital for 1965 were reduced significantly (from $6.4 billion in 1964 to $3.5 billion in 1965), attributable chiefly to the voluntary program and secondarily to the increased domestic demand for capital. Yet these gains were in the short term; they could not be repeated. Direct investment capital outflows in 1965 were almost $1 billion higher than in 1964. All totaled, the fourth quarter's outflow of direct investment capital was $368 million. Thus the long-term impact of the program on direct investment could be expected to be minimal, as indicated in Table 3.

The payments deficit worsened during 1966 and 1967. Measured on a liquidity basis, the 1966 deficit was $1.3 billion, while on an official reserve basis there was a slight surplus of $225 million. In 1967, the liquidity basis deficit was $3.575 billion. Calculated on the official reserve basis, the deficit grew to $3.398 billion. In 1967 the administration again tightened the voluntary corporate guidelines: the ceiling on direct investment outflow plus overseas retained earnings (averaged for the two years, 1966–67) was lowered to 120 percent of the 1962–64 base years (from 135 percent in the 1966 program).[79] A large increase in the deficit occurred in the fourth quarter of 1967, causing the administration to impose a mandatory capital control program on January 1, 1968.[80]

There is a contrast between the results of the bank and corporate voluntary programs. The bank program achieved the Federal Reserve's goals for each of the three years of the capital restraint program. The outflow of short-term capital was successfully restrained; long-term bank loans were substantially reduced, as were "other claims," primarily those of nonbank financial institutions. This resulted in the reduction of the growth rate of U.S. private capital outflow from the peak years of 1963–64 by a small amount in 1966, although not at all in 1967. The growth component of capital outflow lay in the corporate direct investment account. As Table 3 indicates, during the three years of the voluntary program direct investment outflow increased steadily.

Although direct investment growth continued, the overall contributions of the reporting 708 corporations to the U.S. balance of payments did improve, from

$15.1 billion in 1964 to $18.6 billion in 1966. The Treasury Department reported that "Most of the significant growth expected in 1967 can be attributed to continuing improvement in exports and net direct investment transactions." But, the report continued, "participating companies, as a group, were well under the specific direct investment target. They also [are] expected to remain considerably below the tighter 1967 target."[81]

In conclusion, the voluntary program was a short-run success. It reduced short-term outflows and repatriated substantial amounts of short-term funds held abroad. It was a long-term failure, however, since it was not able to reduce the important category of direct investment outflow. Voluntary restraint did not prove an effective means of controlling direct investment outflows.[82]

Between 1965 and 1967 growing business opposition to the voluntary programs focused on the government's attempt to further restrain direct investment and to increase direct investment return flows. As the opposition grew, the new outflow of direct investment increased, as a variety of legal avenues for outflows existed. The government faced the choice of dismantling the voluntary program and paying the consequence of a likely disruption of the international financial system or transforming the voluntary program into a mandatory one.

The experience of the voluntary programs illustrates the complex interests of transnational capital. Capital itself did not develop a unified analysis of the balance of payments and an alternative program until 1966. When developed, this program differed markedly from that of the Johnson and later the Nixon administration. A second aspect of complex interests is illustrated in the vague and diverse proposals by business organizations and representatives of individual firms regarding alternative U.S. politico-military global strategies to significantly reduce the government account deficit. This vagueness suggests that many individuals formulating these proposals understood the dilemma that a rapid reduction of the U.S. global apparatus would have long-term negative consequences for TNBs and TNCs; yet, a failure to reduce the government account deficit would limit their immediate profits and their global competitive position.

The division between state and transnational capital was played out in the context of the politics of international fiscal crisis. This division appeared within transnational capital itself during the first nine months of the voluntary program. By 1966 the majority of corporate and financial opinion viewed state political and military expenditures for global social capital and social expense as too burdensome on business. The unique quality of the global fiscal crisis under a fixed-exchange regime was that there proved to be no alternatives to either capital controls or a major reduction in the government account, short of radically reordering the international monetary system by devaluing the dollar and perhaps establishing a floating rate system. Even had business's proposal to substantially contract the domestic economy been implemented, there was little guarantee that it would have sufficiently promoted exports and reduced imports to eliminate the payments deficit over the long run. In fact, long-term substantial recession would have minimized U.S. exports, especially to the European states which would have been forced to contract their economies. Business–government divisions over politico-military global strategy as a means to reduce the government account deficit were inevitable, given the private appropriation of foreign investment profits under a fixed-exchange rate system. The government account had to remain in deficit; the question was by how much. The capital control program was the state's answer: it would remain in deficit to the degree required by military and political global conditions. Capital would have to sacrifice.

This sacrifice is the heart of the political differences between state and transnational capital over how best to resolve or at least manage the global fiscal crisis. These important divergences between the state and the majority of transnational capital reveal an underlying economic nationalism within international business in the defense of its perceived interests. Although significant benefits accrued to U.S. international business from U.S. civilian and military foreign assistance and the maintenance of troops abroad, this proved to be only one important aspect of transnational capital's several contradictory interests. In terms of the balance of payments, business objected to having to shoulder the costs of financing the deficit. Yet it alone consistently produced dollar reserves adequate to subsidize the state's global activity. Thus, an important source of the state's autonomy from capital lay in its different structural links with the world's monetary system than those of capital.

The voluntary programs began as a weak attempt by the administration to structure markets and to mediate capital's interests through informal corporate-business cooperation. The corporate program failed to reduce the increase of direct investment outflow despite the increased use, and concomitant growth, of Euromarket financing for new corporate investment, especially in Western Europe. In spite of the innovative growth of alternative Euromarket financing sources for U.S. TNCs and TNBs, TNC direct investment grew. When "voluntary" state mediation of capital's interests failed, the mandatory capital control programs achieved in the short run what the voluntary programs could not: the effective structuring of capital's interests from above through state intervention. Yet both programs resulted in long-term strategic failures, for in spite of state attempts to control capital and markets, global financial and market innovation undercut the state's capacity to achieve its ends. Throughout the voluntary program's duration, TNCs increased direct investment in the advanced industrial countries while TNBs expanded their offshore activities. Capital voted with its pocketbook.

5. The Mandatory Capital Control Program, 1968-1971

The payments deficit

In late 1967, after tightening regulations for the 1968 extension of the voluntary capital control program, events convinced the Johnson administration to replace the voluntary program with a mandatory one more restrictive of direct investment. In an immediate sense, the administration was acting in response to the wave of speculation against the dollar brought on by the sterling crisis and eventual devaluation of the British pound on November 17, 1967. This resulted in a large loss of U.S. gold in the last six weeks of the year due to British liquidation of U.S. government agency bonds and other portfolio holdings. The U.S. gold loss also increased the U.S. liquidity deficit. These events, combined with the deteriorating balance of payments for nonmilitary goods of almost $1 billion, simultaneously eroded the traditional U.S. export surplus and increased net capital outflows in the fourth quarter of 1967.[1]

The Treasury Department characterized the problem as follows:

> The British devaluation of sterling has reinforced the urgency of the need to improve the U.S. balance of payments. The British move created uncertainty and unrest in the international monetary system and doubts about the future stability of the dollar . . . in large part because of the persistence of large U.S. deficits.[2]

Measured on an annual basis, the fourth quarter's liquidity deficit was almost $7 billion; for the year 1967, the actual liquidity deficit was about $3.5 billion. Aside from the sterling-related speculative attacks on the dollar, two main factors accounted for the significant growth of the deficit. First, the net outflow of direct and other forms of investment increased in the fourth quarter alone from $500 million to $1 billion, partially as a result of fears generated by the sterling crisis that there would be further capital restrictions. Second, there was a decline in the U.S. trade surplus. Due to the asynchronization of the business cycles in Europe and the United States, the U.S. inflationary boom increased U.S. imports, while the concurrent European and Japanese recessions retarded the growth of U.S.

exports. For the year 1967, the balance of goods and services declined from 1966 by about $304 million.[3] This resulted in a decline of $700 million in the fourth quarter's goods-and-services account. (The decline in the nonmilitary portion of the goods-and-services account was even larger, but was partially offset by military goods transfers within Europe.)

While the immediate reasons for implementing the mandatory programs were the events of late 1967, there was a more fundamental problem: the growth of Vietnam war–related expenditures and other foreign military aid programs was the main long-run factor.

The Vietnam deficit

The impact of Vietnam-related spending on the U.S. payments balance had direct and indirect aspects. Vietnam war spending directly increased the payments deficit an average of about $1.6 billion annually between 1967 and 1969, and slightly more in 1970. (Outside of Vietnam itself, these dollars were held primarily in Japan, Hong Kong, and other Southeast Asian countries and came mostly from expenditures for personnel.) For the same period, the direct costs of the total overseas military account drained an annual average of above $3 billion net in balance of payments terms.[4] Vietnam war–related spending was acknowledged by government and nongovernment sources as a main reason for the 1968 mandatory program. Most observers realized that the U.S. payments deficit was neither caused by the war nor would it disappear after the war's end; but the war was an important factor in the exacerbation of the payments deficit and became a catalyst for capital controls.[5]

The indirect effects of the Vietnam war on the deficit included both the purchase of goods to be used as inputs in U.S. military production and the deterioration in U.S. net exports. The latter resulted from war-stimulated inflation and from the supply bottlenecks in those sectors of production most affected by increased military spending. Leonard Dudley and Peter Passell estimated in the first category a 1967 net payments drain of between $580 million and $1.2 billion, which they assume typical of the years 1965 through 1969. They estimated the war's effect on the U.S. trade position as a net dollar payments loss of between $1.2 and $1.4 billion. The net dollar drain associated with direct Vietnam war expenditures was placed between $3.5 and somewhat over $4.0 billion annually between 1965–1970.[6] It was not until mid-1967 that the Johnson administration instituted measures to restrict the domestic budget deficit and to bring the rising inflationary impact of the Vietnam war under control. The income tax surcharge was not passed until 1968. Thus for three years the war's inflationary impact on the domestic U.S. economy had continued unabated. This was conscious policy on the part of the Johnson administration. David Halberstam describes the Johnson strategy to finance the war in the critical year of 1966:

The [Joint Chiefs of Staff] . . . wanted a wartime footing which included traditional wartime budgetary procedures—invariably meaning higher taxes—they lost that fight in July 1965. . . . Johnson would not give accurate economic projections, would not ask for a necessary tax raise, and would in fact have *his own* military planners be less than candid with *his own* economic planners. . . . The reasons for Johnson's unwillingness to be straightforward about the financing were familiar. He was hoping that the worst would not come true, that it would remain a short war, and he feared that if the true economic cost of the war became visible to the naked eye, he would lose his Great Society programs.[7]

It is likely that the inflationary effects of the war could have been minimized had taxes been increased in 1965 or 1966. By 1967 the damage was done. Johnson's decision to pursue both the war and the Great Society while unsuccessfully demanding a loose Federal Reserve policy in 1965 and 1966, and refusing to increase taxes, provided crucial fuel to the payments deficit after 1967. The war did not limit Johnson's domestic economic plans until 1968, when he simultaneously placed a ceiling on troops committed to Vietnam for political, military, and, for the first time, economic reasons as well.[8] The negative impact of the Southeast Asian war on both the increase of the payments deficit and the decline of the trade surplus prompted transnational capital and the European NATO countries to increasingly question the means of financing the war as well as the U.S. role as world policeman.

The Vietnam war's effects on the balance of payments was felt by Europe in two major ways. First, the deficit pressured the United States to attempt to obtain greater subsidization of its European forces stationed in countries with a payments surplus, especially West Germany. While this had been a longstanding bone of contention between the United States and the NATO allies since the late 1950s, it now became a form of asking the Europeans to partially subsidize the exchange costs of the highly unpopular Vietnam war.[9] President Johnson's 1968 New Year's Day speech called for negotiations between the U.S. and the European surplus countries to find means to finance the added exchange costs of U.S. troops in Europe. The Treasury Department's *Blue Book* made this explicit:

> Ways must be found to neutralize the foreign exchange costs of military expenditures in the common defense. We must find ways to work constructively with our allies on bilateral and possibly multilateral arrangements designed to neutralize the foreign exchange consequences of the location of our military forces and those of our allies. The determination of the share a nation should bear in helping to meet the economic assistance requirements of our community of nations cannot be resolved solely on the basis of domestic resources or budgetary considerations.[10]

A second, more indirect way that the payments deficit affected the relations between the United States and Western Europe (and Japan) was through the export of U.S. inflation to Europe by means of the Eurodollar system. With the announcement of the capital control program on January 1, 1968, Johnson dispatched two high-level officials on a mission to Europe and Asia to explain the new program and to enlist support for it. The result, according to one commentary, was that "the Europeans and other nations will help—but only up to a point." This point would be defined by the United States not pressing "too hard" for trade concessions and accepting that there was little prospect for obtaining greater compensation for U.S. troops stationed in Western Europe or in Japan.[11]

The mandatory program

The controls over capital export were put into operation on New Year's Day by Executive Order No. 11–387, under authority of section 5(b) of the 1917 Trading with the Enemy Act, which enabled the President in time of national emergency to regulate financial transactions in the best interest of the nation. Technically, violation of the controls was a criminal offense. (Although indictment and punishment were extremely unlikely, business leaders grew increasingly distrustful of the administration's war policies.)[12]

Johnson's strategy, like that of previous attempts to control the U.S. deficit, was rooted in the priorities of the Great Society and a Keynesian faith in state capacities. The deficit could be eliminated only through expanding the economy while continuing, and if necessary intensifying, global military commitments, including those in Southeast Asia. Simultaneously, the Bretton Woods system was to be maintained. This necessitated a cooperative approach with Europe and Japan to achieve a stable world monetary system. The payments surplus countries would have responsibility for bringing their surpluses closer to equilibrium, although means for achieving this were neither clearly formulated nor acted upon for fear of disrupting NATO and possibly "deGaulleizing" Europe.[13] With the exception of the anti-inflationary income tax surcharge, the strategy continued the "do everything" philosophy of the earlier years of the Johnson administration. Treasury Secretary Fowler reemphasized this in early 1968:

> Depressing the American economy was an unacceptable solution to our imbalance of payments. . . . The United States must seek a solution to the payments imbalance through the expansion of the world economy rather than through the severe contraction of its own and consequently the world economy.[14]

The mandatory capital control program aimed to reduce the net U.S. capital outflow without inhibiting the growth of U.S. direct investment. The difference was to be made up by TNC reliance on foreign capital and especially Eurocurrency markets. Consequently, much of the mandatory capital control controversy involved debates about the significance of shifting the locus of direct investment financing. This often technical debate was part of the broad political and economic questioning of government intervention in the internal affairs of corporations and financial institutions (as well as about the impact of off-shore Eurocurrency financing on the U.S. balance of payments). In spite of the capital controls, the Johnson administration made clear its intentions toward TNCs: "The U.S. government seeks in countless ways to enlarge the freedom of opportunity for multinational corporations operating overseas."[15] The program's aim was to balance the growth of net capital export financed direct investment against the stability of the dollar, rather than to restrict the growth of direct investment as such. The Treasury Department's *Blue Book* stated that "the United States clearly must moderate the outflows of private capital, weighing carefully the eventual yield such outflows will bring [given] their immediate foreign exchange costs."[16]

The balance of payments program seemingly attacked the deficit problem on a number of fronts. Most immediately, it severely restricted U.S. capital outflows to all countries, especially to Western Europe, and simultaneously increased repatriated profits from past direct investment. It tightened the voluntary bank lending program and instituted standby authority to make the program mandatory if necessary. The program aimed at reducing the payments deficit by saving $1 billion in direct investment outflows and $500 million in bank lending restraint. The program also hoped to save an additional $500 million through restricting "nonessential" travel by U.S. citizens outside the Western hemisphere. (This feature of the program was extremely unpopular and after some months was dropped by the administration.) A further attempt was made to trim government overseas expenditures by $500 million, mainly through reducing the exchange costs of U.S. troops in Europe. (This met with failure as well, since the European NATO states were unwilling to absorb the greater exchange costs for U.S. forces. Some minor agreements were reached to finance the U.S. deficits temporarily, as had been done in the past, e.g., prepayment on military sales contracts and purchase of long-term Treasury bonds by NATO countries.)[17] Since few reductions in the travel or governmental expenditures accounts actually occurred, the immediate burden of the balance of payments program fell entirely upon TNCs and TNBs.

In addition to these immediate measures, three more long-term strategies were proposed. (In fact, all three had been proposed since 1960.) First, Johnson called for various programs to promote exports, such as increased government financing and more effective overseas insurance. Although later enacted by Congress, these had only a marginal impact. Second, Johnson promised to act on longstanding business proposals to begin negotiations with the surplus countries on lowering the nontariff barriers to trade. This was especially aimed at European border taxes on goods and at the value-added tax imposed by Germany and other countries. From these negotiations Johnson hoped to save an additional $500 million in the payments account. Third, Johnson proposed to increase foreign travel in the United States.[18] In all these proposals, the strategy of the administration was traditional. In the words of the Treasury Department's *Blue Book*: "The keystone of a sound international financial position for the United States and the dollar is a substantial trade surplus." Yet only in mid-1967 did the Johnson administration propose the income tax surcharge to slow the massive inflow of imports by decreasing effective aggregate demand, thereby raising the U.S. trade surplus. But the surcharge was too little, too late, and it was viewed as an unpopular war tax.[19] In sum, as in the past, all these long-term measures failed to gain momentum or have an impact on the payments deficit. Consequently, the single operational measure of the 1968 program was to be the capital controls.

Limits on direct investment

The mandatory program established the Office of Foreign Direct Investment (OFDI) as a permanent bureaucratic entity under the auspices of the Department of Commerce. (This indicated that although it had been announced as a "temporary" program, the new capital controls were to be only as temporary as the U.S. payments deficit.) Direct investment was defined to include net capital outflows from the United States plus earnings retained by U.S. foreign incorporated subsidiaries of U.S. corporations, less those capital transfers made with the proceeds of long- or short-term borrowings of the direct investor abroad. Thus, quotas on each corporate entity required remittal of a minimum proportion of overseas earnings, while simultaneously enabling a subsidiary to expand through the use of foreign borrowing, expanded depreciation allowances, and other technical means of financing capital expenses.[20]

The OFDI program divided the world into three areas or "schedules," "in order that the impact of the restrictions would be most severe on certain countries in Western Europe and least severe on the less developed countries." Schedule A countries included the underdeveloped nations; Schedule B covered Ireland, Australia, Japan, the United Kingdom, Spain, New Zealand, and Canada (the latter was shortly exempted from all the regulations). Schedule C included all the developed countries of Western Europe and South Africa. For Schedule A countries the base "historical allowable" for direct investment was set at 110 percent of the annual average in the base period, which was 1965–67. Since the base years of 1965–67 had been the first two years of the voluntary program, the new schedule consequently restricted those corporations that had complied most fully. Schedule B countries' allowable was 65 percent of the base period, which permitted them to maintain their traditional reliance on U.S. capital exports deemed "essential for their economic growth and financial stability." Schedule C countries were prohibited from any net transfers of capital from the United States for direct investment purposes.[21] The OFDI program affected all U.S. direct investors above $100,000 per year, requiring about 3,400 firms to submit quarterly reports. Of these 3,400 corporations, the 700 largest accounted for approximately 90 percent of all direct investment between 1965 and 1967. The program required repatriation of short-term assets to the historical base period level, thereby admitting that the voluntary program had been inadequate.[22]

During OFDI's first year there were few reforms in the original regulations. There was a means of obtaining relief from the regulations through a specific authorization process. Some 1,300 authorizations were requested during 1968; the overwhelming majority were granted in some form.[23] Under the revised program announced in June 1969, three additional areas of liberalization were granted. First, the minimum allowable was raised from $200,000 to $1 million. This exempted 2,600 of the almost 3,400 investors from quarterly reporting, thus reducing the paperwork for smaller firms and for the OFDI. Second, direct investors were offered an alternate basis for calculating earnings which would permit them to ignore the base period 1965–67. This allowed firms with low base-period investments to increase their current net direct investment outflows. Third, the liberalizations also allowed those firms still using the base-period method some margin to shift allowances within Schedule A to Schedule B or C, and from Schedule B to Schedule C. This resulted in some increase in net investment outflows to the more advanced countries.[24] In 1970 the OFDI regulations were again relaxed, increasing the minimal allowance from $1 million to $5 million, providing that the additional $4 million be used in a Schedule A ("less-developed") country. Other liberalizations aided smaller or rapidly growing firms in Schedule C countries as well as firms involved in exploration for natural resources.[25] The impact of liberalization was felt by small and growing firms which had come late to direct investment; there was minimal impact on the largest 700 TNCs subject to OFDI regulations, which accounted for over 85 percent of the total direct investment. Hence these TNCs criticized the liberalizations as token gestures.[26]

The voluntary foreign credit restraint program

The 1968 balance of payments program continued the voluntary foreign credit restraint (VFCR) for banks and nonbank financial institutions, administered by the Federal Reserve, instituting new restrictions and tightening old ones. Banks, for instance, were to reduce lending to nonresidents from 109 percent to 103 percent of the 1964 base period. The new program focused more sharply on Western Europe, requesting banks to reduce outstanding short-term loans by 40 percent during 1968 and to refrain completely from renewing longer-term loans. The goal was $500 million savings in balance of payments: $400 million by banks and $100 million by other financial institutions. The new VFCR program proved to be effective in part because it was relatively simple to administer and in part because the 1969 domestic recession would tighten credit conditions. U.S. banks became net borrowers from Eurodollar sources rather than lenders to Europe.[27] Between 1968 and 1971 the VFCR achieved its stated objectives: the reduction of bank loans to "normal" levels and the maintenance of short-term credits to foreign institutions at limits previously established to meet the requirements of "necessary balances."[28] Although not popular with financial institutions and often publicly attacked, the VFCR program did not cause as much controversy as did the restrictions on direct investment. This chapter, then, will focus primarily on the OFDI program.

Johnson and Nixon: The evolution of the OFDI program, 1968-71

Candidate Nixon made the OFDI control program, announced, as it was, in a presidential election year, a significant focus during the 1968 presidential campaign, especially among business circles. During the campaign Nixon accepted the policy recommendation of his advisor on balance of payments, Gottfried Haberler, a conservative Harvard economist and expert on international finance, to put an "end to the self-defeating controls" on foreign investment "at the earliest possible time." While this was no clear timetable, the business community interpreted this to mean that Nixon would immediately begin to phase out the controls once in office. Statements by Haberler widely publicized in the business press upon Nixon's election confirmed this image of an administration committed to removing the controls.[29]

Once elected, however, Nixon assembled his Council of Economic Advisers and immediately adopted the strategy of his predecessor: the controls were to be maintained with only minimal revisions. This was done in spite of business pressure to set a timetable for the controls' abolition, Nixon's own campaign promises, and the laissez-faire dispositions of Nixon's closest economic advisors—George Schultz, Herbert Stein, and William Simon.[30]

Ultimately, the difference between the Johnson and Nixon administrations centered on underlying strategy for dealing with the entire balance of payments deficit, rather than on the control programs themselves. Johnson and his advisors, influenced by the 1963 Brookings study, had maintained the strategy passed down from Eisenhower to Kennedy: the dollar could be stabilized and its gold value maintained, and the deficit could be ended through an increased trade surplus and an expanding economy. Nixon's strategy was one of benign neglect: no serious effort would be made to correct the fundamental problems of the dollar, yet no dollar devaluation would be implemented. Benign neglect aimed to force other currencies to realign themselves upward against the dollar and to adjust to each other's levels, rather than devalue the dollar.[31] Benign neglect, a new form of official optimism, necessitated that the capital controls remain in effect.

The justifications given for the OFDI and VFCR programs by the Johnson and Nixon administrations were remarkably similar, as indicated in statements by Johnson's and Nixon's respective appointees as Director of the OFDI, Charles E. Fiero and Don C. Cadle. Evaluating the first year of the OFDI, Fiero responded to the criticisms from TNCs and TNBs. He defended the program against the charges that it had slowed the growth of U.S. overseas investment and adversely affected U.S. exports. He justified the program's channeling of direct investment expansion into foreign capital markets on the basis that the program was short-term and would allow for "more fundamental improvements in our balance of payments position." In opposition to the corporate consensus, he concluded that "there is no certainty that current foreign borrowings are entirely at the expense of future gains." By the end of 1968 there was near-unanimous corporate and financial agreement that either controls should be abolished or a specific timetable should be set for their phase-out. The proposed alternative to deal with the deficit was a restrictive monetary and fiscal policy mix to halt inflation by promoting a managed recession. Fiero argued exactly the contrary:

> Domestic economic policy . . . cannot be constrained by tight credit and high interest rates for balance of payments purposes should conditions at home call for relaxation. Without controls, however, such a relaxation presents the risk of substantially larger capital outflows.[32]

The position of both administrations was that the control could and should be dismantled only "as soon as" payments conditions would permit. The Nixon strategy was expressed by Don C. Cadle, new Director of the OFDI, in a candid statement before the National Industrial Conference Board shortly after assuming office:

> The Administration is dedicated to phasing out capital controls as soon as possible. Nevertheless, the small 1968 balance of payments surplus is not indicative of fundamental payments equilibrium sufficient to justify immediate termination of the Program.
>
> Though we in OFDI share the Administration's commitment, and doubtless your own desire, to terminate direct investment controls at the earliest date feasible, that date would not now appear to be in the immediate future. Therefore, "living" with the program remains very much a matter of current importance.[33]

In April 1969 the Subcommittee on Foreign Economic Policy of the House Foreign Affairs Committee held widely publicized hearings on Concurrent Resolutions 85 and 86, calling for the termination of foreign direct investment controls "at the earliest possible date" and labeling them an "unwise and harmful economic policy." The resolutions stated that the "short term has already expired"; that the temporary controls had served their purpose and would be counterproductive were they to be maintained in effect.[34] The Nixon administration, in office only three months, opposed the resolutions. Cadle, the primary administration representative at the hearings, responded to the criticism in the same manner as had the Johnson administration. "To dismantle capital controls at once," he argued, "in the face of a possibly substantial balance of payments deficit in 1969 could well shake confidence in our currency." He continued:

> There have been requests for a definite schedule according to which the foreign direct investment program would be phased out. The difficulty in setting such a schedule is the difficulty inherent in predicting the speed with which fundamental improvements can be made in our balance of payments.[35]

Responding specifically to corporate criticism, Cadle maintained that "the available evidence does indicate that the alleged adverse effects of the program to date are unfounded or are probably not as substantial as alleged [by most business groups and representatives]." He warned that the risks of "hasty" removal of the controls were high, in spite of the tightened domestic credit conditions in early 1969 which would limit capital outflow if the controls were lifted in any case:

> President Nixon has already taken the first step in phasing out capital controls [that is, "liberalizing" them]. Yet, prudence dictates that the dismantling process be carefully measured and conducted in conjunction with the success of measures to cool the domestic economy and to improve other balance of payments accounts.[36]

Thus, the Nixon administration's position was essentially similar to Johnson's during the voluntary program and the initiation of the mandatory program. The OFDI's future was tied to a fundamental improvement in the payments situation. The program was temporary, but without a timetable. When questioned by Democratic representative John Tunney of California, co-sponsor of Resolutions 85 and 86, as to how temporary was "temporary," Cadle responded:

> With regard to how temporary is "temporary," I cannot really answer that question. To be perfectly frank . . . this is what gives us pause with regard to the concurrent resolutions. We are not certain what they mean with regard to how soon is "soon."[37]

Yet fundamental improvement in the payments situation proved to be impossible given the fixed dollar-gold exchange rate system and domestic political-economic priorities, specifically the increasing exchange costs of the Vietnam war. Only after two successive devaluations of the dollar, in 1971 and 1973, were the controls to be phased out. Eliminating the controls prior to the global currencies' revaluation would have led directly to a world monetary crisis, as waves of dollars would have flooded the European surplus countries. No administration wanted to deliberately court an event with such risky international consequences. The benign neglect strategy skirted the risk of courting a currency crisis which would have required dollar devaluation rather than foreign revaluation. In theory the upward revaluation by surplus countries relative to the dollar could maintain dollar stability and the fixed dollar-gold exchange.

Opposition to the controls: An alternative strategy

Against the consistent maintenance of the capital controls by the Johnson and Nixon administrations, firm opposition developed among TNCs and TNBs. It might be expected that corporate opposition to the controls, which had grown since 1966, would take the form of initial organization in 1968 against the OFDI, as it had in 1962 against the Revenue Act. This, however, did not occur. Initial corporate and financial reaction to the mandatory program was in fact similar to its first reaction to the voluntary program in 1965: early skeptical cooperation, rather quickly transformed into articulated opposition. The absence of initial opposition was noted by observers at the time. *The Wall Street Journal*, for instance, commented that business had been "muted and cautious" in its opposition, relying instead on the objections from both liberal and conservative economists. It editorialized:

> As for the business community's seeming reluctance to speak up so far [January 1968], we suppose that is the more or less traditional stance. In the current case, though, the traditional could well be violated, on the grounds that the planners in Washington are playing dangerous games with the economy and simultaneously revealing more clearly than ever their authoritarian political basis. . . . It's not time for anyone who cares about his country to keep quiet.[38]

Writing in *The Wall Street Journal* against the controls, John Kenneth Galbraith entitled a lead article "Plea to Business: Make Yourself Heard." Galbraith worried that the industrial and financial community would not realize or be able to act in its own interest to stop the OFDI program. "It is the myth," he argued, "that this interest is always in view and both rationally and powerfully pursued."

> What is often considered conservatism in the business and financial community is more often cowardice in asserting clear and even overriding interest.
> Now it can no longer be doubted that the American business and financial community faces a disaster of the most compelling proportions. The fruits of great and strenuous private efforts and of the most carefully conceived public policy extending over the last several decades are about to be extinguished.[39]

Thus, the most consistent and early opposition of the OFDI came from academic economists and from the business press, especially *The Wall Street Journal*, which viewed the controls as part of the growing "authoritarian statist attitude" in the United States. To its dismay, the business community was not speaking up in its own self-interest.[40] The *Journal* and other business media explicitly viewed themselves as surrogate representatives for the major corporations and corporate policy groups which chose to remain silent during the first months of the OFDI program.[41]

The restrained initial corporate and financial opposition may be explained by two main factors. First, after 1966 there was a general consensus by transnational capital that the dollar crisis was real and that something had to be done, although the government's policy was not to its liking. Under tremendous government pressure, capital accepted direct investment expansion through foreign financing by using the Eurodollar escape valve.[42] Second, initial business acceptance may be accounted for by the very structure of the OFDI. Staffed by bankers, corporate lawyers, and economists, the Office intended to be sensitive to the problems of individual firms by granting numerous exemptions from specific regulations. While few executives wished to be associated with the program the first reaction of many was that the mandatory program would not change their firm's investment plans for that year. Commented a Du Pont official: "We aren't at all shattered by President Johnson's decision . . . we have been operating our own voluntary balance of payments program, restricting our dollar outflow."[43]

Corporate executives concerned with their ability to carry on day-to-day operations as usual developed a "go along to get along" attitude in order to benefit from OFDI largess. (Such attitudes, however, were criticized by many businessmen.[44]) Commented *Business Abroad* in early February 1968: "The way the program will be administered is vitally important since . . . the thrust of the written regulations was to rule everything out and then permit certain transactions by granting exemptions and authorizations."[45] Thus the OFDI bureaucracy came to play a role for U.S. TNCs similar to the one that the Federal Reserve had been playing since 1965 for TNBs. The corporate criticism of the program that was made was shouldered by corporate policy and research organizations, rather than by individual corporate executives as in the past. Many attributed this to the desire not to be singled out for hostile action by the OFDI.[46] There is no evidence that patriotism played a role in muting corporate and financial criticism of the controls. Throughout the Vietnam war era, significant business criticism of government military policies continued unabated, as did criticism of the government's macroeconomic and payments policies.

With the unexpected announcement of the mandatory program on New Year's Day, 1968, it was at first unclear what the regulations would mean and how individual corporations were expected to comply. The President's speech, summarized *The Wall Street Journal*, "provoked criticism from bankers but drew more guarded reactions from top industrialists." Commented William F. Buckley, chief economist and vice-president of Chase Manhattan Bank, the controls "may help in the short run, but they don't fully come to grips with the heart of the problem." The American Bankers Association had "deep misgivings about resort to even temporary direct control to reduce international payments deficit[s]." The ABA, however, agreed to cooperate with the program.[47] An indicator of eventual corporate and banking reaction to the program came three days after its announcement when the Balance of Payments Advisory Committee, formed during the voluntary program and composed of corporate and financial leaders, publicly opposed the OFDI program in particular and the balance of payments program in general. Although the committee did not resign, for fear of increasing speculation against the dollar, a special meeting of the committee concluded that the "Administration's adoption of the program over the group's objections placed them, individually, in an untenable situation." The committee removed itself by "redesignating" its work and renaming itself to extricate its members "as gracefully as possible from further involvement with the Administration's balance of payments activities."[48] Underlying the largely negative reception by large firms was a basic distrust of government policies and especially its balance of payments policies. A survey of 300 of the leading corporate executives published in February 1968 indicated that the great majority were not only disturbed by the U.S. payments balance, but that "in a rare 100 percent agreement, they blame the government's policies relating to foreign and military spending, domestic expenditures and export programs for the crisis." J. Ward Keener, chairman of General Electric, and member of the now-transformed Advisory Committee on Foreign Direct Investment (formerly the Balance of Payments Advisory Committee) articulated the sentiment: "The government's latest move to "cure" our balance of payments deficit is still another example of using band-aids to treat a mortally wounded man." Typically, Keener placed the blame for the deficit on military and foreign aid spending. Keener concluded with reference to the control programs:

> In placing mandatory controls over private foreign investments—which have consistently developed surpluses—the government is killing the goose that lays the golden eggs and permanently weakening the American industrial structure.
>
> I am convinced that we cannot afford the cost of maintaining such large military forces, families and military services abroad, especially in Western Europe.[49]

Similar sentiments were expressed in relation to Johnson's commitment to the Vietnam war by some pragmatic corporate doves. The president of Leeds and Northrup Co. commented: "Our foreign policy must be much more realistic than it has been in the past. We need to consider whether or not the United States can continue to fight foreign wars of this [Vietnam] nature, regardless of our attitude toward the moral issues."[50] Important representatives of capital were beginning to view the Vietnam war itself as an important cause of the deficit. Reactions to the control program were also closely tied to a general view of the importance of government overseas expenses. Concluded the president of Rexall Drug and Chemical Company: "End foreign aid, buy American and end the Vietnam war."[51]

Walter B. Wriston, president of the First National City Bank of New York (later Citibank), stated that the balance of payments program amounted to exchange controls which would never work effectively. The February issue of the bank's *Monthly Economic Letter* refrained from calling for ending the controls. (It would come to adopt that position in December 1968). It pointed out that the program could work "if . . . coupled with firm and adequate monetary and fiscal action and wage self-discipline." Its main fear was that the capital controls would be the prelude to the "spread of direct controls over international trade and investment." In the growing international climate of protectionism, the U.S. capital controls added to that spirit: "International economic liberalism is on the defensive."[52] Views parallel to Wriston's were expressed during early 1968 by important business organizations and representatives. *Business Abroad* summarized the common theme: "The Action Program may produce good numbers, but it won't solve our payments problem. Unless accompanied by an effective anti-inflationary policy at home, it will only make the problem worse."[53]

The U.S. Council of the International Chamber of Commerce agreed that the capital control program was "not directed toward the root cause of the deficits," because still remaining to be accomplished were a reduction in government spending and a tightening of domestic monetary policy. In congressional testimony, the president of the National Foreign Trade Council argued similarly: "The controls which have been placed on the direct investor can only serve to make it more difficult for business to make a positive contribution to our admittedly critical balance of payments situation." Yet neither organization called directly for an end to the OFDI program. In a like vein, at a meeting of the National Industrial Conference Board, a speaker warned assembled corporate leaders: "Efforts to balance our national accounts by reducing American private investment, will, if continued for long, weaken the growth of foreign earnings on investment. We are simply buying time—and trouble—on our current course."[54]

The Research and Policy Committee of the Committee for Economic Development issued a statement highly critical of the Johnson administration's financing of the Vietnam war. The report viewed the capital controls as a wartime measure, the result of an economy mismanaged since 1965. It suggested that the controls were a poor substitute for responsible fiscal, monetary, and tax policies. Yet the CED viewed the controls as necessary. The restoration of free capital movements was conditioned upon minimizing the foreign exchange costs of the war.[55] The CED's critique of the control programs was more moderate than that of any other representative of large capital, including those of many individuals on the CED's Research and Policy Committee.[56]

Most business leaders viewed the mandatory program as an evil with which they must live, as they had viewed the voluntary program before it. They stressed its temporary and emergency character, suggesting that by the end of 1968 it should be abolished. However, this position was not accepted by all representatives of large capital. In February 1968 the Machinery and Allied Products Institute (MAPI) and the president of ARMCO Steel Company took exception to the "necessary evil" view. MAPI argued that the OFDI program was protectionism in reverse:

> It is an attack on the ability of American industry to maintain and improve its position in international trade. It is a give-away to the competition. As for Europe, it is almost tantamount to a forced retrenchment of American industry's position in Europe.[57]

MAPI recommended "a prompt return to a voluntary system affecting direct investment abroad," in spite of "certain misgivings about even a voluntary system." (This was to be the most common alternative to the OFDI program mentioned by corporate leaders by late 1968.[58]) It was necessary to end the OFDI program because, according to a MAPI statement:

> In all candor, we have no confidence that government has a determination to end this program of mandatory controls at the earliest possible date. . . . The judgment made here—which we believe to be widely shared in the business community, although not widely articulated—is underlined and strengthened by a conviction that there is no strong will to use this control program on a very short-term basis, and to replace it at a very early date with something that makes more sense from a long-range standpoint.[59]

Corporate opposition becomes public

It was just after the November 1968 presidential election that important sectors of capital went public in their opposition to capital controls, pinning their hopes on President-elect Nixon's promise to phase out the program. The First National City Bank of New York called in December 1968 for immediate dismantling of the program. Speaking for the business community as a whole (which it declared had "accepted the controls as a crash program on the strength of Administration assurances that they would be temporary"), the bank called for the "self-defeating controls" to be lifted. Controls tend to proliferate, the bank declared, "far beyond the confines delineated at the time they were imposed."

> They have proved costly to the U.S. economy; abroad they have created ill-will towards the United States; they are contrary to all the United States has been striving for in freeing trade and payments between countries; and they are contrary to the world's long-run interest in having scarce capital move to places where it can be used most productively.[60]

During the first months of 1969, opposition to the OFDI and other capital controls mounted, culminating during two congressional hearings held by the Joint Economic Committee and the House Committee on Foreign Affairs. G. A. Costanzo, Executive Vice-President of the First National City Bank of New York, recommended terminating all controls in 1969 rather than waiting until the "underlying imbalance is corrected." He pointed out that the financial innovation of the Eurodollar market undermined the controls' impact on the overall U.S. balance of payments by increasing "the demand for dollars abroad for short-term borrowing and for capital investment." He continued:

> This demand has been met by answering increases in the supply of dollars in the Eurodollar and Eurocapital markets. The additional dollars have come in part from the United States . . . there have been outflows of funds which would not have occurred if the additional demands for dollars abroad had not been artificially created by our own controls.[61]

Costanzo's alternative was simple: tight fiscal and monetary policy ("above all") should solve the payments problem as well as halt domestic inflation.

During testimony before the House Foreign Affairs Committee, a dozen representatives of the largest TNCs and TNBs called for immediate termination of all the capital control programs: the IET, VFCR, and OFDI. This was in striking contrast to the Nixon administration's strenuous argument for maintaining the controls. The representatives of large capital responded with their usual advice: rely on tight fiscal and monetary policy.[62] Despite the unanimous support among TNCs and TNBs for eliminating the controls, there was no agreement as to how long the phase-out process should take. Some argued for immediate elimination, suggesting that there would be minimal adverse effect on capital outflow due to the then-prevailing high interest rates. Others argued more cautiously that the phase-out should occur throughout 1969 and into 1970. All agreed, however, that an absolute timetable should be established.

Throughout 1969 capital pressured for termination of the controls. In April the National Industrial Conference Board held a financial conference during which all the speakers opposed continuation.[63] The Conference Board *Record* published as a lead article the text of a speech by John J. Powers, Jr. which was highly critical not only of the present program but also of the "process of policy making" which had led to the program's beginning in 1961.[64] In November the National Foreign Trade Council called for an end, since "such controls can no longer be justified as temporary restraints to meet an immediate balance of payments emergency."[65] Corporate opposition to the controls, although ineffectual, would continue until the devaluation of the dollar in August 1971. It became evident after mid-1969 that the Nixon administration was determined to continue the controls in spite of its campaign promises and over the continued objections of all sectors of business. Increasingly, business would return to the problem as "living with" the controls. That business was able to do so despite its strong objections was a result of its continuing ability to maintain overseas investment through foreign borrowing.[66]

The basis of transnational capital's criticism of both the Johnson and Nixon administrations' balance of payments strategy was its objections to loose monetary and deficit fiscal policy and to elements of foreign policy which it thought too expensive—aspects of NATO and the financing and scale of the Vietnam war. While the divergence between business and the administrations over these issues was significant, it is noteworthy that neither individual TNCs and TNBs nor various business policy organizations lobbied for sweeping changes in particular international monetary policies—policies then under active debate and continuous review. A general silence pervaded with regard to the Bretton Woods system, the changes in currency exchange rates, going off gold, and the policy of "benign neglect." Rather, a spectrum of more limited TNC and TNB policy criticisms and alternatives emerged, from the moderate CED to the more severe IEPA, under the Johnson administration in 1968 and the Nixon administration in 1969. In spite of these criticisms, neither the Johnson nor Nixon administrations applied severe restrictions to contract aggregate demand and slow economic growth. This reluctance to employ classical solutions to persistent payments imbalances as advocated by transnational capital was rooted in the political priorities necessitating economic growth and the Keynesian faith in its achievement.[67]

Thus both the Johnson and Nixon administrations were hesitant to apply monetary and especially fiscal policies which would significantly contract aggregate demand. This unwillingness was the outstanding point of conflict between the state and transnational capital.

In 1968 the CED recommended a moderate tightening of monetary policy, increased taxes (in addition to the 10 percent income tax surcharge), and a reduced federal budget. Of all TNC and TNB organizations, the CED position came closest to those of the Johnson and Nixon administrations. The CED proposals, however, were sufficiently more moderate than those of other sections of corporate and financial capital to indicate that the CED did not reflect business opinion as a whole.[68] The ABA argued more forcefully than the CED that reduction in aggregate demand, left unspecified, was necessary for the balance of payments. (The CED restricted itself to a critique of inflation, which it attributed solely to the financing of the Vietnam war.) The ABA suggested that U.S. "efforts to adjust her economy so that deficits no longer occur have not involved material changes in aggregate demand." The ABA did not wish to trigger depression, but rather "to slow the rate of growth of the [U.S.] economy relative to the rates of growth in principal trading partners."[69] It proposed the classical remedy:

There are obvious costs from the use of general instruments in terms of some increase in unemployment, but the effects are not catastrophic and, except in the case of the harshest combination of policies, the effects are well within recent historical range.[70]

Sentiments similar to these were reflected in a 1969 editorial in *The Wall Street Journal*. It called for a "deep recession," if necessary, to counteract the payments deficit and inflation and criticized the Nixon administration for not directly confronting these two interrelated problems.[71]

A second area of division between the state and transnational capital concerned the costs of empire. Some of the criticism in this area by TNBs and TNCs focused on the efficiency of U.S. military and foreign aid and U.S. troops stationed abroad. This criticism was not controversial since it recommended only cost-saving actions. The second, highly controversial, aspect concerned overall strategy. The concern of many corporate executives and some policy groups, in the words of N. R. Danielian of the IEPA, was how to maintain existing levels of foreign and overseas military expenditures given that they were seen by the government as "irreducible." The fear was that the state's logic would mean the private sector "must be sacrificed," if only temporarily.

> One might even agree to this view, as a national necessity. But what worries me is how we are going to maintain these programs, over the long pull, if we undercut our earning power in the private sector.
>
> . . . It goes to the very heart of the ability of the United States to maintain its power position in the world. [Like Great Britain's, our] difficulties are not due simply to lack of competitiveness in international commodity markets. Her difficulties are due, on the one hand, to loss of investment income, and on the other, to government expenditures abroad beyond her earning power. If we are not careful and balanced in our military and economic policies in the next decade, we may find ourselves in a similar situation.[72]

The IEPA warned that a withdrawal of private sector investment or a slowing down of the rate of its expansion would be the long-term result of maintaining the present apparatus of world empire. Since this was unacceptable, it was necessary to redefine the NATO alliance and the alliance with Japan, particularly the funding of U.S. troops abroad. For the IEPA, the issue was not financial but political: how to share the cost "in such a way as to eliminate the impact on the U.S. balance of payments." It concluded:

> If our allies in Europe still refuse to go along with equitable sharing of these costs, then we should be prepared to reduce these expenditures unilaterally. It is not likely that either the Soviets or the NATO countries will even agree to this or make it easy for us if we make the solution conditional upon their agreement and reciprocity.[73]

Similar warnings came from the MAPI, which called for realistic goals in foreign policy in order "to avoid sapping the strength of the private sector in the pursuit of short-term goals to the point where there will ultimately be no alternative to a sharp, involuntary reduction in international commitments to the detriment of the country."[74]

General criticism of foreign political and economic policy was not restricted to the economic nationalist position within TNCs and TNBs. The American Bankers Association, for instance, questioned both the financing of U.S. troops in Europe and the very necessity of those "large numbers of troops."[75] The ABA position was similar to the IEPA's in its assessment that

> the cost in withdrawal of private interest abroad threatens to undermine the progress to be obtained by continuing present military and aid strategy. Additionally, failure to show the Government's willingness to make major policy changes casts doubt on all parts of the balance of payments program and the dollar itself. *In such circumstances, it may be recommended that some parts of our present Government programs abroad including military forces be reduced consistent with our obligations to our allies.*[76]

The criticisms by transnational capital frequently focused on U.S. financial relations with its allies. Senator Jacob Javits, always a conscientious spokesman for large and especially financial capital, criticized the costs of U.S. troops in NATO countries in 1971:

> Our government, in my judgment both administrations, has been much too short on this issue. They have hardly been indignant at all. Instead they have engaged in high-level fancy negotiations in which everybody was so charming to everybody else that nobody knew what it was all about.[77]

In short, moderate corporate policy organizations and economic nationalists alike made serious criticisms of foreign policy related to the payments crisis and capital control programs. Added to the disagreements between state and capital over fiscal and monetary policy, some of the most central issues of the late 1960s and early 1970s caused further division. Aspects of this were embodied in the 1971 report of a blue-ribbon commission to the President, the Williams Commission (named for its chair, Albert L. Williams, Chairman of the Finance Committee of IBM). In its report, *United States International Economic Policy in an Interdependent World*, the commission called for a "new realism" to confront the economic problems which had developed from "the overseas responsibilities the United States has assumed as the major power."[78] The call for a new realism, a greater emphasis on economic nationalism, would be reflected in the protectionism of Nixon's 1971 New Economic Policy. Such realism would come to be the theme of the 1970s. The capital controls reflected a realism of a different sort: a realization by the state that it could not simultaneously pursue the maintenance of empire, unlimited global expansion of TNCs and TNBs, and Keynesian policies at home. Even if Keynesianism were to be minimized or completely eliminated as the guiding philosophy of domestic economic policy, the apparatus of empire would still conflict with the free movement of capital under circumstances of slow- or no-growth economies in the advanced industrial states.

Conclusions

The mandatory capital control program continued and strengthened state intervention in markets, especially financial markets. One result was the increased importance of what became informally known in business circles as the "Eurodollar escape valve." This was partly purposeful state policy, as had been Treasury Secretary C. Douglas Dillon's 1963 attempt to stimulate European financial markets. In 1968 the purpose was to use the Eurodollar market to finance a significant proportion of U.S. global direct investment, which otherwise would have been financed directly from U.S. capital markets and from the domestic resources of U.S. TNCs, thereby worsening the payments deficit. The Eurodollar escape valve, by allowing an alternate source for financing foreign investment, lightened pressures to dismantle the capital controls.

The Eurodollar escape valve was not without high cost, however. U.S. policy contributed to growth of the innovative Eurocurrency system. The IET had promoted the internationalization of commercial and investment banks. The mandatory controls now forced U.S. TNCs to internationalize their financial sources as well. In these ways, state intervention was stimulating market innovation. As TNBs and TNCs became more dependent on new financial markets, their interests were transformed. Increasingly they had a direct stake in the internationalization of finance: this was, ironically, in reaction to restrictive policies by the United States and other states to protect their "national interest." The short-run effect of the Eurodollar escape valve was to mute, but certainly not silence corporate and financial opposition to mandatory control programs. The long-run effect, to be discussed in greater detail in the following chapter, was twofold. First, the Eurodollar escape valve promoted a large foreign dollar overhang—the foreign dollar debt owed to international financial institutions by U.S. TNCs. Second, the innovation made Eurocurrency markets larger and more efficient, allowing for more effective speculation against the dollar in the foreign exchange markets. Thus the controls were admittedly a tactical success, permitting alternate sources of financing and muting opposition to politically tolerable ranges, while promoting alternative routes for corporate expansion. The controls were, however, a strategic failure: this was evident in the speculative currency crises of 1967, 1969, and 1970, and in the ultimate collapse of the Bretton Woods system in 1971. By promoting the use of the Eurocurrency escape valve, U.S. state intervention buttressed financial innovation which in the long run contributed to the collapse of the dollar–gold exchange standard.

The divisions between international capital and the Johnson and Nixon administrations over the mandatory program continued the debate over the voluntary program. As with the voluntary program, business opposition focused on three issues. First, sustained criticism was made of existing government fiscal and monetary policies, with capital arguing instead for consistent tight money, higher interest rates, and budget surpluses. Second, capital called for a reduction in the external costs of the U.S. apparatus of empire, especially in foreign aid and foreign military assistance. Increasingly, business opposition to the Vietnam war became linked to the payments deficit as both symbol and proximate cause of U.S. global overextension. Third, an increasingly anti-European, anti-internationalist economic nationalism appeared among international business organizations, expressed in journals and statements. In addition to these large areas of divisions, the introduction of mandatory capital controls reintroduced debates over the specific impact of the voluntary and mandatory programs on the pattern of U.S. direct investment growth—debates similar to those in the early 1960s over the 1962 Revenue Act's original proposal to eliminate foreign tax credits. The significance of these differences is that the majority of business opinion crystallized around the conclusion that domestically, Keynesianism was not working, and that internationally the costs of U.S. hegemony were too high. Between 1968 and 1971 the domestic and international threads of the Keynesian coalition became unraveled. In this historical period, the widespread advocacy among TNC and TNB executives of state-initiated recession to assist with balance of payments is noteworthy. During 1967 and 1968 riots and rebellions in Black communities peaked in both intensity and number, while the mass base of the antiwar movement expanded tremendously. Yet the majority of articulated corporate and financial sentiment argued for state-induced recession to protect the dollar.

The alternative policies advocated by capital were not adopted by the Johnson and Nixon administrations; their domestic and foreign political costs were perceived as too high. The controls were maintained intact until the dollar's initial devaluation in August 1971, and liberalized thereafter until 1974, when they were finally abolished, after the dollar's second devaluation in 1973. Ultimately, what was to be more significant than the political actions taken by TNBs and TNCs in opposition to the capital controls were their day-to-day actions in restructuring international finance through financial innovation. This story is told in the following chapter, which analyzes the contradictory impact of the voluntary and mandatory programs on the U.S. and the global economy, on the continued expansion of U.S. TNCs and TNBs, and on the U.S. balance of payments through 1971.

6. The Contradictory Consequences of the Capital Controls

This chapter traces the impact of the three successful capital control programs, described in previous chapters, on the international financial and monetary system from 1963 through the collapse of Bretton Woods in 1971. We shall pay special attention to the growth of the Eurocurrency system, the most significant financial innovation of this period. The state's attempt, for balance of payments reasons, to restructure the interests of transnational corporations and banks had created new market opportunities. Ironically, the ensuing global financial innovations would provide an extranational base from which to challenge national banking and financial regulation, particularly after the mid-1970s. The growing challenge to state financial regulatory capacities by innovative banking and financial institutions, both from within and without, directly undermined state monetary policy. The internationalization of financial capital, which may be seen as a manifestation of what I call the dialectic of state intervention and market innovation, deepened the internationalization of those very problems which the U.S. capital controls had originally addressed. Chief among these was the decline in U.S. state capacity to direct its domestic economy, and hence to maintain the coalitions upon which its political power rested.

The first brief section of this chapter focuses on the immediate consequences of the Office of Foreign Direct Investment (OFDI) program on the rate of foreign direct investment and on capital accounts in the U.S. balance of payments. The second substantive section of the chapter analyzes the contradictory consequences of the three control programs on the U.S. balance of payments and on the world financial and monetary systems.

In order to appreciate these consequences, this discussion will provide a technical, and necessarily difficult, overview of the debt overhang, interest rates and the impact of currencies' valuations on the U.S. balance of payments. The concluding remarks of the chapter furnish a summation of these developments.

Immediate consequences of the OFDI

At the center of the OFDI controversy were two interrelated, but separable issues: the impact of the program on the rate of growth of overseas direct investment and

Table 1

**U.S. Net Capital Outflow—Europe[4]
(in millions of $)**

Year	1960	1961	1962	1963	1964	1965	1966	1967	1968	1969	1970
Net capital outflow	962	724	868	929	1,388	1,479	1,834	1,458	1,001	1,209	1,904

the direct and indirect impact of the program on the U.S. payments balance and its various accounts. The intent of the OFDI program was not to limit the rate of direct investment expansion. Various U.S. government agencies have concluded in retrospective studies that the rate of direct investment growth, worldwide and in the three scheduled areas, was not slowed. Concluded one study: "The Program does not seem to have significantly restrained expenditures for foreign plant and equipment."[1] Other data support this conclusion. Worldwide U.S. direct investment increased steadily between 1960 and 1970, from $31.9 billion to $78.1 billion, despite the existence in the latter half of those years of the voluntary and mandatory control programs.[2] More significantly, U.S. direct investment in Europe increased from $6.7 billion in 1960 to $34.5 billion in 1970.[3] New U.S. capital outflows to Europe, in spite of the control programs, showed an overall, though uneven, increase, as Table 1 suggests.

The growth of direct U.S. investment in Europe was greater than the net U.S. direct investment capital outflow, the difference due to U.S. foreign subsidiary overseas borrowing. During 1968 there was a decrease in direct investment (defined by the OFDI as net capital transfers plus foreign borrowing), which became significant evidence to those opposing the program. However, the decrease proved to be both a temporary response to the new OFDI and part of the general slowdown in direct investment in all the advanced countries, including Canada, which was exempt from the restrictions.[5]

Thus it appears that the OFDI did not reduce the rate of total direct investment in Europe or in the world, although it did shift the locus of financing, and thereby marginally raised costs.[6] Whether there might, in the absence of the controls, have been a faster rate of expansion after 1965 remains unanswered.

While it may be said that between 1968 and 1971 the OFDI only marginally affected the growth of direct investment, it is more difficult to assess the controls' impact on the balance of payments as a whole. The effect of the mandatory program on the capital account, specifically on the direct investment account, was complex. The program did significantly slow down both the net outflow of direct investment capital (in payments accounting terms) as well as so-called "regulated direct investment" (that is, in OFDI-defined direct investment terms). The two sets of figures are calculated differently, so that they cannot be

Table 2

Regulated Direct Investment, 1965–70
(millions of $—OFDI defined direct investment—1970 estimate)[7]

	1965	1966	1967	1968	1969	1970
Total all schedules						
(excluding Canada)						
Transfers of capital	3,080	3,387	3,360	2,321	3,427	4,520
Reinvested earnings	1,058	1,109	934	1,129	1,530	2,250
Direct Investment	4,138	4,496	4,294	3,450	4,957	6,770
Deduction for use of proceeds	(48)	(634)	(582)	(2,209)	(2,603)	(2,972)
Regulated Direct Investment	4,040	3,862	3,712	1,241	2,354	3,378
Schedule C						
Transfers of capital	1,284	1,553	1,409	739	1,304	1,539
Reinvested earnings	1,177	275	205	191	604	753
Direct Investment	2,461	2,828	1,614	930	1,908	2,292
Deduction for use of proceeds	(65)	(446)	(366)	(972)	(1,510)	(1,582)
Regulated Direct Investment	2,396	2,382	1,248	(42)	398	710

Note: Definitions of terms as used by OFDI:

Transfers of capital: net transfers by direct investors to their incorporated and unincorporated affiliated foreign nationals associated with changes in direct investors' equity or debt interests in such affiliates. Also includes: indirect transfers of capital made in connection with parallel and triangular financing arrangements and 'deemed' transfers made under special arrangements with OFDI officials. (Repayment of long term foreign borrowing obligations previously used to reduce 'positive' direct investment is treated as a transfer of capital. Thus it is not comparable with the balance of payments accounting category 'net U.S. foreign direct investment'.)

Reinvested earnings: direct investor's share of earnings after foreign taxes of its incorporated affiliates, less dividends declared, before deduction from those dividends of withholding taxes paid to foreign governments.

Deduction for use of proceeds: The 'use' of foreign borrowing to reduce regulated positive direct investment under the OFDI program. This means actually expending the proceeds in making transfers of capital of 'allocating' the proceeds against positive direct investment, provided they are repatriated to the United States by the end of the year in which the allocations are made.

Regulated direct investment: The sum total of the above, on which basis the program may be evaluated.

directly compared except for trends.

From Table 2 it is apparent that "regulated direct investment" (that is, direct investment outflow from the United States, calculated to include borrowing and reinvested earnings) declined substantially worldwide, most rapidly in Europe. Similarly, Table 3 shows that the net outflow of direct investment capital in Europe (in balance of payments accounting terms) also reached a low in 1968 but increased steadily thereafter, so that by 1970 U.S. worldwide direct investment outflow exceeded the 1966 level. The outflow to Europe was reduced substantially by the OFDI program, from a high in 1966 of $1.4 billion and in 1967 $1.2 billion, to $374 million in 1968. Thus the goal of reducing the capital account by $1 billion worldwide in 1968 was exceeded by a reduction of $2.3 billion. This, however, was due to a variety of extraneous factors, including a recession in West Germany and tight money in the United States. In 1969 the program was again somewhat below target, while in 1970 the outflow was at preprogram levels, about $3.3 billion.[8]

Long-term consequences of the capital controls

While the OFDI program only marginally restricted U.S. TNC expansion in the short run, more profound consequences of all the capital control programs may be found in the changes in the international financial and monetary systems during the last half of the 1960s and throughout the 1970s. The U.S. controls were one catalyst for the internationalization of finance. Arthur F. Brimmer suggests that the transformation of the largest U.S. commercial banks into TNBs during the late 1950s and 1960s "altered the flow of funds, changed the distributional impact of monetary policy, and placed strains on the traditional instruments of central banking." As a consequence of these alterations, the domestic U.S. financial system was more "open to the influence of foreign financial developments than was the case . . . in the early 1960s."[9] The growth of the Eurocurrency system has been remarkable: from about $9 billion in 1964 to $1.4 trillion in late 1981.[10] This massive growth of international liquidity came to haunt state policy makers throughout the late 1960s and 1970s. This section focuses on three long-term consequences of the capital controls during the 1960s and early 1970s: the debt overhang problem and effective U.S. monetary policy; the growth of interest rate wars; and the effect of the Eurocurrency system on the U.S. balance of payments.

Debt overhang and the diminished power of
U.S. monetary policy

The imposition of the Interest Equalization Tax (IET) in 1963 was a substantial impetus for the growth of the Eurobond market, which provided long-term financing primarily to foreign corporations and state agencies which had pre-

Table 3

U.S. Direct Investment Income and Outflow:
Net Balance of Payments Accounting 1968–71
(in millions of $)[11]

	1968	1969	1970	1971
a. Direct Investment Income*				
World	6,264	7,084	7,906	9,297
Europe	994	1,115	1,538	1,785
b. Direct Investment Outflow (−)				
World	−3,025	−3,060	−4,445	−4,526
Europe	−620	−967	−1,262	−1,348
c. Total (inflow): net (a−b)				
World	3,239	4,024	3,461	4,771
Europe	374	148	376	437

*Includes fees and royalties.

viously been served by the New York capital market. After the voluntary capital control programs were established in 1965, U.S. TNCs as well began to use the Eurocurrency system for alternative financing. As U.S. and non-U.S. TNCs looked to the Euromarkets to provide long- and short-term financing, as well as for the lucrative and highly liquid investment of surplus funds, U.S. TNBs quickly opened branch offices in London and elsewhere to serve their U.S. and foreign customers. In 1968 the imposition of the mandatory capital control programs increased the number of TNCs and TNBs borrowing from and lending to the Eurocurrency system. This "Eurodollar escape valve" provided relief from the U.S controls, but at the cost of the build-up of long-term debt owed by foreign affiliates of U.S. TNCs and TNBs. The debt overhang came to have a significant impact on U.S. ability to manage the balance of payments deficit, eventually negating the strategic goals of the control programs. To understand the crucial importance of the Eurocurrency system in this process and its links with the U.S. economy, a brief overview of the sources and uses of Eurocurrency funds during the 1960s is essential.

The Eurocurrency system grew from about $9 billion in 1964 to $71 billion in 1971, as narrowly measured by the Bank for International Settlements (BIS). More realistically, by 1971 the Eurocurrency system's net size was about $145 billion, as measured by the Morgan Guaranty Bank's more inclusive standards.[12] Between 1964 and 1971, the United States and Canada became net users of Eurodollars (comprising 70–80 percent of the Eurocurrency market), while Western European and other countries became important suppliers of funds. TNBs used the U.S. inflow of Eurodollars to counteract the Federal Reserve Board's tight money policies in 1966 and during 1968–69. While Eurodollar inflows increased during this period, outflows grew as well. In 1969 the United

States alone supplied $4.1 billion, in 1970 $4.5 billion, and in 1971 $6.1 billion. A large proportion of these U.S. outflows were deposits by U.S. TNCs of funds raised in European financial markets, through the channels of U.S. banks.[13] Thus an important factor on the source side of the Eurodollar market was the growth in outstanding liabilities of U.S. banks to their own foreign branches. During the tight money year of 1966, U.S. banks, in order to improve their reserve position with the Federal Reserve, increased their liabilities to their foreign branches from $2.8 billion (on July 27) to $4.0 billion (on December 28). This constituted a significant inflow of Eurodollars, which made a circular trip from U.S. banks to the Eurodollar market via TNBs' branches, returning via the same branches to the U.S. head offices. U.S. TNBs' liabilities to their foreign branches increased overall from $1.0 billion in 1964 to $15.5 billion in 1969.[14] The consequence was increased interest rates on both sides of the Atlantic, enabling U.S. TNBs to counteract U.S. monetary policy, as will be detailed in the following section. In this period, U.S. TNBs were important users of as well as lenders to the Euromarket, as financial intermediaries for final nonbank users, and in their own right to counteract U.S. credit restrictions during tight money times. The most important of these latter instances were in 1966 and 1968–69, when U.S. resident banks, through their foreign branches, borrowed heavily in the market. In 1968 alone, the use of Eurodollar funds by U.S. TNBs almost doubled.

Eurodollar liquidity enabled the largest U.S. banks to increase their reserve positions with the Federal Reserve Board to a degree that vitiated the government's tight money policies. They could consequently expand their loans and with them the monetary base of the domestic economy, directly countering Federal Reserve policy which was attempting to halt an inflation due especially to the Vietnam war and the resulting growth of imports. The Eurodollar market enabled U.S. TNBs to circumvent the impact of Regulation Q's interest-rate ceilings used to control the credit-creating capacity of the U.S. banking system. Through their foreign branches, the banks were able to minimize the impact of Regulation Q while at the same time integrating their overseas branches more fully into a worldwide banking system. This circumvention led to a worsening of the balance of payments deficit.[15]

U.S. TNCs were also large users of Eurodollars. Prior to the 1965 voluntary program, Eurodollars primarily financed trade. The control programs forced TNCs to borrow Eurodollars as a source of short- and long-term capital. While there is no comprehensive data on TNCs' Eurodollar borrowings, the sources and uses of funds for TNCs' subsidiaries reveal the changes in their financial structure. Between 1967 (the first year for which data are available) and 1971, U.S. affiliates increased short- and long-term liabilities, to a great extent by borrowing Eurodollars, from $9.4 billion to $14.9 billion. Affiliate liability to foreign, mainly Eurobank, institutions increased from $2.5 billion in 1967 (27.1 percent of total investment funds) to $5.9 billion in 1970 (40.3 percent), decreasing to $5.0 billion (34.3 percent) in 1971. At the height of the borrowing, 40 percent of

Table 4

Total Outstanding Borrowing by OFDI Subject Corporations[16]
(millions of $)

1965 and prior	1966	1967	1968	1969	1970	Outstanding as of 12/3/70
13	59	32	259	378	1,530	2,271

the total funds for affiliate expansion in all industries came from long- and short-term liabilities abroad.[17] The impact of the capital controls on foreign borrowing by U.S. TNCs is evident in Table 4 which indicates short-term (under one year) borrowings from foreign banks.

Thus U.S. TNC subsidiaries increased liabilities faster than total assets, giving rise to a large debt overhang. The OFDI estimated it to be between $0.8 and $3.0 billion in 1971.[18]

Consequently, between 1965 and 1971 U.S. domestic credit markets became increasingly interdependent with the Eurocurrency system undermining government restrictions on credit and money and exerting an upward pressure on interest rates. After the capital controls, U.S. TNCs were able to continue to expand European investment, in large part due to the existence and growth of the Eurocurrency system, and the expanded role of U.S. TNBs in that system. But the cost of this form of expansion was a growing debt overhang, a direct result of the U.S. capital control programs. Ironically this exacerbated the long-term U.S. balance of payments deficit since much TNC short-term borrowing was rolled over into effective long-term debt at its end of term. The overhang was financed through the Eurodollar markets. (The impact of the debt overhang on the U.S. balance of payments will be examined in detail below.) The Eurocurrency system contributed to the persistent rise of interest rates in the advanced countries and interest rate wars among them, as each government attempted to maintain its fixed exchange rate in the face of rapid short-term capital movements across borders.

Interest rate wars

The second major result of the capital controls was the competitive raising of interest rates, as national monetary authorities attempted to protect their currency and economy from foreign exchange fluctuation and speculation. The controls contributed directly to the raising of rates in two ways. First, by stimulating the growth of the Eurocurrency system, they permitted the more efficient working of foreign exchange mechanisms through increased velocity in the circulation of a fixed stock of currency, thereby amassing a large pool of highly liquid funds capable of flowing across borders. Second, the controls encouraged dollar in-flows to the United States while reducing outflows in order to reduce the deficit, as measured on a liquidity basis. This served as an incentive to raise U.S. interest rates for reasons of balance of payments, in order to attract foreign dollar holdings. A more detailed examination of the linkages between Eurodollar and U.S. interest rates illustrates these points.

The interest rate differential between Eurofunds and national money markets linked the Eurodollar market to various national economies. National interest rates had always been both directly and indirectly interdependent. The Eurosystem offered increased velocity and decreased market transactions costs, making it more efficient than the national market. Eurodollar interest rates for lenders were always higher and for borrowers always lower than in the United States and other national money markets, since operating costs were lower and there was no legally required reserve fund to be held by a central bank. These efficiencies assured an ever-growing supply of Eurofunds, while increasing demand was assured by tight short- and long-term world money.[19]

Prior to the 1965 U.S. capital controls, the relation between the Eurodollar rates and the U.S. money market was expressed in the differential between Eurodollar rates and U.S. interest paid on time deposits and money market securities.[20] This interest rate differential insured that large amounts of both U.S. and foreign dollars would be invested in the Eurodollar market rather than in various money market instruments in the United States, most importantly in Certificates of Deposit and Treasury Bills.[21] Before 1965, the higher interest rate payable on Eurodollars was a partial function of the global supply of dollars resulting from the U.S. payments deficit. This was channeled into the Eurodollar market by European central banks' policies, which encouraged the private holding of U.S. dollars. Consequently, on the supply side of the Eurodollar market, prior to 1965 the higher rates of return on Eurodollars insured the growth of the market.[22] Euromarkets were then directly dependent on U.S. markets and interest rates.

Critical in the development of the post-1965 Euromarkets was the changed relationship between national and Eurodollar interest rates. This relationship enabled the Eurodollar market to develop after 1965 as an independent international short-term capital market. While linked closely to the overall conditions in the dominant U.S. market for dollars, the Eurocurrency system became more than a foreign extension of it.[23] E. Wayne Clendenning concluded in 1970: "It is primarily these [U.S. capital] restrictions that now provide Eurodollar rates with their independence from U.S. rates."[24] The severing of the direct link between U.S. and Eurodollar interest rates contributed to the independent role of the Eurodollar market in the competitive raising of national interest rates after 1965.

As the Eurocurrency system grew in size, its interest rate structure had a more direct and independent impact on national monetary policies. During the 1960s, monetary policy was used by states to correct balance of payments deficits or surpluses. High interest rates attempted to attract foreign currency and to discourage domestic outflow and thereby reduce deficits. Before 1965, when U.S. rates were lower than international ones, outflow of short-term capital had a negative impact on the balance of payments measured on a liquidity basis. This caused U.S. monetary authorities to increase the interest rate. For instance, in 1962–63 the United States chose a policy of high interest rates to counteract the growing deficit on long- and short-term portfolio capital accounts. In turn, this increase pressured upward the Eurodollar rate.[25] The velocity and magnitude of short-term capital flows responding to interest rate differentials increased with the growth of the highly liquid Eurodollar market and of the global supply of dollars. This encouraged the competitive raising of national discount rates, as central banks attempted to protect their economies from more efficient free-market forces of international short-term capital. This monetary protectionism was the forerunner of the 1971 dollar crisis.

Official monetary policy often gave rise to a defensive form of interest rate increases. In order to sustain an effective domestic monetary policy and prevent outflows of short-term capital, it was necessary to raise central banks' discount rates to equal or surpass global competitive rates, especially in the Eurodollar market. This would initially aid in financing a payments deficit, but at the long-term cost of expanding the domestic supply of money and credit, as foreign funds would flow in to take rapid advantage of higher rates. Thus the traditional logic dictating that high interest rates always discouraged credit expansion became perverse, as high national rates attracted additional funds from abroad, whether in the Euromarkets or in national money and capital markets. West Germany in particular, with its traditionally low inflation policies and relatively high interest rates, experienced this perverse effect between 1966 and 1973.

In conclusion, the growth of the Eurocurrency system after the 1965 controls heightened interest rate competition among central banks as they attempted to maintain their capacity to implement macroeconomic policies. The Eurodollar escape valve prompted by state intervention did provide immediate relief for U.S. TNCs and TNBs from U.S. capital restrictions, but at the long-term costs of global monetary disorder and decreased capacity of the state to control its economic environment through monetary policy.

The Eurocurrency system effects on
the U.S. balance of payments

The third major consequence of the capital controls was the rapid growth of the Eurocurrency system. A critical effect for U.S. policy in turn was the Eurocurrency system's negation of the strategic aims of the capital controls themselves, namely, stabilization and correction of the balance of payments deficit. Assessing this impact of the Euromarkets on U.S. payments is difficult, partly because necessary data is lacking and partly because of the inherent complexity of the new global financial movements. One can, however, appreciate the important role of the Eurocurrency system in the destabilization of the world monetary order by pinpointing significant incidents during the late 1960s and early 1970s.

Before addressing this issue, it should be stressed, first, that the U.S. payments deficits were an important early contributor to the Eurocurrency market's rapid growth in the early 1960s, although the market responded to other factors in the innovative world of international finance.[26] Second, the capital controls provided an impetus for the development of the Eurobond market (an important sector of the Eurocurrency system) as an alternative source of external long-term finance initially for U.S. TNCs. The Eurobond alternative strengthened the vehicle and reserve roles of the dollar, as the Eurobond market did not have the destabilizing potential of the larger and more volatile short-term Eurodollar market.[27] After 1967, the Eurodollar market as well did not depend primarily on the U.S. payments deficit for its growth but was also more directly stimulated by the U.S. capital controls.

The impact of the Eurocurrency system on the U.S. payments deficit after 1965 rides on the question of the Eurodollar market's effects on speculative pressures against the dollar. If the Eurodollar market increased demand for the dollar for private, nonofficial use, then, at least in the short run, it eased the U.S. payments balance. But in the long run, these holdings proved a potential threat to the dollar since they could be sold to official monetary authorities. In official hands the dollars would add to claims on the U.S. gold supply. Since the Eurodollar market thus expanded the total external dollars supply, it made the dollar that much more susceptible to speculative waves, as in fact occurred in 1967, 1968–69, and 1971. On the other hand, if the Eurodollar market acted as a substitute rather than a supplement for dollars which might otherwise have been supplied from the United States, the effect would—again—be either negative or positive, depending on the sources which held the dollars and on the means of accounting used to calculate the U.S. payments balance. Eurodollar market substitution for U.S. dollars depended on Eurodollar interest rates being high, which occurred as a result of a shortage in available capital in various national money markets. When international rates declined, money became easier and there was repayment of previous debts to the Eurodollar market, as happened in 1970 and 1971. What at one point was substitution rapidly became supplementation.[28]

Before proceeding further, it is useful to recall the means used to calculate the U.S. payments balance. Depending on whether the liquidity or the official settlements basis is used, the impact of the same transactions on the Eurodollar market could have an opposite effect. The liquidity basis treats the movement of private short-term capital, including commercial bank funds, differently depending on whether the action is initiated by a U.S. resident or a nonresident. Private foreign claims on U.S. banks and money markets are treated as a settlement item if they are short-term and liquid, whereas private U.S. claims on foreign banks and money markets are classified as a capital outflow item. Thus there is an inherent asymmetry to the liquidity basis which, however, is inherent in the dollar's unique role as the primary global reserve and transaction currency.[29] The official settlements basis distinguishes payments items that are capital flows from those that are settlement ones, depending on whether or not they are held by other foreigners and international institutions. Thus all short-term capital flows are treated symmetrically whether or not they are liquid, and whether they are transacted in the United States or abroad.[30] The official settlements basis balance would be improved by a flow of dollars from foreign central banks and into foreign private holdings, as occurred, for instance, in 1967–68. The liquidity balance would be hurt by the same movement. The liquidity basis tends to be most sensitive to dollars held in private hands abroad and therefore is a better indicator of possible speculative ends to which those dollars might be put via the foreign exchange mechanism. The official settlements basis tended to be most sensitive to potential gold drain from the United States by foreign governments holding dollar claims on U.S. gold.[31]

The complex effects of the Eurocurrency system on the deficit and on global monetary conditions can be illustrated by examining a few specific instances of the impact of the Eurodollar market on the U.S. payments balance and the related status of the dollar. In 1966 and 1968–69, high Eurodollar interest rates resulted in an unusually large differential between them and the return on U.S. short-term money market instruments (three-month Treasury bills, negotiable certificates of deposit, and prime commercial paper), thus drawing funds from the U.S. and foreign national markets into the Euromarkets. A substantial proportion of these funds came from European central banks. The result was a leveling out and in some cases actually a decrease in, official dollar reserves. This was recorded as an improvement in the official settlement basis of the U.S. payments balance. In this case, the Eurodollar market indirectly contributed to easing the U.S. deficit, if calculated on the official settlements basis.[32] Through its expansion of international liquidity, the Eurodollar market removed dollars from official holdings. A greater proportion of international trade could then be financed by Eurodollars without recourse to the official reserves of governments. The expansion of the Eurodollar market also increased the circulation velocity of private U.S. dollar holdings by causing dollar balances held in the United States to be switched from time to demand deposits and by expanding the means whereby these dollars could be lent and borrowed internationally. This too relieved the pressure on official reserves, supporting the U.S. Treasury's goal of assisting in the creation of non-U.S. money and capital markets.[33]

What complicates the analysis of the impact of the Eurodollar market in the 1968–69 period is that the flow of funds from and to the United States was circular. The Federal Reserve Board's Regulation Q placed an interest rate ceiling on all domestic deposits, providing strong incentives for U.S. depositors to place funds in the Eurodollar market. As U.S. residents' claims on foreign institutions mounted and as liquid liabilities to foreign branches of U.S. banks increased, a circular flow through TNBs' foreign branches developed. Thus Eurodollars contributed to the deficit measured on a liquidity basis and to the resulting divergence between it and the official settlements basis of calculating the balance of payments.[34] In 1969 the official settlements basis showed the payments balance to be $2.7 billion in surplus, while the liquidity basis showed a deficit of $7.2 billion. U.S. tight money policies tended to push up Eurodollar rates while at the same time increasing the demand for Eurodollars, which required a further increase in U.S. interest rates to accomplish the original policy ends, by necessity drawing off official reserve funds. Consequently the growing U.S. deficit was increasingly financed by private dollar holdings and less by central bank holdings, temporarily easing the demand against the U.S. gold supply. At the end of 1967, foreign central banks held $15.6 billion in external liquid dollars, while $15.7 billion was held abroad in private hands. In 1968 foreign central bank holdings declined to $12.5 billion, while foreign private holdings increased to $19.4 billion. In 1969 foreign central bank holdings decreased further to $11.9 billion, while foreign private holdings surged to $28.2 billion.[35]

The positive effect in 1969 on the deficit, even on the official settlements basis, was short-lived. While the dollar gained strength on the foreign exchange markets in 1969 due to this surplus, both this apparent strength and the temporary payments surplus were at the cost of a huge short-term, volatile foreign debt. The debt's repayment began in 1970, accompanied by an easing of U.S. domestic monetary policy. These actions resulted in the swamping of European money markets with U.S. dollars, creating an upward pressure on most European currencies, a downward pressure on the U.S. dollar, and the necessity of central bank intervention to protect the existing exchange rates. This resulted in an increase in the U.S. 1970 and 1971 deficits on both the liquidity and official settlements basis.[36] Evidence for this abrupt turnaround is that while the short-term external debt of the United States rose over the whole decade, the components of the debt varied. The proportional division of the flow of funds between central banks and private sources from 1967–69 reversed itself in 1970–71. This laid the ground for the dollar crisis of August 1971 and, with it, the end of the Bretton Woods system. U.S. indebtedness to foreign branches of commercial banks decreased from a high of $20.4 billion in September 1970 to $17.0 billion in December 1970, $14.0 billion in March 1971, and finally a low of $13.2 billion in June 1971. During the same period, central banks' dollar holdings, which had previously declined, rose to record levels: $21.7 billion ($17.8 billion of which was in liquid form); $23.9 billion ($20.1 billion liquid); $28.7 billion ($25.1 liquid), and $35.3 (liquid n.a.). The pressure on the dollar became overwhelming, and in August the gold–dollar link officially ended, and the dollar was devalued.[37]

The events of 1967 through 1971 indicate that whether measured on a liquidity or an official settlements basis, the long-term impact of the Eurodollar market on the U.S. payments balance was to increase U.S. external debt by facilitating and expanding the vehicle and reserve role of the dollar. Private and central bank debts were interchangeable, so that both liquidity and official settlements measures of the U.S. payments balance were necessary to indicate the specific forms of debt overhang. The central mechanism of the interchange from private to official debt holdings was the Eurodollar market. Thus, the increase of Eurodollars and, consequently, of international liquidity endangered the stability of the dollar, given speculative fears that the U.S. balance of payments deficit would not improve or could even worsen. Dangerous speculation against the dollar, the immediate reason for the August 1971 crisis, arose out of the United States' inability to eliminate the deficit, which reflected the real rather than the monetary forces at work in the U.S. economy and behind it, the structure of U.S. global hegemony.[38]

In conclusion, between 1967 and 1971, the Eurodollar market had a destabilizing effect on the dollar as the main reserve currency and a long-term detrimental effect on the U.S payments balance. The Eurodollar system exacerbated the deficit and made it less responsive to the means undertaken by the U.S. government to reduce it, most importantly, the capital controls. This vicious circle was completed as the capital controls contributed to the growth of the Eurocurrency system. The capital controls also engendered a debt overhang which further directly contributed to the U.S. payments deficit and indirectly further diminished the effectiveness of U.S. monetary policy. The growth of the Eurocurrency system facilitated interest rate wars among the advanced capitalist states and between each state and the Eurocurrency system, as states attempted to protect both existing fixed-exchange rates and domestic macroeconomic policies from the impact of currencies' valuations and short-term capital flows.

The August 15, 1971 decision to cut the dollar's value from gold, thus ending the Bretton Woods system, was brought about by the massive speculation against the dollar. Although between 1971 and 1973 there were attempts to maintain the fixed-exchange rate system apart from gold, the breakdown of the Bretton Woods system ushered in the collapse of official governmental control of exchange rates and the concomitant decline of a global monetary system organized by governments themselves and by international organizations of their own creation. In place of this system, the private sector forces of financial innovation came to dominate the exchange rate system (with state central banks sporadically intervening through heavy foreign exchange transactions) and control the majority of international capital flows. The dialectic of state intervention and financial innovation was thus exemplified by growth of the private sector-dominated international monetary system after 1973 and in the central institution of that system, the Euromarket. Freed from direct state intervention, the Euromarkets furthered financial innovation in penetrating the U.S. and other domestic economies in the 1970s. The next chapter examines futile U.S. government attempts in the late 1970s and early 1980s to limit and regulate the Euromarket's expansion.

7. U.S. Attempts to Regulate the Eurocurrency Market, 1979–1980

The global financial revolution of the 1970s deepened the already contradictory relations between the U.S. state and U.S. transnational banks and heightened the internally contradictory interests of the TNBs themselves. The U.S. government's initiatives in 1979 and 1980 were intended to slow the rapid growth of the Eurocurrency system, and to directly regulate U.S. and other TNBs' Euromarket activity. They marked the first multilateral attempt to structure international financial markets and bring their operations into conformity with national bank regulatory laws and policies.

The 1979–80 Eurocurrency regulation initiatives were motivated by concerns similar to those spurring the capital controls a decade earlier. After 1973, the U.S. balance of payments no longer was the prime indicator of global monetary instability, since the managed float greatly extended the system's tolerance for large payments deficits. Currency speculations, massive and usually short-term capital flows, and international liquidity became the new central indicators of weaknesses in the post-1973 system. The attempts to control the Eurocurrency system illustrate the dialectic of financial innovation and state intervention: the ubiquity of financial regulation—required for the control of monetary and credit flows—breeds innovation and re-creates a basis for divisions between the state and global financial capital, engendering further intervention. The strategic failure of Eurocurrency resolution and the growth of unregulated global money and credit markets is the story of growing state incapacity in financial and monetary management.[1]

The first section of this chapter discusses these attempts at international bank supervision in light of the 1978 dollar crisis. It also analyzes the intellectual policy context as the background against which the government, academic, and TNB Eurocurrency control debates occurred. The second section presents the Federal Reserve and Treasury Department control proposals. The third discusses TNBs' responses and the eventual failure of the regulatory proposals. The fourth concludes with a discussion of the relation between global financial innovation and trends toward domestic financial deregulation.

International bank supervision and the 1978 crisis

In the debates about Eurocurrency regulation, at stake was the ability of the state to conduct monetary policy in response to the proliferation of financial innovations. Never before had the ability to expand liquidity been located to such a degree outside the territory of the state that nominally issued the reserve and transaction currency of the international monetary system. These debates can therefore be seen as either a prelude to the assertion of state sovereignty over monetary, credit, and debt policy instruments or the beginnings of the collapse of state monetary authority over the economy. The former would require that state control of financial institutions and markets both mediate TNBs' interests and protect markets from their own destructive potential, while the latter would imply the breakdown of the state's mediating abilities and the decline of state regulatory capacities.

U.S. Federal Reserve and Treasury Department officials—spurred by the rapid slide of the dollar during the summer of 1978, which culminated in the dollar crisis of October—changed their approach to the Eurocurrency system. U.S. official interest in increasing coordinated supervisory powers over Euro-banks had originated in the 1974–75 near financial panic, which had prompted coordinated actions by U.S., Western European, and Bank for International Settlements (BIS) officials. These actions had attempted to standardize procedures and open channels of intergovernmental communication in order to prevent a recurrence of the bank failures and currency runs of 1974–75. But this informal crisis-prevention coordinating activity, the forerunner of the U.S. Eurocurrency regulation initiatives of 1979 and 1980, could not prevent the massive decline of the dollar in the late summer and autumn of 1978; it proved to be a fair-weather strategy. The failure of informal regulation and supervision in the face of disagreements between the U.S. and European (especially West German) governments in the fall of 1978 caused the U.S. government to propose more formal, nationally based but globally coordinated Eurocurrency regulations.

Bank supervision: 1974–1978

In 1974 representatives of the Group of Ten (G-10) advanced industrial nations plus Switzerland and Luxembourg had formed what subsequently would become known as the Cooke Committee, operating under the auspices of the BIS. It was formed in immediate response to the 1974 failure of the British-Israel Bank, which had ignited a controversy between the United Kingdom and Israel about which government had supervisory authority over the bank's affairs. The committee attempted to establish broad principles for international banking to which national authorities would conform in their own supervisory practices. It attempted neither to standardize diverse national banking laws and regulations nor to investigate particular banks' activities. The committee tried to locate the lacunae in bank supervision and to establish an informal intergovernmental "early warning system" to alert national authorities in the event of banking system problems which would insure that no TNB could escape supervision by a national authority. The Cooke Committee's impact was primarily informal: it regularized contact among national bank authorities and provided coordinated direction for ongoing national regulatory reforms.[2]

In October 1977, the Commission of the European Economic Community (EC) published a working paper that argued for EC-wide standardization of bank supervisory practices. Opposition from EC private sector banks and from the Bank of England, the major Eurocurrency center, convinced the commission to adopt the more general and informal approach of the Cooke Committee. A "Group de Contact" was formed to carry on the work of the commission. In December 1977, the first EC Banking Coordination Directive was adopted to informally coordinate supervision by national authorities.[3]

Similar coordinated actions occurred in the United States among the Federal Reserve Board, the Office of the Comptroller of the Currency (OCC), and the Federal Deposit Insurance Corporation (FDIC). In 1977, the Committee on Foreign Lending of the Federal Reserve Board recommended revisions in the supervision of international bank lending. All U.S.-based TNBs were required by the end of 1977 to report to the Federal Reserve Board their "country risk" status every six months, along with their foreign lending exposure on a country-by-country rather than on an aggregate basis. Country risk was defined as the potential risk arising from the economic, social, legal, and political conditions in each country to which banks had lent funds. By 1979 similar procedures were required by the OCC and the FDIC.[4]

These efforts at global TNB supervision by U.S. agencies, by the EC Group de Contact, and by the Cooke Committee emphasized country risk supervision and the coordinated and regular exchange among supervisory agencies of more general information. There was no standardization of international supervision, nor even of the information exchange itself. For instance, Swiss banking retained its privileged character, thus ensuring a gap in information on those TNBs with Swiss accounts. Until late 1978 these three agencies did not publicly discuss Eurocurrency regulation or control, but concentrated exclusively on supervising foreign bank lending. Their efforts assumed that control of market participants' riskiest activities would moderate or control Euromarket instability. Markets were not seen as having an existence separate from their participants. There were three problems with this approach. First, not all TNBs' home offices were located in nations represented on the Cooke Committee. Second, and more importantly, as coordinated regulations proliferated, most Eurobanks established shell branches or subsidiaries in the Cayman Islands, the Bahamas, Panama, or other unregulated off-shore centers. Third, even had information been completely coordinated, it remained questionable whether new data in the hands of national supervisory authorities would or could produce prudent practices by the banks themselves.[5]

Concern about the prudential aspects of Eurobank practices, noted by the Cooke Committee, was reinforced by the Basle Accord of December 1975, which established the principle (however vague) of a parent bank's moral reponsibility for its subsidiaries and branches. Simultaneously, a country's bank was to maintain supervisory responsibility for all banks registered within its borders. Thus, prudential supervision and regulation were logically intertwined with monetary regulation, since the growth of nationally interpenetrated commercial banking networks made the movement of credit across national borders more immediately responsive to small changes in credit demand and to interest rate differentials. In the United States, the concern of the Federal Reserve and the Treasury Department about the prudential aspects of Eurocurrency operations became closely related to the U.S. attempts to "stabilize" the Eurocurrency system, which began in January 1979.[6]

U.S. and West German concern over the growth rate (twenty percent per annum) of the Eurocurrency system, which would lead to attempts to restrict and regulate the market's growth beyond the previous informal supervision and information exchange, were intensified by the dollar's massive decline in the fall of 1978. Between August and October 1978, the dollar declined against the leading world currencies, especially the mark, Swiss franc, yen, and French franc. The last week of August saw the dollar decline 2.4 percent against the Swiss franc, 1.4 percent against the mark, and 1 percent against the French franc in one eight-hour period. Similar panic selling gripped the foreign exchange markets during the week of October 30. The West German government refused to support the dollar by further foreign exchange intervention during late October 1978. Therefore, on November 1 President Carter approved a program designed to rescue the falling dollar. The program raised U.S. domestic interest rates, increased the Federal Reserve discount rate from 8½% to 9½%, established a $30 billion support fund for Federal Reserve foreign exchange intervention, and took a variety of technical measures to restrict domestic credit and decrease the global supply of dollars.[7]

The importance of the 1978 dollar crisis was that, for the first time in the postwar era, other states forced the United States to restrict its expansionary domestic economic policy. This reflected the relative decline of U.S. hegemony in the international system and the concomitant rise of independent European monetary policies, symbolized by the formation of the European Monetary Union in that year. The contrast, for example, between U.S. actions in 1971 and 1973, when the Europeans and Japanese were forced to go along with U.S. monetary initiatives, and in 1978, when the United States was forced to respond to the dollar's decline and European state actions, was striking. The November 1 program attempted to lower the 8 percent underlying inflation rate at the cost of

possible recession. Strong-currency states attempted to limit the dollar's inflationary impact on their domestic economies by maintaining their own tight
monetary and fiscal policies and slow growth.[8] The decline of the dollar in
foreign exchange markets during the late summer and fall of 1978 increased
pressure on central banks, including those of the oil-exporting nations, to diversi-
fy their official reserves away from dollars and to other strong currencies or
baskets of currencies. This diversification away from dollars by both official and
private holders increased pressure on the dollar, further destabilizing the monetary system. The near-panics of August and October 1978 raised in dramatic
form the specter of a massive and rapidly growing offshore dollar market that
was necessitating U.S. domestic economic contraction to protect its currency.

The 1978 dollar crisis sharpened the imperative for controlling foreign exchange markets through some form of control or regulation of the Eurocurrency
system. If the system could be stabilized and its growth rate substantially reduced, the offshore production and circulation of stateless dollars could be
curtailed, in turn stabilizing the dollar. Thus, in sum, the proposals for regulation
of the Eurocurrency system first made public in early 1979 had their origins in the
dollar's decline in autumn 1978, in the refusal of West Germany to support the
dollar or loosen its fiscal and monetary policy, in the formation of the European
Monetary Union, and in the failure of informal supervisory practices. The
November 1 plan did not halt the decline of the dollar (although it did slow it);
nor did it significantly stabilize exchange rates nor end official reserve diversification away from dollars. The 1979 Eurocurrency controls would be proposed in
the context of these failures.

International monetary disorder and policy debates

The broader context of the U.S. Eurocurrency control proposals was the intellectual policy debates about the origins of international monetary disorder generally
and, specifically, the nature of the Eurocurrency system. These debates necessarily involved technical issues and are presented below in some detail.

U.S. proposals to regulate the Eurocurrency system resulted from the perception of policy makers that central banks and other regulatory agencies were
increasingly unable to implement policy. U.S. Federal Reserve and Treasury
Department officials started from the assumption, noted by Richard Sayers, that
"the essence of central banking is discretionary control of the monetary system."[9] As the U.S. monetary system became more directly linked with the global
monetary and financial system, and as those systems underwent substantial transformation during the 1970s, U.S. Federal Reserve officials concluded that the
global monetary system could not be left to free market forces alone. U.S. central
bankers came to view the growth of the Eurocurrency system with varying
degrees of concern, especially in the context of rapid domestic financial innovation and global instability.[10]

However, economists, financial analysts, and policy makers ascribed the instability of the financial and monetary systems during this period to a large variety of often conflicting factors. Among the most important were the post-1971 transition to a floating-rate system; the growth of Third World and other global debt, with accompanying payments and adjustment problems; OPEC oil surpluses; national economic rivalries among the advanced nations, resulting in divergent or ineffectual national monetary and macroeconomic policies; the growth of state deficits; and the slow growth of all the advanced industrial economies. Thus, while most economists and policy makers assumed increased financial and monetary interdependence during the 1970s, they differed on its specific consequences for national monetary policy and for central banks' capacities for prudential regulation. As Alexander Swoboda suggests, there was indeed a "bewildering" tangle of intersecting issues and problems.[11]

Below I sketch a few major policy controversies as they influenced the 1979–80 attempts by the U.S. Federal Reserve and Treasury Department to regulate the Eurocurrency system, and I interpret these controversies in terms of their policy intent, that is, as composing a general ideological influence on policy.[12] I divide the controversy into three overlapping areas: the significance of the floating-rate system in relation to the growth of the Eurocurrency system; the varying analyses of the strengths and weaknesses of the Eurocurrency system itself; and finally, the policy implications of these analyses.

The breakdown of the Bretton Woods system and the *ad hoc* emergence of the dollar-based floating-rate system rejuvenated the decades-long debate on the desirability of fixed versus floating rates. This controversy would merge with the Eurocurrency control debates over the role of the Eurocurrency system in "greasing" the foreign-exchange markets, for such "greasing" affected national monetary and macroeconomic policies inasmuch as they increased currency instability.[13] There were two critical issues at hand: the degree of national economic interdependence under floating rates and increased currency substitution, and the extent of national economic political costs of increased interdependence. Thus the financing of a nation's balance of payments, a central problem under the Bretton Woods regime as discussed previously, became transformed into primarily a foreign-exchange and interest-rate problem.

The degree to which these adjustment problems constrained autonomous national monetary and macroeconomic policy was widely debated, as was the impact of floating rates on international and national liquidity, its distribution, and consequences for inflation.[14] Ronald I. McKinnon argued that the received wisdom among most academic economists and macroeconomic policy makers lagged behind the internationalization process, predicated as it was on nationally insular economic models. These models either assumed nationally limited financial and commodity arbitrage with foreign institutions (i.e., classic Keynesian and older monetarist models) or focused on a global monetarist view—the maintenance of separable demand functions for each national money, which are assumed to be stable. McKinnon suggested that the floating-rate system increased international switching among convertible currencies, making more difficult a central bank's task of stabilizing exchange rates and adjusting the domestic money supply to support official foreign exchange interventions.[15] He argued that "international currency substitution destabilizes the demand for individual national monies so that one can't make much sense out of year-to-year changes in purely national monetary aggregates [for] explaining cycles in purely national rates of price inflation." He pointed to the explosion of the world's money supply in 1971–72 and in 1977–78, in which "speculation against the U.S. dollar was combined with exchange interventions by foreign central banks [to prevent the dollar from failing] that directly expanded money supplies in Europe and Japan. . . . The impact on the world price level was unambiguous." In sum, "speculation in favor of the dollar in 1980–81 imposed unduly sharp deflation on the world economy, just as speculation against the dollar in 1971–72 and again in 1977–78 fueled the two great inflations of the 1970s."[16]

For McKinnon, the floating-rate system necessitated official intervention in foreign exchange markets and the abandonment of domestic interest rate targets. (This policy approach was embodied in the Federal Reserve Board's October 1979 monetarist reorientation.) The increased openness of national economies due to floating rates required increased multilateral cooperation among central banks to adjust domestic money supplies to correspond to each country's foreign-exchange market interventions; such cooperation aimed at maintaining key currencies' real purchasing power and, consequently, relatively stable trading patterns.[17] Given floating rates, the Eurocurrency system had come to play a vital role in facilitating foreign exchange and, thereby, trade. The main problem of the Eurocurrency system under a floating-rate regime was not too much destabilizing speculation but too little, McKinnon argued, since speculators were unwilling to take the long-term risks that would facilitate market stability. Thus "the problem seems not to be one of excessively destabilizing speculation, but rather one of the absences of speculation over time horizons longer than a day or two."[18] The issue was not currency risk as such, but the more serious problem of potential bank solvency or liquidity crises.

Whereas McKinnon was critical of the long-term viability of floating rates, at least in the absence of effectively coordinated multilateral central bank policies, another important policy current, articulated by Thomas D. Willett, tended to favor a floating rate system, primarily because it minimized global liquidity. He argued, in any case, against the importance of international liquidity as a major cause of national inflations. Furthermore, he suggested that although excess global liquidity under the Bretton Woods system may have been a major contributor to national inflations, the adoption of floating rates minimized such a recurrence.[19] The impact of this debate over international currency regimes on policy makers' perspectives on the Eurocurrency system hinged on the degree to which a floating system increased or decreased national economic autonomy.[20]

If the relationship of the Eurocurrency system to different exchange rate regimes provided a context for policy making in the late 1970s, the debate about the Eurocurrency system itself became a specific focus. The fundamental reason for the massive expansion of the Eurocurrency market, according to D.F.I. Folkerts-Landau, was "the increase in the opportunity cost of the noninterest-bearing reserves domestic banks are required to hold against their deposit liabilities, as well as from the reduction in the risk and cost of long-distance financial transactions." This expansion led to the loss of autonomous national control of monetary and credit aggregates. Two consequent concerns were the potential for inflation, or alternatively for rapid deflation, and the soundness of the global, and hence the domestic, banking system.[21]

At the heart of this controversy was the degree of national insularity from global financial integration that was needed to achieve national policy goals. Jurg Niehans, staking out an extremely benign interpretation of the Eurocurrency market's impact on national policy, suggested that the long-term decline of financial transaction costs speeded up desirable financial innovation; national authorities should see the Euromarkets as "harmless," indeed, as an efficient, near-perfect market. However, national authorities typically reacted with attempted regulation because of the ideological power of "obsolete models" of monetary theory, which assumed that the Eurocurrency system, to a degree, created money. Niehans suggested rather that the rapid growth of the Euromarkets, and similar rapid financial innovation in the United States, led to the decline of traditional bank money, and consequently to the appropriate decline of central bank reserve requirements.[22]

In contrast to Niehans, Alexander Swoboda argued a middle ground. Although agreeing with the majority of academic economists that the Euromarkets created little if any new money and credit, he stressed that this minimal role in money creation did not rule out potential problems. He pointed to the matter of efficient or equitable credit distribution among various types of financial intermediaries and to the prudential soundness of the then rapidly growing interbank markets. This position was generally supported by Willett and McKinnon.[23]

While the debate of the early 1970s about the markets' credit creation produced a consensus that they created little new net credit, the Eurocurrency debate among academic economists shifted in the mid-1970s to focus on the degree of liquidity created by the Eurocurrency markets, and how this affected their interbank and prudential aspects.[24] Some came to believe that the lengthening of the maturity transformation between bank assets and liabilities inherently resulted in the substantial growth of global liquidity. Thus even stable, aggregate global monetary growth might not assure stable global liquidity expansion. Jane Little, for instance, argued that between 1973 and 1978 Eurobanks created greater net global liquidity "in terms of maturity transformation for the non-banks than had hitherto been indicated" by various studies. This was accomplished without varying the volume of loans available to nonbank end users, "by modifying the maturity structures of . . . assets and liabilities," with some shortening of maturities on the liability side of the balance sheet, but primarily with the lengthening of maturities on the asset side. The consequence was that "some borrowers are able to obtain funds for a given maturity at lower cost than they otherwise would. As a result, some investments occur which would otherwise not have been economically feasible."[25] Short-term Eurocurrency deposits, especially due to OPEC's high liquidity preferences in the late 1970s, were used on a massive scale to finance bond and other long-term loan placements whose overall maturities bore little relationship to the structure and duration of the interbank deposits. Eurobanks assumed that a rapidly expanding deposit base would provide an adequate underpinning for this procedure, avoiding liquidity crises. Eugene Versluysen concluded that a bank's "individually sound management principles can nevertheless result in collective illiquidity."[26] A Bank of England analysis concluded similarly: "An active inter-bank market may therefore increase the scope for behavior which seems prudent at the level of the individual bank, but seems less so when the whole picture is examined."[27] Folkerts-Landau concurred that additional international liquidity is created through "external depository financial intermediaries' practice of sustaining a greater degree of maturity transformation in their balance sheets than do the domestic depository financial intermediaries."[28]

In contrast, in an article which examined the Eurocurrency system under fixed-exchange rates, John Hewson and Jurg Niehans argued that the maturity structures of claims and liabilities of Eurobanks to nonbank end users had little if any impact on nonbank liquidity through positive maturity transformations, and "thus creates very little liquidity to the non-bank sector." They noted, however, that central bank operations in Eurocurrency markets might have produced quite different results than those of private actors. Central banks' Eurocurrency deposits increased global liquidity for the nonbank sector in a manner parallel to the Federal Reserve purchase of Treasury bills by its Open Market Committee; consequently, it was not the Eurocurrency markets themselves but the policies of central banks that had expanded liquidity.[29] (This related to the controversy, discussed below, about the creation of global base, or high-powered, money and the growth of official monetary reserves.)

The concern over maturity transformation was closely related to apprehensions about the growth of the interbank market which stressed the solvency and prudential integrity of Eurobanks. This growth raised the possibility of growing destabilization of the system due to the pyramiding of interbank deposits. The longer the chain of interbank deposits, wrote George W. McKenzie, "the longer the maturity and/or the greater will be the risk associated with each succeeding deposit," until a bank's liquid liabilities (initial bank deposit) supported increasingly illiquid assets. There was, consequently, an ever-present potential for liquidity crises or, in the worst case, a serious solvency crisis for banks that participated heavily in the interbank market.[30] Similar evidence during the late

1970s and early 1980s came from a Group of Thirty survey of Eurobanks, which concluded that "a majority of banks feel that interbank activity may be becoming more risky because of a change in the composition of the market (an increasing proportion of interbank borrowing being done by second and third tier banks)."[31]

Many observers thought that the central banks' practice of holding some proportion of their currency reserves in Eurodeposits increased the global monetary base, exacerbating concerns about Euromarket prudential and solvency problems and liquidity expansion. According to McKenzie, the monetary base was composed of "the sum of securities held by the central banks and its net international liquidity position (foreign-currency assets plus gold minus foreign-currency liabilities . . .)."[32] The Eurocurrency system did have substantial liquidity expansion potential to the degree that central banks held monetary reserves in the form of Eurocurrencies, thereby expanding their domestic monetary base. After the 1971 dollar devaluation, most of the advanced industrial states had agreed, under pressure from the Bank of International Settlements (BIS), to reduce or eliminate official reserves placed in the Eurocurrency system. Nevertheless, as Willett pointed out, with the rapid growth of petrodollars and other petrocurrencies, official holdings of foreign exchange by 1977 (in billions of Special Drawing Rights [SDRs]) were some 201 billion, of which about one-third (70.3 billion) was in Eurocurrencies (of which 58 billion was in Eurodollars).[33] Thus, while in general the Eurodollar market made only a minor contribution to raising the expansionary potential of international reserves, a possible exception could inhere in the central bank depositing of reserves. Swoboda noted:

> The observation that some 30 to 35 percent of total foreign exchange holdings are held in the Eurocurrency markets lends support [to these arguments, but] the impact should not be exaggerated [since this estimate is derived] from the assumption that these Eurodollar reserves serve as a source of high-powered monetary base supporting a multiple expansion of domestic money. To the extent that a significant part of central bank deposits in the market originate in oil-rich countries [about one-third] this assumption is unlikely to hold.[34]

The concern about the growth of the global money stock through official reserve depositing in the Euromarkets was an important factor to both policy makers and to TNBs in the controversy about Eurocurrency control.

This variety of analysis lent itself to an equal variety of mutually opposing policy implications. Three main policy currents emerged: "benign neglect," as advocated by Niehans and adopted as the dominant policy of the Federal Reserve in the early and middle 1970s; what McKinnon called benign attention, which stressed the significant domestic effects of Eurocurrencies to be remedied by interest rate and other market adjustments to influence foreign-exchange rates and capital flows[35]; and, finally, the regulatory-supervisory approach, which also stressed Eurocurrencies' significant effects, adopted by the Federal Reserve and the Treasury Department, in conjunction with the benign attention adjustment approach, after 1978. In general, there were two fundamental concerns in attempting to control or adjust to the Eurocurrency system: macroeconomic policy and bank solvency. Macroeconomic policy goals included greater stability of the international financial and monetary system (although this obviously included bank solvency as well) and the implementation of domestic monetary policy. Bank prudential and solvency issues included concerns about the efficient and prudent interaction of national and international financial markets, the equitable treatment of various financial intermediaries, and the distribution of global liquidity.

McKinnon, for instance, supported the Federal Reserve shift in November 1978 from benign neglect to benign attention. This shift took the form of massive, emergency foreign-exchange intervention to support the dollar and "allowing the American monetary base to contract commensurately with this intervention." Federal Reserve action recognized that "instability of money demand is now rife because credibility in the rule [of slow, steady money supply growth] is lacking, international currency substitution has become commonplace, and fringe banks and money market funds are offering competing forms of money . . . [which necessitated] an additional governor on the short-run rate of base money creation in the United States."[36] McKinnon argued that the logic of the 1978 emergency intervention should be expanded into general practice through increased cooperation among U.S., West German, and Japanese central bankers. They would adjust their respective domestic money supplies to correspond to each central bank's intervention in the foreign-exchange markets, thereby smoothing the dollar–mark and dollar–yen trade values in order to maintain what McKinnon calls "a rough purchasing power parity."[37] Coordinated action would aim to bring "the world's supply of convertible money under control through a mutual nonsterilization pact *and* agreed-on rates of domestic credit expansion by each of the three central banks." While this proposal was organizationally and economically rational, it ignored the increased economic and political pressures in all three countries toward rivalry and protectionism in both trade and money, especially evident during periods of slow growth or recession.[38]

Willett made similar recommendations for cooperative international surveillance of global monetary aggregates in order to minimize excess international liquidity. He suggested that the International Monetary Fund (IMF) should supervise this process. Allotting greater importance to SDRs as a reserve asset would enable the IMF to play a stronger role in determining when official intervention and balance of payments financing were desirable. This increased IMF role was to include the regulation of official borrowing on private international financial markets. Yet Willett recognized realistically that such a proposal would require a significant alteration in political alliances, as it would cede national authority to a U.S.-dominated intergovernmental agency.[39]

The political tenuousness of his proposal for international surveillance implicitly necessitated a fall-back position that paralleled McKinnon's national adjustment approach. (Neither McKinnon nor Willett directly acknowledged any political or economic consequences for various national economies of the fall-back national adjustment approach, such as slower economic growth and increased unemployment. Nor did they confront the consequences of failed attempts at international central bank cooperation. But it was exactly such failures that provided the impetus for U.S. proposals to regulate the Eurocurrency system in 1979.) Swoboda advanced a similar national adjustment approach, which would have moderated growth in the domestic component of the monetary base; moderated creation of international reserves by limiting the use of national currencies as foreign exchange reserves; revised domestic monetary targets to take account of off-shore markets in particular national currencies; and, finally, unified "regulations and reserve requirements affecting domestic and off-shore bank lending and borrowing."[40]

The Federal Reserve Bank of New York maintained a consistent position after early 1979 that contrasted sharply with most academic policy analyses. In 1982 it summarized that position, arguing that the national adjustment approach was necessary but not sufficient to counteract the Eurocurrency market's impact on U.S. monetary reserves. The policy was insufficient because it was not possible to know what proportion of Eurodollars (whether held by U.S. residents or foreigners) to take into account or even to which measure of monetary aggregate (M-1B, M-2, M-3) a selected proportion should be compared. Based on this reasoning, the Federal Reserve and the Treasury Department adopted a three-part strategy in 1979: a modified adjustment approach, along the lines McKinnon, Willett, and Swoboda had recommended; a multilateral attempt to coordinate an imposition of requirements on the Eurocurrency market; and finally, an attempt to coordinate systematic collection of global Eurocurrency data among the Group of Ten's central banks. This last part of the strategy was necessary to implement a national adjustment approach.[41]

The final relevant context of these policy debates was the impact of the rapid growth of U.S. domestic financial innovation. The consequences paralleled those of global innovation: a decline in control and regulatory functions of central bank institutions and a decreasing distinction between money and credit. Yet the control of money required strict limitations on the availability of short-term, large-scale finance credit. The growth of short-term credit was primarily responsible for the rising proportion of debt to real wealth in the U.S. and world economies which characterized the high inflation–low growth pattern of 1970s and early 1980s economic development. The result of these developments was the emergence of what I call a three-tiered U.S. monetary system. The first tier consisted of traditional bank money and credit, regulated by the Federal Reserve Board and the Comptroller of the Currency, insured and relatively stable. The second tier was composed of the new debt and credit institutions, uninsured and unregulated, offering substantially higher yields on investments and often greater investment liquidity. The second tier was the domestic equivalent of, and increasingly directly connected to, the third tier, which was the international private sector financial system, primarily the Eurocurrency system. The third tier was linked with the first tier through the participation of TNBs and with the second tier by supplemental access to global credit sources unrestricted by Federal Reserve Board controls. The second tier was as well directly linked to the third and the first tiers through growth of Eurocurrency and interest rate futures.

This three-tiered monetary system increased monetary instability due to the lack of control over short-term financial growth. Competing credit markets with differential yields on parallel investments increased the likelihood of runs by investors searching for the highest returns. This was the domestic equivalent of foreign exchange speculation. There were two related monetary consequences of this massive financial innovation. First, both domestic and international short-term credit and debt markets were increasingly unstable. Second, in order for a central bank to effectively implement a restrictive monetary policy, it would now have to constrict credit more strenuously, pushing the economy near the edge of a major debt deflation. This has occurred five times—in 1966, 1969–70, 1974–75, 1978–79, and most recently 1981–82. The existence of two unregulated and rapidly expanding tiers in the monetary system created pressure on central government institutions to further deregulate the relatively declining first tier of official money and credit institutions. It also provided a powerful base from which to argue that existing unregulated international markets, primarily the Eurocurrency system, should remain unregulated in order to effectively compete with domestic financially innovative markets, and *vice versa*. Thus the tendency to equalize regulatory environments among the three tiers was very strong, deregulating the first tier to better meet the competitive challenges of the unregulated second and third. This became the central argument of TNBs against the Eurocurrency regulatory initiatives.[42]

Regulation ventured: Federal Reserve and Treasury Department strategy

The Department of the Treasury and Federal Reserve Board initiatives to regulate the Eurocurrency market in 1979 and 1980 responded to three factors: the instability of the international financial and monetary systems, the shift toward benign attention, and the increasing pressure to deregulate and restructure U.S. financial institutions given the new wave of domestic financial innovation. The logic of unrestricted financial institutions in global markets brought economic and political pressure to bear on nation states to deregulate their own domestic financial systems in order to equalize regulatory environments.

The Carter administration's response to financial innovation would be to propose moderate global regulation tempered by a significant degree of domestic deregulation. The failure of the effort at global regulation underscored the weakening both of the efficacy of domestic monetary policy and of the U.S. capacity to mediate TNBs' interests. This latter was indicated most clearly between 1978 and 1980 by the explicit, contradictory demands of U.S. TNBs. On the one hand, they wanted restrictive domestic credit and monetary policies to limit inflation, stabilize growth, and protect the dollar; on the other, they opposed all attempts to regulate Eurocurrency markets abroad and demanded more rapid and far-reaching financial deregulation at home. But this desired equalization of domestic and global regulatory environments through domestic deregulation would have made the desired state exercise of monetary restraint more complex and difficult. Given increased internationalization, the state's capacity to control financial and monetary institutions was already weakened, even when such control was in the long-term interests of TNBs themselves.

In early 1979 officials of the Department of the Treasury and the Federal Reserve Board began publicly and privately to test the climate of U.S. and world opinion (especially among German, French, and British central bankers). They floated various proposals to influence or directly regulate the Eurocurrency system in order to slow its rapid growth. What was striking about the Federal Reserve's and the Treasury Department's analysis of the Eurocurrency system was their stress on both the credit creating and liquidity potential of the Eurocurrency system. The emphasis on credit creation stood in sharp contrast to the views of the majority of academic analysts, who, as noted previously, no longer considered net additional Eurocredit as significant. However, many academic economists did share official concern about the problems of equitable credit allocation and distribution, as well as about liquidity and bank prudential concerns. Official policy analysis, however, contained its own dilemmas. The Federal Reserve itself was divided about the impact of the Eurocurrency system on the domestic and international financial and monetary environment. G. William Miller and Paul Volcker of the Federal Reserve agreed early, along with Under-Secretary of the Treasury for Monetary Affairs Anthony M. Solomon, that the Eurocurrency system's growth necessitated some sort of control. Until at least May 1979, Volcker and Miller were opposed within the Federal Reserve by Henry C. Wallich, who then took a more restrained view of the Eurocurrency system's impact; his public turnabout came between May and June.[43] In reaction to U.S. probes, many TNBs and leading business publications began to publically question a central and nearly universally established tenet of state financial and monetary intervention: that the state can and must control the supply of money and credit, that money does not manage itself. The 1978 dollar crisis had raised speculation as to whether the United States was about to reimpose capital controls. Indeed, there had been some consideration of this course by the Carter administration but no action was taken.[44] In early 1979 Solomon delivered a well-publicized speech in London on the state of the international monetary system, in which he referred to the joint action of the U.S., Japan, Germany, and Switzerland to support the dollar against speculative attacks. Arguing that this type of multilateral coordination could and should set a precedent for greater "large scale [state] intervention" to stabilize foreign exchange markets under circumstances of "serious disorder," he went on to suggest for the first time that there should "perhaps" be similar multilateral steps to "strengthen official influence over [the Eurocurrency] markets." In addition to improving information about the markets, such steps would avoid repeating what Solomon perceived as the ineffectiveness of the U.S. capital controls of the previous decade. He stopped short of calling for state regulation of the Eurocurrency system, suggesting instead that "consideration can usefully be given to whether steps might be taken to bring banks operating in the Euromarkets more completely and explicitly under the regulations and supervision of *national banking authorities*." He explicitly recognized that such multilateral action—whether supervisory or coordinating, whether informational or regulatory—"can raise highly sensitive issues of national sovereignty."[45]

National sovereignty issues had already arisen during informal and formal supervisory central bank actions. The proposed formal Eurocurrency controls, which would require a high degree of information-sharing, would have increased tensions over these national sovereignty sensitivities. These concerns were viewed in 1979 during a series of multilateral consultations among central bankers to discuss the problems posed by consolidated bank supervision. Consolidation meant that a bank's assets and liabilities would be aggregated on a global rather than on a country-by-country basis, enabling the parent central bank to effectively analyze a bank's prudential soundness. Consolidated supervision raised two important national sovereignty issues. The first concerned the microeconomic supervisory role of central banks. If, as lenders of last resort, central banks were to ensure the prudential soundness of their TNBs on a global basis, the central bank would require disaggregated data on TNB operations in all countries, as the United States had begun to require. Thus, for instance, traditional closed Swiss bank accounts would have to be revealed to foreign state authorities. Concerning the Eurocurrency markets, consolidated supervision meant the centralized collection of data on individual TNBs' Eurocurrency operations, which had been closed to central state or multilateral enumeration even in the United States.[46] The second issue concerned the regulatory, macroeconomic role of a central bank, its ability to conduct traditional monetary policy. Solomon raised the point in May 1979 at the *National Journal* International Trade and Investment Conference: "We should consider whether additional measures are needed to help assure that the Euromarkets do not work to erode domestic money and credit policies, and that the markets themselves remain strong and capable of fulfilling their intermediary function." Solomon suggested that a minimum reserve requirement for Eurocurrency deposits be "considered." To be deposited with the respective central banks, it would simultaneously strengthen the Eurosystem and the effectiveness of national and international monetary policies. This proposal went substantially beyond either country-risk or Euromarket supervision.[47]

Although Eurocredits to end-users were then only a fraction of total funds raised in domestic banking markets, this fraction was rapidly growing and causing an expansion of global and domestic liquidity. This net addition to global money and credit was of concern to both Treasury and Federal Reserve officials. In May 1979 Wallich estimated it to be about $100 billion of truly "stateless" money.[48] To mitigate the potential inflationary impact of "stateless" money on the economy, a national adjustment approach, as previously described, was adopted in early 1979 by the Federal Reserve. The specific amount of domestic monetary constriction was to be coordinated with the emergency credit restrictions of November 1, 1978, which had been adopted as part of the response to the October 1978 dollar crisis. This reflected Federal Reserve and Treasury Department officials' changed perception of the Eurocurrency system; they increasingly stressed the system's potential to destabilize U.S. policies. The Federal Reserve began to implement a national adjustment approach by adjusting downward its money supply targets to take into account net Eurocurrency additions to U.S. liquidity. Wallich suggested that the Federal Reserve had only two options to counter this net addition: interest rate increases (in theory slowing "domestic" additions to the money stock) or some quantitative regulatory control. Since Eurocurrency net additions to world liquidity would increase, Wallich was clear that "the need for the Federal Reserve to exert greater interest rate pressure on the home market in order to offset expansion of the Eurodollar market is likely to increase in time."[49]

This interest rate approach, as outlined in the section above, was the domestic response to Eurocurrency growth favored by TNBs. However, it had negative consequences that troubled Wallich. Eurofunds were funneled through the largest, most concentrated TNBs, located in regional centers of the domestic money and capital markets. Hence tighter domestic monetary policy via higher interest rates would disproportionately contract the "local" domestic economy, increasing economic and financial concentration. In the long run, concentration would decrease state capacity to implement effective monetary, debt, and credit policies. To the degree that TNBs maintained access to Eurocredits, and to the degree that Euroliquidity expanded, there would be an institutionalization of abnormally high U.S. interest rates. If the U.S. rates remained high, Eurocurrency rates would follow, and other nations would raise their own rates in defense.[50] Such defensive interest rate wars did serve to protect domestic economies from imported inflation and national currencies from speculative pressures but at the cost of slow or no real economic growth, along with increased financial concentration due to lopsided access to Eurocurrency credit.

In response, Wallich and other officials proposed to distribute access to credit more equitably. In addition to interest rate adjustment, other policies could help equalize the competitive and regulatory conditions between the Euromarkets and domestic markets. This meant moving in one of two directions: either, as favored by TNBs, the elimination of domestic reserve requirements, effectively bringing the Eurocurrency system home or, as favored by the Federal Reserve, the imposition of reserve requirements on Eurobanks. In 1979 Wallich thought the situation was rapidly reaching extreme proportions: "Over time, as the Eurocomponent of the total market for any currency expands, control over the aggregate volume of money and credit may altogether slip from [monetary authorities] under these circumstances."[51] To Wallich, the implication was clear: reserve requirements would function as a tax upon Euromarket actors, discouraging participation, even though it would provide an incentive for further financial innovation.

> Reserve requirements or other restraints could be expected to drive some financial activity into other markets, such as those for bonds and commercial paper, where costs would be lower [than either domestically or in controlled Euromarkets]. In the last analysis, overexpansion in all markets can be restrained only by sufficiently high levels of interest rates. But this overall restraint should occur within the context of greater competitive equality between the Euro- and the domestic markets.[52]

Wallich and the Federal Reserve's strategy was to develop preemptive regulations which would avoid a future need for capital controls. A national adjustment approach, as had been attempted in late 1978, would raise domestic interest rates—thereby constricting all markets in response to Eurocurrency developments—but would do little to eliminate interest rate differentials among U.S., other national, and Eurocurrency rates. Costly credit and money would be maintained for extended periods with little guarantee of controlled declines of credit and borrowing levels. Interest rate wars among financial centers would intensify and, in Wallich's words, "this might then lead to controls over the movement of capital in order to cope with such developments." Wallich's strategy attempted to "develop techniques that will keep the expansion of the Euromarkets manageable, without placing domestic markets at a disadvantage and without recourse to controls."[53]

The central concern of the Federal Reserve and the Treasury (contrasting sharply with that of most academic analyses) was with the Eurocurrency system's growth making a net addition to global credit that could, as Wallich suggested, "come to equal or exceed domestic creation of money and credit."

> It would take severe restriction in domestic markets . . . to bring about a given amount of restraint in the Euromarkets. . . . It must be expected that as more restraint is exerted in domestic markets, some of the domestic demand will shift to the Euromarket and be met there, although at rising rates. In time, therefore, the Euromarkets are likely to pose a mounting threat to domestic monetary policy.[54]

Wallich's statements were striking: he stressed that given the 1978–79 25 percent per annum rate of Euromarket growth, Eurocredit would overtake the creation of domestic credit within a foreseeable period, effectively eliminating state monetary policy. The result was a paradox for the international monetary policy of central banks: to be effective on the global level required conflict with the dominant financial institutions which were their domestic political constituency for conservative domestic policy. Effective monetary policy would now necessitate multilateral coordination and direct state intervention in financial markets. In the pursuit of stable, noninflationary economic growth and free markets, policy makers advocating tight monetary and credit policies turned their attention to centers of financial innovation. Consequently, economic conservatives and former private sector bankers, such as Paul Volcker, were driven in the pursuit of conservative macroeconomic goals to oppose the desires of TNBs.[55]

TNB opposition to regulation

The Eurocurrency regulation proposals were made public in early 1979; throughout the year and into early 1980, U.S. Treasury and Federal Reserve officials met with their counterparts in Western Europe to explore multilateral actions. In early May 1979, Iowa Republican Congressman James Leach introduced in the U.S. House of Representatives the Eurocurrency Market Control Act of 1979, on which hearings were held in June and July. Had it been passed, the bill would have had little effect on U.S. policy for its main provision merely instructed the Chairman of the Federal Reserve Board to consult with financial officials and central bankers of foreign states to establish reserve requirements on all Eurocurrency deposits.[56] Nevertheless, although defeated in committee after hearings, the bill focused congressional attention on the Eurocurrency system.

Opposition to the bill came from TNBs as well as from the Treasury Department. The banks argued that such policy was bad policy; the Treasury Department argued that the bill rubber-stamped existing policy and was an unnecessary congressional intrusion on executive prerogatives.

According to Leach, the bill would restore state control over monetary policy as well as eliminate the competitive advantage held by the larger international banks over local and regional banks. He saw TNBs' Eurocurrency activities as one aspect of a trend toward financial concentration and innovation which threatened smaller banks and other financial institutions that lacked access to global, and in many cases to national, capital. The proposed reserve requirement on foreign and domestic deposits became the central issue in the hearings. It was at this time, mid-1979, that U.S. government proposals to European countries began to focus on Eurobank reserve requirements, and discussion in the business press at the time emphasized this. The debate over the nature and proper function of reserves held by a central bank illustrated the contemporary crisis even in long- and well-established banking practices amidst financial internationalization and innovation. (While not all advanced industrial states have required reserve maintenance, those that have not have had functionally similar regulations such as liquidity ratios.)

In opposition to the reserve requirement proposals in the Leach bill and concurrently being pursued by the Treasury Department and the Federal Reserve Board, transnational banks offered a counter-proposal. This would speed the growth of Euromarkets whether located abroad or at home, the latter in the form of an International Banking Facility (IBF) in New York City. The IBF would enable TNBs to operate in the United States without reserve requirements, state and local taxes, or interest rate ceilings for all their foreign, Eurocurrency-based business. TNBs saw the IBF as a step toward the elimination of reserve requirements and interest rate ceilings for domestic banking. While TNBs wanted to use the IBF as a wedge for deregulation, Federal Reserve officials saw it as a way to make the best of a bad Eurocurrency situation. In June 1980, Anthony M. Solomon, now newly appointed as President of the New York Federal Reserve Bank, argued that given the rapid growth of the Eurocurrency system he " would prefer to see a return of the Eurodollar business to the U.S. and foreign-based deposit and loan business serviced from U.S. shores. [The IBF] would enable U.S. banks to handle foreign business onshore, free of the Fed.''[57] The creation of what Solomon called International Banking Free Trade Zones would not open the doors to domestic deregulation, but would insulate domestic banking from IBF "Euro" banking within the United States. The Federal Reserve approved such international facilities in June 1981.[58]

In contrast to TNBs' desires for entirely unregulated IBFs, the Federal Reserve's original IBF plan was formulated in such a way as to pressure the United Kingdom into agreeing to internationally coordinated bank supervision and also to limit the then rapid growth of non-European offshore banking centers (e.g., Caribbean shell banks and the Asian dollar market). The Federal Reserve had refused to approve IBFs between 1977 and 1979, although under pressure to do so from U.S. TNBs. Only in 1979, as an attempt to augment its negotiating position with the Bank of England, did the Federal Reserve reactivate the IBF proposal. Significantly, it linked its proposal to stringent bank reporting requirements (Federal Reserve forms FRY-7 and FRY-8F), which would have required submission of consolidated financial settlements, full reserve disclosures, records of loan losses, and detailed financial statements for all related bank subsidiary and branch companies, including information on shareholders, directors, and financial officers. This would, in theory, have challenged both the London and the offshore Eurodollar markets, while simultaneously increasing and centralizing in Federal Reserve hands reporting requirements for all banks operating in IBFs.[59] But foreign central banks objected that such an increase in the Federal Reserve's supervisory powers would violate the understandings, embodied in the Basle Agreements of 1975, that the primary responsibility for bank supervision resided with a TNB's domestic regulatory authority.[60] Faced with strong objections from commercial banks, the Bank of England, the Bank of Japan, and the Deutsche Bundesbank, the Federal Reserve significantly modified its original negotiating position.

During the 1979 congressional hearings on the Leach bill, William Janeway, vice-president of the New York investment house F. Eberstadt and Co., summed up the issue of state regulation of banks:

> The evidence of history is overwhelming. Left to their own "prudence," private bankers operating for profit will once a generation jeopardize the savings of their depositors and the stability of the economic system by borrowing too much too short and lending too much too long. Reserve requirements and liquidity ratios function as direct reminders of that which truly prudent bankers do not forget: If death is nature's way of telling you to slow down, bankruptcy is the market's way. Indirectly, as well, reserve requirements and liquidity ratios are a prime vehicle for the exercise of surveillance by monetary authorities, allowing some margin of warning before push comes to shove.[61]

Janeway's perspective was confirmed by TNB representatives testifying at the hearings and in the business press. The most articulate spokesperson for TNBs was Dennis Weatherstone, vice-president of Morgan Guaranty Trust Co., a leading Eurobank. Weatherstone's argument, similar to the benign neglect approach advocated by Niehans, was extremely simple: it made no sense to impose controls on the Eurocurrency market because capital would in that case innovate, finding other routes to avoid state control. Since the Eurocurrency system was not the cause of capital flows, but merely their most efficient means of transmission, controlling the Euromarkets would only lead to the use of other such means. Nor, Weatherstone suggested, could Euromarket controls avoid exchange rate instabilities, since other avenues, including traditional on-shore foreign lending, would develop to fill the void of an overregulated Eurocurrency system. The solution he advocated was to equalize regulatory environments by "eliminating reserve requirements on domestic time deposits. A side benefit of this in the United States would be to help restore the competitive position of banks vis-à-vis the ever growing—and, I should add, uncontrolled—commercial paper market."[62] In addition, Weatherstone called for the removal of interest rate ceilings on domestic banks, then set by Regulation Q. He concluded that "a far more fruitful approach to dealing with the rapid growth of money and credit in the Euromarket would be to eliminate the regulations and controls which contributed to the growth of the market in the first place."[63]

The TNB position was summed up by William S. Ogden, executive vice-president and chief financial officer of the Chase Manhattan Bank: "If it works, don't fix it." A statement from the New York Clearing House Association, composed of twelve of the largest U.S. and British TNBs, argued that imposing reserve requirements would "constitute a burdensome and unnecessary interference with a well-functioning international market." H. Robert Heller, vice-president for international economics at the Bank of America, suggested from a somewhat different perspective that since most Eurocurrency liquidity creation was not of money but of credit, the former could be regulated and "perhaps" subjected to controls, while the latter should not.[64] In effect, the results would be the same since distinguishing between money, near-money, and credit was increasingly both conceptually and legally problematic in the new domestic credit and debt institutions and in the Eurocurrency markets.[65]

Two vice presidents of Citibank expressed TNBs' contradictory interests in a *Foreign Affairs* article surveying the events of 1979–80. They suggested that

> market reactions have taken the play away from the authorities yielding economic consequences as untoward as they were unexpected. Perhaps 1980 should be called "the year of the markets," to underline this emergent phenomenon. So far, its economic consequences have been unfavorable—in Britain, the United States, and the world at large.
>
> In the advanced industrial nations the frustrations of government and central banks are part of a larger phenomenon: not only interest rates and exchange rates but also inflation, business activity, and employment have passed beyond the authorities' control. Broad economic management, whether in the traditional Keynesian, "fine-tuning" mode or in the up-to-date form of monetary targets, seems to have reached a dead end.[66]

In sum, throughout the Eurocurrency control debates of the late 1970s, TNBs, demanding rapid deregulation of U.S. domestic banking and finance, used the growth of the Eurocurrency system as a stalking horse. United States moves toward decontrol (e.g., the establishment of IBFs and the 1981–82 wave of domestic financial mergers) weakened traditional state mechanisms to control money and credit and to regulate banks, making the implementation of macroeconomic policy more difficult. The traditional conservative impulse to control money, credit, and debt—through a slow and steady increase in the money and credit supply in times of low inflation, and through constriction in times of high inflation—ran up against the specific demands of transnational bankers. In the financial sector, advocacy of deregulation increasingly came into conflict with effective monetary and credit policy. Adequate state response would necessitate what the authors characterized as a disciplined stabilization program modeled on those of Japan, West Germany, and Switzerland. As the largest economy and as the issuer of the dominant global reserve currency, the United States had to take the lead by applying the "shock therapy" of stringent monetary control by controlling the reserve base of bank institutions (which would affect monetary aggregates). They concluded: "The way to control the money supply is to control it—i.e., to eliminate other considerations such as the level and stability of interest rates and unemployment that compete with the money target in monetary management."[67] This critique of the Thatcher, Carter, and early Reagan monetary policies appeared to question the general effectiveness of state policy. Yet their call for shock therapy—for politically and economically painful policy—affirmed and demanded the coercive power of an effective state to direct the economy through coordinated monetary and fiscal policy. The critical but unexamined assumption of this sharp economic conservatism was that the state possessed (and, given moves toward domestic and international deregulation, would continue to possess) the capacity to effectuate such policies. It was ironic, though significant, that two vice-presidents of a leading TNB should advocate that state monetary policy be implemented through controlling the reserve base of banks, for this was what the Eurocurrency regulatory proposals intended. Yet the proposals were resisted by TNBs as a disruption of well-functioning and self-regulating global markets. TNBs' opposition to the Eurocurrency regulation proposal and their simultaneous near-unanimous support for tight domestic monetary policy suggest the ubiquity of these contradictory and complex interests regarding monetary policy. The 1979–80 Eurocurrency debates illustrated the conflict between TNBs and the Department of the Treasury and the Federal Reserve Board, even in the pursuit of a conservative cooperation. The two vice-presidents' article, which made no mention of the debates on the impact of the Eurocurrency system on domestic monetary policy, was a prime example of TNB myopia.

Conclusion

The state impulse toward internationally coordinated regulation of the Eurocurrency system had run out of steam by early 1980. U.S. and West German efforts had made little headway in financial centers benefiting from Euromarket locations, such as London, Luxembourg, and Switzerland. Unilateral action, even by the United States for the dollar component of the market, would have been counterproductive in the absence of appropriate state intervention to ensure continued investment and production.

The 1979–80 Eurocurrency proposals, as a multilateral attempt to influence the growth of the Eurocurrency system, have three major implications for state regulation of global financial markets. The first is that such international agreement among states requires a high degree of multilateral cooperation, as recognized by Ralph Bryant:

> The problem of competitive disparities among nations' regulatory environments that bias the location and types of financial intermediation is manifestly an *international* problem. The United States cannot effectively act on its own to improve the situation. Unilateral imposition by the Federal Reserve of reserve requirements on the Eurocurrency liabilities of the foreign branches of U.S. banks . . . would merely chase most . . . business away from U.S.-controlled banks. . . .

If progress is to be made in diminishing the competitive disparities, an unprecedented amount of international cooperation will be required. Nations that benefit from the existing disparities . . . will somehow have to be persuaded to participate in reducing them.[68]

Specific future controls will have to prevent the development of further financial innovation (such as Eurocommercial paper). Without major power realignments in the global interstate system, failures are likely to persist, since certain states have a vested interest in remaining Eurocurrency centers. Economic rivalry among advanced states strengthens these divisions.

The second implication of the Eurocurrency control efforts is that global regulation, whether unilateral or multilateral, requires strengthened domestic intervention. The logic of attempted multilateral regulation of capital in the face of repeated failure is, consequently, not merely further attempts but increased national control. Yet stringent national control of investment, production, and finance not only presupposes political movements and coalitions for such control, but the ability to find alternative means for such control and alternative methods for the organization of social and economic life.

Thirdly, capital neither likes control, even in its own self interest, not tolerates it for long periods. Rather, controls breed continual innovation. Financial innovation has typically been the basis for growth and development throughout capitalism's history, but at the cost of long-term build-up of debt and increased speculation. The latter, in a variety of forms, has led to panics, financial and monetary instability, and, ultimately, to debt-induced depression. Intervention to stabilize, guarantee, and subsidize markets has been the usual contemporary state response to potential financial and monetary disasters, each time beginning a new cycle in the dialectic of market innovation and state intervention. TNBs' failure to confront the domestic and global implications of monetary and financial global nonregulation is noteworthy. This myopia, a result of TNBs' complex and contradictory interests, provoked comment by Jelle Zijlstra, Chairman of the Bank for International Settlements (BIS) and former Dutch finance minister, in reference to separate BIS proposals for Eurocurrency controls in 1979: "Banks are not very fond of controls, and consolidated reporting would extend the long arm of the central banks to their affiliates. But bankers do not always know what is in their best interests."[69]

8. State Policy Formation and Business Interests

A central theoretical concern of this study has been to locate the various grounds for state autonomy from transnational capital, especially in circumstances where state policy finds little if any support among various oppositional social groups and politically mobilized forces. Such circumstances clearly reveal the structural roots of state autonomy in relation to capital. I stress two interconnected aspects of the state's relation to institutional capital.

First, the state is integrally tied to an international system in manifold and complex ways, some which have been explored here. The state is not merely a reactor to that system or to domestic political pressures, but an active subject in the creation and re-creation of the international political economy. State structure and state policy matter, for the state is grounded in a larger social system than is transnational capital. This is not only because the state responds to political pressures from below or outside of institutional capital; what is too often ignored is that the economic and geopolitical links of the state to the international capitalist system become an important source for state autonomy.

The second aspect of the state's relation to capital lies in the complex and contradictory "interests" of capital, especially transnational capital. The state plays a critical role in the economic and political formation and mediation of the problematic character of capital and class interests.

Most American social scientists who have written about business and government have adopted one of two views of interests. The first more common one relies on the utilitarian assumption that various social classes, interest groups, and organizations have relatively unambiguous interests. This rationalist-objectivist view suggests that social forces are able to articulate and act on their interests, which are objectively what representatives say they are. A second view of interests claims that it does not really matter what interests may be "objectively"; all that matters is what representatives define as interests and how they act on them. This is a behaviorist and subjectivist view. Both perspectives share the assumption that interests are clear, readily articulated, and relatively coherent. On this basis, numerous theories of the relation between business and government have been constructed.[1]

This book develops an alternative thesis: the interests of capital in general and transnational and conglomerate capital in particular are complex and internally contradictory. This contributes to the state's capacity, and indeed sometimes its necessity, to operate independently of capital. It is an important reason why powerful economic institutions sometimes do not get what they want from government.

State capacity

Recent neo-Marxist analyses of the state which emphasize its relative or potential autonomy from capital improve upon previous interpretations of state power as directly beholden to capital or to a particular section of capital, usually finance.[2] Yet most of them define what the state is not; only a few attempt to go beyond negative statements to specify what the state "must" do. James O'Connor, for instance, suggests that the state must reproduce the social relations of capital, maintain legitimacy, and promote capital accumulation by providing what he terms *social capital* (state expenditures directly and indirectly reproductive of capital) and *social expense* (nonreproductive costs of social control). He does not, however, explain how this is actually accomplished or why it is necessary. O'Connor does not explore the political process of social capital formation. He assumes that there are functional necessities of the system which impel the state to develop policies reproductive of the system as a whole, even if such policies may lead to what O'Connor terms "fiscal crisis."[3] Fred Block and Claus Offe, to mention only two examples, suggest specific mechanisms through which what they take to be the rationalization and control tasks of the state are performed, but neither has undertaken empirical and historical studies to test his hypotheses.[4] Most studies that highlight the relative and potential autonomy of the state from capital rely on a social conflict explanation for those state policies they identify as being not supported by, or actively opposed to, capital.[5] They tend to overlook the contradictory nature of capital's "interests" as a source of independent state action.

What is the state? I take the state to be a bureaucratic, administrative institution which encompasses a complex web of often feuding interests that are in some cases beholden to outside social forces or classes and in others are primarily internal to the state. The state is a bureaucratic institution maintaining a monopoly of legitimate violence, capable of structuring social interests, although constrained by markets and organized political forces. The state plays a socially hegemonic role linked to the role of ideology as an active formative social force. Finally, the state maintains military, political, and important aspects of economic sovereignty within the international state and economic system.

The U.S. state is comparatively more fragmented and decentralized than the states of other advanced industrial societies; yet it is neither uniformly decentralized nor uniformly bureaucratic. In terms of its capacities for economic intervention, the U.S. state's mechanisms range from the relatively unbureaucratic settings of the Department of the Treasury, the Federal Reserve Board, and the Office of the President, to the massive bureaucracies of the departments of Defense and Commerce. The few state agencies directly responsible for the formation of U.S. international monetary policy and specifically for administering capital controls are quite centralized and not highly bureaucratic.[6]

The state is an active historical subject, whose actions matter in the composition and activities of classes, markets, interest, and institutions both within its national territories and in the world system as a whole.[7] Yet the state is not free to choose any action; it is constrained by another powerful political, economic, and social actor—capital. Charles Lindblom has observed that the mutual dependence of state and capital creates a "duality of leadership." The leading positions within the most powerful state institutions in the United States are held overwhelmingly by individuals from corporate and financial occupations. Yet the underlying forces which define the state apart from capital impel them, as state managers, to act quite differently than they would in their corporate and banking roles.[8]

National sovereignty, which the state manifests,[9] has two crucial elements: politico-military and economic. The organization of state military action and the balance of global politico-military forces have their own logic not reducible to the economic role of particular institutions. The capital controls, for instance, were not originally directly related to U.S. global military strategy, but they became intertwined with it after the Vietnam war escalation in 1965. U.S. state politico-military policies after 1965 increasingly conflicted with the stable workings of the world economic system, and with the expansion of U.S. TNBs and TNCs in particular.[10]

In the global interstate system, the nation-state organizes and implements its own international and domestic economic agenda in accordance with its unique politico-military role. State sovereignty in the economic realm, especially in times of either prolonged or sharp economic crisis, may well yield policies which differ from capital's actions and policy prescriptions. This is illustrated not only by the capital controls themselves, but by the basic strategies of top-level U.S. policy makers throughout the 1960s and 1970s. The defense of the Bretton Woods system, the conflicts between various presidents and corporate and banking officials over politico-military policy, and the conflict between transnational banks and both the Federal Reserve Bank and the Department of the Treasury over the implementation of monetary policy, all provide important examples of attempts to defend state economic sovereignty. Above all during this period, the state's concern with maintaining its economic sovereignty involved the international balance of payments. The balance of payments epitomizes the state's necessity to manage its own fiscal house in order to maintain its solvency. Persistent balance of payments difficulties exemplify the state's inextricable position in the interstate system.

The constraints placed on the state by business institutions and markets have two primary dimensions. The first is the direct and indirect political influence exerted by powerful economic institutions. This has been extensively studied. The second aspect has received less attention. The working of markets and the international system (both economic and politico-military) affect and often limit the more traditional influence of private economic power. As the state is affected by markets and the international system, it attempts to structure the institutions and interests of capital in accord with prevailing economic ideologies.

The history of the capital controls and international monetary policy between 1960 and 1980 suggests that even those state managers most ideologically sympathetic and attuned to TNC and TNB expansion were compelled in their roles as state managers to restrict and channel free capital flow for reasons of state. These politically informed economic policies respond to relatively short-run U.S. state interests, most importantly the balance of payments and the maintenance of domestic economic growth, and to the geopolitics of the U.S.-dominated international monetary system. The collapse of the Bretton Woods system from 1971 through 1973, and the continued domination of the dollar from 1973 through 1980 structured a course of action of the U.S. state. The rapid internationalization of capital, beginning in the 1950s, led to the increased fragmentation of transnational capital's interests vis-à-vis the U.S. state. This is indicated, for instance, in the divisions within individual TNCs and TNBs and between their various "representative" organizations concerning macroeconomic and geopolitical policies. The basis for these divisions among TNBs and TNCs themselves, and between them and the government over an extended period, raises the question of the fundamental nature of the interests of large corporations and banks.

Business "interests"

The concept of interests is one of the most widely used in social science. My use of it differs substantially from most uses. I take interests to be essentially socially constructed, and thus they cannot be comprehended apart from the ideologies which inform them. Interests are not necessarily a natural or direct reflection of social or class situation, nor are they inherent in social structures. The process of interest construction is conflictual, it is the stuff of political and economic action, and behavior on the basis of interests—rational, calculating action—is itself constituted from multiple possibilities in social situations.

This conception of interests breaks with the Benthamite utilitarian tradition which argues that interests reflect rational calculation as the means toward the maximization of some goal, usually money and power. Most orthodox Marxists (although not always Marx himself) adopt similar assumptions regarding class interests. The Marxist and Weberian traditions alike posit the pursuit of interests as a natural or ideal-typical logic of a system, whether capital or a bureaucratic organization. Both approaches suggest that interests inhere in an individual's, group's, or class's relation to the social structure or in the institutional structure itself. In contrast to this rationalist approach to interests, I propose that the immediate behavior of individuals, classes, or social groups cannot be derived from such assumptions. This is especially the case in regard to the interests of classes and complex organizations.

While my argument here is aimed primarily at the rationalist-objectivist assumptions of the Weberian, orthodox Marxist, and utilitarian traditions, it also implies a criticism of most pluralist, realist, and statist perspectives[11] which do not seriously attempt to relate interests to social structure but see interests as being purely subjective, whatever the actor proclaims them to be.[12] Interests have both objective and subjective aspects. These are interwined and complex, reactive and creative. In short, interests are dialectical, so that contradictions reemerge each time a solution is found for a problem.[13]

In sum, clear-cut interests—whether of corporations, states, or class formations—do not emerge automatically from class position or organizational structure, but are constructed on the basis of political, social, and ideological conflict. Once interests become institutionalized, they are apt to take on a life of their own, interacting with other institutions and classes. In this study, interests are found to be constituted in the interplay between the state and capital, and between the state and the international system, rooted in a socioeconomic structure with multiple possibilities for interest construction. Conflicts between the state and transnational capital are one essential ingredient in the formation of what are often taken, *ex post facto*, to be class-wide or national interests.

The dialectical formulation of the concept of interests can be illustrated with reference to the modern corporation. A number of studies have questioned the assumption that a concept of rational calculated interests adequately explains the behavior of the large business institutions.[14] Raymond Bauer, Ithiel de Sola Pool, and Anthony Dexter, for instance, argued that in the case of tariff policy in the 1950s, interest groups and diversified business firms did not necessarily act rationally or serve their own interests. Assuming rationality of the actors obscures critical theoretical problems and blocks from view "critical information about the structural parameters that in fact determined how people saw their interests, to what they attended and therefore how they behaved."[15] Self-interest, they conclude, is not an objective fact, especially in the case of the large firm: "the aspects of the conception that varied included *whose* self-interest, in light of which *facts*, and over *what period of time*."[16]

Theodore Lowi draws a similar conclusion regarding corporate positions in the 1950s congressional tariff debates. "Many of the leaders of the largest firms refused to generalize at all and remained actively inactive throughout the decade because their firms were too diversified to have a clear-cut interest. . . . (Many) typical large firms . . . left their individual managers to lobby as they saw fit."[17] Phillipe Schmitter continues this line of reasoning, suggesting that an interest group, firm, or even class may not comprehend its interests. The process Schmitter designates as interest mediation shapes interest perception. Interest group associations, he argues, "not only may express interests of their own, fail to articulate or even to know the preferences of their members, and/or play an important role in teaching their members what their interests should be, but also often assume or are forced to acquire private governmental functions of resource allocation and social control. Representation (or misrepresentation) may be only one of the activities of these associations, occasionally not even the most important one."[18]

This suggests that the state takes on an active role in developing interest consciousness and often in structuring interest groups themselves. Charles Anderson develops the notion of political design in a corporatist system, arguing that the state often will "define and channel the relationships of groups to the policy-making process. . . . [Policy makers] delimit group formation and competition, 'license' legitimate representative bodies, and may even create interest organizations."[19] While this corporatist model is not fully applicable to the United States (except during the first New Deal), the crucial point is that a state institution can attempt to thrust its notion of interest upon a particular class, class fraction, or interest group. Conversely, what is true of the state in relation to the units of capital holds as well for the "representative" organizations of the business community in relation to individual units of capital. A clear example is the comment of the President of the U.S. Chamber of Commerce regarding the apparently anomalous financial contributions of large corporations to liberal pro-labor Democratic members of Congress during the 1980 elections: "Business should quit trying to buy access (to Congress) and start buying a new forum for private enterprise. A lot of companies are putting their narrow, selfish interests ahead of the broader interests of the business community."[20] The struggle over realizing interests is thus the struggle over defining what constitutes interests.

What many analysts take to be the objective interests of firms, as articulated by firm representatives, are in fact strategic organizational and political choices drawn from what is a typically broad range of possibilities. The larger the scope of business enterprise, the greater the realm of choice of strategy and the resources to attain the chosen end. Yet a broad realm of choice does not usually lead to long-term, far-sighted economic, political, or social vision on the part of transnational managers. Most of the evidence in this study confirms Fred Block's observation that "ruling class" consciousness is rarely higher than business confidence—what works for profits and stability in the relative short run. If confidence is low, corporate and banking managers search for some other ideology, technique, or explanation of what works.[21] Leonard Silk and David Vogel offer substantial evidence for this view based on their extensive private discussions with top-level corporate executives.[22] I argue that the diverse positions taken by managers and by representative organizations cannot be fully explained as simply the result of the provincialism of managers with limited experience outside of their occupational purview. Rather, TNBs and TNCs present inherently contradictory interests.

These contradictory interests can be traced to four sources: the contradictory logic of capitalism as a whole; the nature of profit; the nature of complex organizations; and the role of ideology. The economic logic of capitalism has always contained a contradiction between the logic of the individual firm and the imperatives of the system as a whole. One example from the present study will illustrate the point. In the late 1970s, TNBs and other powerful corporate and financial actors called on the Federal Reserve Board and other government agencies to pursue a tight monetary policy to limit inflation and stabilize domestic and global economic conditions. Reducing debt and credit, minimizing the U.S. international trade imbalance, increasing U.S. exports, and stimulating productivity were seen as important interrelated goals. Yet TNBs simultaneously demanded a program of financial deregulation, along with a policy of noninterference in the Eurocurrency markets and permitting Eurocurrency transactions in certain U.S. free banking zones. These steps implied the growth of credit, debt, and new forms of money and consequently would decrease the capacity of the government to stabilize and control monetary aggregates. The two sets of recommended policies—limiting monetary growth and deregulating financial institutions—would likely have opposite results. Furthermore, qualitatively greater state intervention in international financial markets to confront global economic instability would logically have necessitated greater domestic intervention, since unregulated international markets tend to spill over into domestic regulated ones. Thus, TNBs' interests were ultimately contradictory: business expansion and global competition called for deregulation, while economic stabilization and traditional monetarist anti-inflationary policies required more regulation of money and credit. Stabilization of the financial system as a whole conflicted with the ability of individual TNBs to compete profitably and to expand domestically and globally.

A second source of the complexity of a firm's interests lies in the problems of defining profit. Most economists assume that large banks and corporations are predominantly, if not exclusively, economic actors which instrumentally employ noneconomic strategies to realize their own best estimate of their economic interests. A core of rationality, guided by profit, is seen as the driving force within the prototypical firm. This argument is too narrow, for it does not explain why a firm may make decisions not in its economic interests. It can, however, be argued that while firms are primarily economic actors, they are intrinsically political, organizational, and ideological entities as well. Consequently, the firm cannot be understood as a purely economic actor in the classical sense. There is no purely economic logic which determines its behavior. Even if profit should be the guiding light for a firm's actions, there are few clear-cut criteria by which a multidivisional transnational firm or bank may calculate profit, especially over the long term. It is extremely difficult, as management theory informs us, to operationalize a notion of profit.[23] Ideology, culture, organizational politics, and competitive position come to play important roles in the definition of profit.

Thus, an ideal-typical concept of profit as the guiding force begins to decompose into economic, strategic, organizational, and ideological elements.

The third source of complex interests of the firm lies in its being a complex organization. The typical multidivisional firm's interests—even defined as objective interests—are diversified. The brokering of these intraorganizational interests through a management hierarchy creates internal conflict. What were once, in a competitive market of single-line producers, actual markets (and in most economic theory remain so) become internalized within the firm, taking on an increasingly political and organizational character. Firm strategy is not only market-oriented, but must be concerned with the internal markets—the politics of organization—within the firm. The ultimate test of a firm's viability remains the external market. Yet this external market typically acts on the firm through numerous mediations: multidivisional structures, varying control of resources (financial, sales, and productive), diversification, and occasionally the state itself. In sum, the organizational complexity of the transnational firm's interests result from its diversified, multidivisional (consequently multimarket), and transnational form. The resulting organizational flexibility of the firm, although it implies an ability to shape the market forces and politics, also signifies a lack of a single grounded interest within a unified organization. This is reflected in what Stanley Davis refers to as matrix organization theory, according to which transnational enterprises are intentionally structured around bureaucratic units with competing claims, making interests opaque.[24]

The final source of the complex interests of capital is ideology. The ideological roots of contradictory interests are evident in their necessary interpretation, typically in bureaucratic settings, in the making of business strategy. Different perspectives on state intervention, for example, play significant roles in the weighing of interests and the developing of strategies. For instance, Keynesian assumptions informed U.S. balance of payments programs throughout the 1960s, while during the late 1970s, monetarism and the cult of free markets dominated much corporate thinking and led to the move toward deregulation as a strategic preference. (Yet often the intense competition which resulted from deregulation created havoc within industries, such as the airlines industry, and fostered significant corporate pressures toward re-regulation and organized markets.)

These contradictory interests of the typical large firm have a number of implications for the degree of internal coherence among TNCs and TNBs—i.e., the degree of class cohesiveness.[25] They have implications as well for the relation between TNBs and TNCs and the state. The first implication concerns what can be called the problem of representation of transnational capital's interests. Representatives of transnational capital vary from managers of TNBs and TNCs who speak in their firm's or their own name; to various organizations and journals with which these firms are affiliated and which attempt to speak in their collective name; to, in some circumstances, government agencies speaking in a firm's name. Evidence from the present study indicates that, over a two-decade period, on many of the strategic issues of foreign, economic, and military policy, there was little consensus among the various representatives of transnational capital. These differences of opinion and emphasis are the basis for interest mediation. Within many of the corporations and banks studied, several alternative positions might be expressed by different officials, and occasionally even by the same officials in different settings. For example, in the 1960s many corporate officials signed policy statements of the Committee for Economic Development (CED) on balance of payments policy while arguing a different position in congressional testimony. Yet many analysts of corporate politics take the CED to be the most important representative organization for large capital during this period.[26] On closer examination, the CED represented only one important trend among corporations and banks. During the 1960s and early 1970s TNCs and TNBs adopted two primary policy orientations. The International Economic Policy Association (IEPA), a smaller, conservative-nationalist (rather than liberal-internationalist) organization, has been little studied. Yet it "represented" corporations similar and even identical to those which participated in the corporate liberal CED. Further, within their organizational structures were divisions between liberal-internationalist forces and those of a conservative-nationalist orientation.

Recapitulating briefly, the representation of corporate and financial interests is an extremely complex process involving many levels of representative organizations and the statements and actions of corporate and financial managers in many settings and circumstances. Ideology plays an important role in all these settings. This diversity of positions is rooted in the contradictory interests of the firms themselves.

It should be noted that the complexity of interest approach does not lend itself well to (nor does it claim to be) a causal-predictive model of either business or interest group actions, nor of state activity and response. It thus differs in intent from both functionalist and structuralist accounts of social power and the state. What the approach offers is a greater analytic sensitivity to the conflictual interactions of state, markets, and market actors seen in structural terms.

Protecting capital from itself

That "ruling class" consciousness is typically no more than business confidence opens the way for, and often requires, state managers to formulate policy which goes beyond these limitations. In order for contradictory interests to be transformed into more coherent policy, the state must play a mediating role in the formulation of TNCs' and TNBs' interests. To the degree that the state performs this role, there is a possibility for state strength and capacity to remain intact. Because firms' interests are problematic and multiple strategies are possible, state interest mediation may lead in a number of different, logically consistent directions.[27]

The state's response to complex interests took two forms during the period between 1960 and 1980 in terms of foreign economic, especially monetary, policy. The first state response was what I call *interest mediation for capital*. State mediation for capital resembles a corporatist form of the state's relation to business, attempting to guide complex interests and harmonize them with each other. Typically, this means active business participation in state and quasi-state activities, both in policy formation and execution, a form of private government. This study offers some examples, for instance, the presidential appointment in 1965 of a blue-ribbon business commission to oversee and enforce corporate cooperation, based on previous business suggestions for a quasi-governmental voluntary capital issues committee. This interest mediation role performed by the state on capital's behalf dominated between 1960 and 1965, during which time TNBs and TNCs had neither a unified position on balance of payments policies nor specific means to achieve whatever policy might be seen as best. Government officials on numerous public and private occasions articulated for business what a "business" position should be. They were partially successful in developing business positions which had been only vaguely defined and conceptualized. State interest mediation for capital usually responds to one or more of three circumstances: divisions among or within TNCs and TNBs and their representative organizations; a situation in which there appears to be no position or only a highly generalized agreement; and, finally, a situation where contradictory interests are clearly articulated. This study has examined each of these possibilities.

The second state response to paradoxical interests is what I call the process of *interest formation*, where state activity initiates interest-transforming structures, typically over the opposition of dominant business or class groupings—in the case at hand, most of transnational capital. State interest formation occurs typically in opposition to the expressed desires of capital rather than in some form of joint corporatist effort. Interest formation uses state power to structure social interests generally and, specifically, capital's interests as they are rooted in markets. The distinction between state interest intermediation and formation is an analytic one. In practice, the development of particular policies may begin with state attempts at interest mediation yet result in interest-formation activities in opposition to capital's self-representation. Thus interest formation may result from the failure of intermediation attempts or from the different priorities of state and corporate policies, as with U.S. policy after 1965. The capital controls themselves were an instance of interest formation in that they channeled and directed capital, setting the stage for new markets and new means of doing business. One central purpose of the 1963 Interest Equalization Tax, for instance, was to strengthen the European national capital markets at the expense of the New York market, which up to 1963 had been the center of postwar global finance. New York–based transnational banks and investment houses objected that this would benefit European bankers at their expense. But Treasury Department officials (themselves recruited from Wall Street firms) responded that global U.S. state economic strategy necessitated a sacrifice for reasons of balance of payments. Each instance of capital controls exemplified interest formation, in some cases resulting from the failure of prior state interest mediation attempts such as "jaw-boning" business to voluntarily restrict capital exports.

The difference between state interest mediation and state interest formation assists in distinguishing my argument from theories which explain autonomous state action with reference to divisions within and among competing firms, between large and small units of capital, and among different sectors of capital or various geographical regions. In these formulations, the state is usually perceived as a rationalizer or broker attempting to act in an alleged general interest of capital. These formulations both miss the incoherence of capital in general and attribute an objectivity to the state which is often absent. While the state's role in interest mediation or interest formation often attempts rationalization, rationalization rarely results. Contradictory interests do not lend themselves to coherent policy. Those who stress the state's role as rationalizer place too much faith in state capacities and in its knowledge of what proper policy would be.[28]

While there are structural tendencies in the workings of capitalism which place the state in an interest mediating and interest formative position, nothing guarantees that a particular regime or administration will respond to those tendencies. There will, of course, be serious consequences if regimes do not act, but inaction has as many consequences for future structure as does action. I stress this interaction of ideology and structure against what I consider the overemphasis on structure by many who have written about the state. Both Theda Skocpol and Nicos Poulantzas, for instance, although far apart in many ways, effectively remove ideology from their analysis of state and class in attempts to define what Skocpol refers to as a "non-voluntarist" approach.[29] In contrast, I suggest that ideology is crucial in the formulation of state policy and has important consequences in the determination of the future structure of markets, the state itself, social interest groups, and, in certain circumstances, class formations. Keynesianism and monetarism embodied ideologies which played significant roles in shaping the structure of domestic and global markets and interest groups. State policy as an ideological expression is, on the other hand, limited by the structural mechanisms of markets, the bureaucracies of state and private sectors, and social and class conflict.

An example of the constraints on ideology, given the structural interactions of state and markets, is provided by the seemingly contradictory recommendations of Henry Simons. Henry Simons, although a classical economic liberal in the laissez-faire monetarist tradition, nonetheless argued that in order for a truly competitive, laissez-faire economy to operate, "we obviously need highly definite and stable rules of the game, especially as to money."[30] These rules have to regulate banks and issuers of short-term credit very closely in order to stabilize the conditions for effective and stable competition. Simons's observations in

1936 are all the more relevant given the trend toward the internationalization of commercial banking and finance:

> Banking is a pervasive phenomenon, not something to be dealt with merely by legislation directed at what we call banks. . . . It seems impossible to predict what forms the evasion (by financial institutions of state control of official money) might take or to see how particular prohibitions might be designed in order that they might be more than nominally effective. (A better financial structure would be one) in which the volume of short-term borrowing would be minimized, and in which only the government would be able to create (and destroy) either effective circulating media or obligations generally acceptable as hoards-media.[31]

Simons pointed to the ever-present tendency of financial institutions of all types to create various forms of money and near-money in order to circumvent state limitations on official money. This continuous tendency toward financial innovation has historically disrupted the pattern of state regulation of monetary and financial institutions and has often resulted in speculative waves and financial panics. To the degree that state policy has attempted to limit the growth of unofficial money, and near-money, it has usually met with the opposition of financial institutions, even though the typical motivation for state action is to protect capital from the potential destruction of its own free markets.

Max Weber argued that "money" was a social construction by state legislation. The state dictated what he called the currency's "formal validity" and defined its geographical "monetary area" of circulation. Like Simon, Weber assumed the congruence of a money's circulating region with a state's national sovereignty. Recent trends toward the globalization of finance, however, have severed the bonds between the geographical areas of the states monetary sovereignty and the actual area of circulation and production of "its" currency. Consequently, the politics of national monetary management become crucial for comprehending the development of a state's economic "interests," which may often be in opposition to those of TNCs and TNBs. Weber suggests that "The public treasury does not make payments simply by deciding to apply rules of (an ideal) monetary system . . . but its acts are determined by its own financial interests and those of important economic actors."[32] In the period between 1960 and 1980 the financial and monetary interests of transnational capital often diverged from the U.S. state's "own financial interests," most clearly defined by its chronic balance of payments deficit. Due to the increasing internationalization of capital, the state's statutory and regulatory monopoly of the social definition of money has disappeared. Private sector market innovation reduced the state's capacity to legally define money and thereby weakened its ability to make definite and stable rules for the game.

State efforts to restrict markets and financial innovation also have two external sources. The first is the direct and indirect impact of social forces from below, which may induce state action independent from capital. The second is the role of the state in global politico-military relations, often related to state intervention in the domestic economy for "national security" purposes. In turn, the state's "interest" in managing its own economic house tends to promote a concern with managing capital—protecting capital from itself.[33] As evidence from this study indicates, this potential for autonomous action is the case even for the U.S. state, apparently ruled so directly by the managers of TNCs and TNBs.

In response to the restraints inherent in these policies, capital has innovated, especially globally. The most dramatic and significant forms of innovation have been financial, carried on by TNBs and other financial institutions and by TNCs and large nontransnational firms with substantial cash and credit access. The U.S. capital controls, along with the small and highly controlled financial markets in the European states, were the initial impetus during the early 1960s for global financial innovation. Once TNBs and TNCs had achieved an arena relatively free from nation-state restrictions regarding the definition of money and credit and from the regulation of financial institutions themselves, the workings of free financial markets began to threaten the institutions and strategies of states within the inter-state system. International financial innovation, which was by definition unregulated by states, tended to augment pressures on the nation-state, especially after the mid-1970s, to deregulate domestic banking and financial institutions in order to equalize competitive and regulatory environments.

One of the components of the dialectic of state intervention and market and financial innovation is the nature of the interstate system. The capital controls have been interpreted in terms of a conflict between the logic of U.S. state politico-military global hegemony and continued TNB and TNC expansion. Such an interpretation, which Franz Schurmann has called the state's world of "ideology" conflicting with capital's world of "interests," is to a degree correct.[34] State policy throughout the 1960s and 1970s favored the politico-military policies and their economic corollaries against the undirected and unlimited expansion of U.S. TNCs and TNBs. State policy did attempt to channel and structure markets for its own ends. What a simple duality of political versus economic expansion neglects, however, is the degree to which the two are mutually dependent. The interaction of state and markets runs too deep for polarities to capture the fits and starts, and *ad hoc* quality, of state policy. Nor can this formulation capture the complexity of defining the "interests" inherent in capital's expansion and accumulation.

The dialectic of state intervention and market innovation often appears most clearly when new strategic market opportunities occur. For example, there was significant corporate and financial opposition to large increases in military spending during the Korean war and to the "military-industrial" complex in general. In both instances, corporations that would shortly become prime beneficiaries of state military largesse were brought into the new complex in the face of their own skepticism or even opposition to the state-initiated projects.[35] The capital controls described in this study were responses to what state officials perceived as serious global monetary disorder after 1960, even though the existence of a monetary crisis was barely recognized by many banks and corporate managers. Such action meant sacrificing what state managers saw as the short-run interests of TNCs and TNBs by restricting capital outflow in order to protect the ability of the state to pursue its foreign and domestic politics. Any solution to the balance of payments deficit attempted by the U.S. state would have negatively affected some aspects of TNB and TNC operations, even as the deficit affected their ability to expand and profit with state support.

The history of the five capital controls proposed to deal with the payments deficit illustrates that state intervention leads to financial innovation. This first occurred internationally in the Eurocurrency system, and then domestically in the late 1960s and the 1970s. In turn, financial innovation and market activity outside the purview of state regulatory authorities led to the disruption of traditional domestic and international regulation by state agencies, especially in the implementation of macroeconomic policy. Market and financial innovation resulted in increasingly unstable markets. The combination of instability and the incremental loss of control by the nation-state over its traditional macroeconomic policy instruments led to state attempts to restructure these new markets. In this context, there developed a debate between state managers and representatives of capital over what constituted the interests of capital. During the 1960s, this debate was pursued on the terrain delineated by the Keynesian paradigm.

Keynesianism and monetarism as state ideologies

In the debates over the interests of capital and the state's proposals for various forms of capital controls, economic ideology plays a central role. It was through the lens of Keynesianism that the 1960s capital controls were conceived. Keynesianism mediated the dominant interests of global capital, as articulated by various representative organizations and individuals, and the interests of state. The growing problems of Keynesianism as ideology and policy is illustrated by the history of the capital controls from 1960 through the early 1970s.

The Keynesian revolution became enshrined in U.S. macroeconomic policy with the passage of the Kennedy administration's Revenue Act of 1962, although the roots of the Keynesian coalition dated back to World War II.[36] During the 1960s Keynesian thinking dominated the debates about domestic and foreign economic policies. Keynesian policy coincided with U.S. hegemony in the world system. That the United States continue as the world's central banker and gendarme was essential for the realization of its Keynesian objectives.[37]

The triumph of Keynesian ideology in the 1960s had its origins in the reaction to the sectoral rationalization of New Deal state intervention, which emphasized state regulation of production and distribution of goods. This strategy was re-placed by the Keynesian goal of achieving aggregate economic equilibrium through control of the budget surplus or deficit and over money supply.[38] Along-side the shift from regulatory to aggregate interventionism, came the shift from supply to demand-side emphases, in light of the stagnation and turmoil of the Great Depression. The economic and political goals of Keynesianism were full employment, price stability, and steady economic growth. Herbert Stein has characterized Keynesian thinking as composed of three levels of analysis. The first level—which came to dominate among U.S. neo-Keynesians—held that economic equilibrium at full employment may not be achievable through mone-tary measures alone, and must be supplemented by increased government spend-ing and tax cuts. Problems were seen as temporary; state policy would be able to direct the economy back on the path of growth, with few if any structural alterations. Second-level Keynesians believed that the economy was permanently unable to regenerate full employment due to a secular decline in the interest rate (relative to the low return and high risk of holding securities). Thus there would always be a need for governmental deficit spending and measures to stimulate consumption through income redistribution. Third-level Keynesians saw the second level extending into a secular economic stagnation in which full employ-ment could be sustained only through government spending or, more likely, employment.[39] Second- and third-level Keynesians achieved little influence dur-ing the 1960s and 1970s.

Level-one Keynesianism has typically been seen as the polar opposite to monetarism, especially as monetarism became increasingly influential in the United States by the mid-1970s. What should be stressed, however, are their similar origins, approaches, and assumptions. Both perspectives emphasize ag-gregative intervention, which attempts to minimize or bypass any form of direct regulative intervention, such as capital controls for investment rather than pay-ments purposes.[40] In this context, Keynesians and monetarists have shared four basic assumptions about production, markets, and finance. They have recognized that new investment occurs overwhelmingly within the nation-state and responds significantly to state policy. Both have argued that aggregate demand can be managed by the fine tuning of fiscal, monetary, debt, and tax policies for growth, with theoretical "full employment" achieved through the market, although they differ on the correct policy mix. Both have assumed that the state can manipulate interest rates and the supply of credit and money (including state debt), thereby influencing investment and market growth. Finally, until the middle to late 1970s, most Keynesians and monetarists assumed a national economy as their basic unit of analysis, one linked to the international economy by trade. Keynes had written in 1933:

> Ideas, knowledge, science and hospitality, travel—these are the things which
> should of their nature be international. But let foods be homespun wherever it is

reasonable and conveniently possible, and above all, let finance be primarily national.[41]

Level-one Keynesians have used a model of the firm based on Alfred Marshall's classical prototype. There are four Keynesian assumptions about the nature of the firm, as identified by Ronald Müller. First, price behavior is flexible and competitive markets prototypical. Second, firms behave in a similar manner, with no qualitative differences regarding size, structure, and scope of operations. Third, firms' operations are independent and minimally influenced by activities in other nations and other industries; the model is a single-nation, single-industry prototype. Finally, pricing decisions are based on short-run profit maximization, with these profits derived from a single industry and nation.[42] In sum, the assumptions of most Keynesians, and in fact most monetarists, flow out of a certain theoretical model of markets and firms, of competitive prices, and of control over the levers of nation-state power that, once activated, are effective.

Level-one Keynesian ideology stresses aggregate economic intervention, yet to create the conditions for effective policy, direct regulative intervention would have to be undertaken on two fronts. The domestic front involved some form of wage–price guidelines and later formal controls, from the Kennedy era through Nixon's New Economic Policy. The foreign analogs were the capital controls. All attempted direct intervention into markets and supply conditions rather than relying on aggregative demand management; all led to results opposite from their intent. The U.S. capital controls and other foreign capital exchange controls stimulated the internationalization of finance and money capital, primarily through the Eurocurrency system. Wage–price guidelines led to controls, distorting supply conditions and politicizing the wage struggle.[43]

Buttressing Keynesianism as politically viable policy was the post–World War II coalition of organized labor and sectors of transnational capital and national business, supported by academics–policy makers. This coalition began to show serious strains beginning in the early 1960s. The issue was the necessity of sustaining regulative, supply-side intervention to create and stabilize conditions for aggregative, level-one Keynesian policy. Domestic wage–price guidelines and controls and international capital controls were the policies over which the coalition came to founder. By the time Nixon proclaimed himself a Keynesian in 1971, there were few others to support him. Big business's support of the Keynesian compromise, as evidence from this study suggests, was tentative, except in the relatively short periods when things seemed to work smoothly. Transnational capital became summer soldiers, if not in the Great Society itself, then in the macroeconomic policies which made that program possible. As soon as problems developed, business support evaporated. Business was ready to restrict economic growth, court recession to counter inflation, and correct payments imbalances. Corporate leaders were ready to accept the social costs of devaluation, deflation, and recession: high unemployment, slow growth, and social disorder. To a lesser degree, the Committee for Economic Development committed itself to similar positions. ''Full employment'' policy, supported in the abstract by significant numbers of corporate and banking leaders, was quickly forsaken when immediate profitability or stability was threatened.[44]

In the end, state regulation and intervention into supply-side conditions to tame the business cycle and stimulate aggregate demand through control of fiscal and monetary policy were to produce results opposite of what was intended. Increasingly, the credit-money cycle developed autonomy from the industrial business-investment cycle, precisely because the institutions of credit exploded beyond the control of any nation-state. This was the result of policies designed to structure credit markets in the first place, a classic example of financial innovation played out on a global stage.[45]

Keynesian ideology, in making the nation-state its unit of analysis, had taken for granted that state power would be effective. First, as observers have noted, to assume the state's ability to implement fiscal, monetary, debt, and tax policies in a coherent manner and a short time period in order to counteract business cycles was quite unrealistic.[46] The second unwarranted assumption, not widely acknowledged prior to the mid-1970s, was the effectiveness of state power to control policy levers, regardless of the country's relation to the international political economy—this despite the fact that U.S. Keynesian policy developed during a period of increased national dependence on external events.

The primary strategy to correct the payment deficit, capital controls, flowed from both a Keynesian vision of the national economy and the assumption of U.S. hegemonic stability. It was the hegemonic position of the United States in the world system that provided temporary support to the illusion that level-one Keynesian intervention (aggregative where possible, regulative where necessary) would work. To the degree that it was effective during the 1960s, the Keynesian coalition remained intact and provided the basis for the Great Society programs. But a growing dissonance between national economic policies and an increasingly internationalized world economy developed during this Keynesian decade.

The collapse of the Bretton Woods fixed-dollar exchange system in 1971 and the relative decline of U.S. hegemony through the 1970s signaled the beginning of a long-term crisis of state interventionist capacity even for the United States, previously the most insular of domestic economies. As the state's ability to regulate its macroeconomic environment through monetary and fiscal policies was eroded, two dominant responses were formulated. One, strongly influenced by monetarism, suggested that the state should retreat from many macroeconomic responsibilities to some form of laissez-faire. The other response, more related to neo-Keynesianism, argued that coordinated transnational action would be necessary to gain control of the new internationalization of capital. Ironically, some of those proponents identified with laissez-faire have argued most strongly for control of monetary policy instruments, which requires strong state monetary institutions. This reflects the ideological irony of monetarism: in order to create the conditions theoretically necessary for a free market, the state must intervene in money and financial markets. Except for those who have argued that money and financial markets are self-regulating, there has been a dual logic at work in monetarism, reflected, for instance, in the Federal Reserve's 1979 monetarist experiment, which significantly began with combined domestic credit controls and foreign exchange intervention. This dual logic has provided for some monetarists some common ground with a number of Keynesian interventionists. This alliance was evident in the 1979–80 Eurocurrency control activities.

Theories of the state

Economic ideologies such as Keynesianism and monetarism, when transformed into policy, have substantial consequences for the structure of the global political economy, for the relations between capital and the state, and for the context of state attempts at interest mediation and interest formation.

I have argued that business interests, especially those of transnational capital, are complex and often contradictory. Conflict between capital and the state inhere in capital's contradictory requirements and demands upon the state. State policy in these circumstances cannot directly reflect the ''interests'' of business. This results in a complex role for the state in interest mediation and interest formation, as means of protecting capital from itself. State policy results in the structuring of markets and institutionalizing of ideological conflict, which creates a continuous dialectic of state intervention and market and financial innovation. For these reasons, even without direct or indirect social and class conflict from below, state and capital will often not see eye to eye. These dynamics do not occur in each case of state-capital conflict, nor do they eliminate the great degree of state-capital cooperation. They are, however, an important source for the state-capital conflict which is more widespread than has been suggested by the weight generally given to other factors by observers and scholars.

Explanations of state intervention that attribute near-complete autonomy to the state, or, alternatively, ones that view the state as a simple reactor to various social forces and conflicts, miss the nuances and complexities of the state's relation with the institutions of capital, particularly TNBs and TNCs. Capital's contradictory interests, state intervention, and global market innovation constantly interact and mutually constrain even under the most probusiness administration. This view can be further clarified by briefly contrasting it with the two major traditions in the study of the state—statist and social conflict approaches. The following overview of these perspectives is not intended as a survey of the literature but as a brief critical review which will place in larger theoretical perspective the main arguments of this book.

Statism

Statist perspectives begin with the assertion that the state is analytically distinct from society and social forces. The state pursues a notion of the "national interest" which is not reducible to social forces or interest group pressure. Statist analysis tends to stress state military or economic capacities. There are two major schools of statist or realist thought: a *realpolitik*–strategic school, most identified with the work of Otto Hintze, Stanley Hoffman, Hans Morganthau, and Thomas Schelling and a more recent neo-nationalist school, identified with David Calleo and Benjamin Rowland, David Gilpin, and Stephen Krasner. Strategic realism stresses geopolitical and military-strategic power, while the new realism has been more concerned with economic issues. Both approaches analyze issues in terms of the "national interest," which is usually defined normatively as the public good or the public welfare, and at times merely as "preferences of decision makers."[47] For Morganthau, realism means the national interest defined as power: the world is seen in terms of a balance of power. The national interest is rooted in the nature of the interest to be protected, the political environment within which interests exist, and the "rational necessities which limit the choice or ends and means by all actors on the stage of foreign policy."[48] National interests are the "uneasy compromise" between "section" (group) interest and "the national interest rationally conceived" by the "statesman-actor."[49] For reasons of national interest, "all nations do what they cannot help but do: protect their physical, political and cultural identity against encroachments by other nations."[50]

The new realism, which takes a neo-mercantilist or state-centric view of state economic policy, shares the *realpolitik* tradition's definition of national interest. Stephen Krasner defines the national interest simply as "the goals that are sought by the state." Three conditions must be met for national interests to exist: they must be related to "general societal goals"; they must persist over time; and they must have "consistent ranking of importance in order to justify using the term national interest."[51]

The new realism shares with the old a primary concern for the national interest as against the growing forces of global economic power and interdependence. Its concern, however, is with the economic power and integrity of the nation-state rather than with a national interest defined in terms of strategic-military power. David Calleo and Benjamin Rowland write:

> Every modern state is mercantilist in that it accepts the responsiblity for managing the national economy for the general welfare . . . [defined in] broad social, political and cultural as well as economic terms. The state, drawing on its authority as the historic and legitimate expression of the general interests, tries to shape the national economic environment.[52]

Similarly, Robert Gilpin suggests that the unbridled expansion of U.S. international capital is not necessarily in the national interest. He defines national interest as "what its political and economic elite determines it to be."[53] He argues that the U.S. state elite has been too dependent on the economic elite in its view that overseas corporate expansion is identical to the national interest. Corporate and national interests do not and should not coincide. While Gilpin is critical of what he calls the mercantilist model of the world economy, his views are close to his own definition of classical mercantilism, which says that wealth and power—the economy and the state—are identical. Thus, quoting Jacob Viner, Gilpin suggests that in the modern world economy, "international economic relations are in reality political relations. . . . The attempts to create and to escape from such dependency relationships (of economic international interdependence) constitute an important aspect of international relations" for the state.[54]

While Gilpin and Calleo and Rowland have focused on the relation of national interest to the international economy, Krasner has most fully articulated a statist approach to the relations between U.S. TNCs and the U.S. government. Krasner begins by arguing that state and society are analytically distinct. Against Marxist structuralist versions of the state which suggest that the state acts to preserve the coherence of capitalist society as a whole, Krasner asserts that the behavior of the U.S. state "must ultimately be understood not in terms of economic or strategic objectives, but of ideological ones."[55] By this Krasner means that state actions have their own goals which cannot be reduced to "specific societal interests." Krasner points to a series of foreign policies that contradict any notion of a *rational* state acting to protect the capitalist system (e.g., U.S. "passivity" in response to foreign economic nationalism; "irrationalities" concerning military intervention, especially in Vietnam). He criticizes structuralist Marxists accounts of the state for assuming rational state calculation based on social class interests.[56] Krasner admits in passing that if ideology is seen not simply as a direct reflection of immediate class "interests" and structure, but has a "life of its own," then his argument is not distinguishable from a structuralist Marxist position.

In this important respect a dialectical constraint perspective resembles Krasner's position but with the difference that for the former, the "autonomous" role of ideology links the state as an historical subject with society, especially with the structure of markets, economic institutions, and classes. Krasner's point is that the state does not necessarily act rationally from a system maintenance perspective, and in this respect he rejects strategic realist and functionalist Marxist perspectives which view the state as a rational actor. He is correct: policy attempting rationalization is usually not rational in result. Krasner sees state irrationality resulting from ideological world views. This is the basis of unique state interests. In the state's world of irrational ideology, *ad hoc* decision making prevails. Yet Krasner and most other statists have not examined the sources of this irrationality in the state's response to the workings of the international monetary and financial system, to TNCs and TNBs and to global markets. Most state-centric work has not paid adequate attention to state-market dynamics, to the dialectic of state intervention and market innovation. Nor has it confronted the complex nature of transnational capital's interests, although this might significantly strengthen the case for a modified statist approach. State ideology and the pattern of *ad hoc* decisions are important, but they are both cause and effect of the state's relation to markets and financial innovation. Although state policy is constrained by capital and other social forces, it is not reducible to them. Krasner's perspective does emphasize the unique role of the state, its logic of world power, and the role of ideology in the constitution of state "interests."[57] My argument, in contrast to Krasner's consideration of ideology only as it affects state "interests," stresses similar aspects of ideology in the complex and contradictory interests of TNCs and TNBs.

Social conflict perspectives

In contrast to statist approaches, social conflict perspectives analyze state action as a result of the direct and indirect influences of bureaucratic organization and social, usually class, conflict. The central arguments of such diverse traditions as the bureaucratic politics perspectives, pluralism, various elite and power structure explanations, and most neo-Marxist and world system views share a social conflict approach, although they differ on the nature of the social forces. Like most statist work, social conflict perspectives assume a relative coherence in the interests of social classes and interest groups. Consequently, the role of the state in interest mediation and interest formation is minimized or ignored. If these processes were viewed as important, social forces themselves would have to be seen as mediated in relation to their impact on the state.

The bureaucratic politics perspective on state policy formation explains what it sees as the typical incoherence of state action by borrowing from American sociology's critique of bureaucracy as irrational and inefficient. It directly challenges most statist perspectives, which assume that state action is chosen, in Graham Allison's words, "as a calculated solution to a strategic problem."[58] The bureaucratic politics perspective offers a critique of bureaucracy which explains action through the conflicts of state bureaucratic interest groups. While a social conflict explanation, the bureaucratic politics perspective is partially a bridge to statist views, since it is exclusively concerned with state action apart from external social forces. The bureaucratic politics perspective identifies an important locus of policy generation in the politics of organization of the state itself. The state cannot be a rational actor, as many (but not all) state-centric approaches would have it, since policy is generated out of what Allison has called bargaining games, which regularize bargaining along "channels among players positioned heirarchically within the government . . . [who have] no consistent set of strategic objectives but rather according to various conceptions of national, organizational and personal goals, [make] governmental decisions not by rational choice but by the pulling and hauling that is politics.''[59] State bureaucracy is seen as a special case of typical complex organizations; organizational subunits play out their ''interests'' within the state, often mobilizing social interests for intrastate politics.[60]

The bureaucratic politics tradition offers an explanation of the state as an institution, as a complex organization which, in its own terms, seriously takes the control over resources and power.[61] It has been limited, however, by its lack of attention to state interactions with outside sources of power, disregarding in our case, especially, the role of markets and of capital. The bureaucratic politics paradigm also is limited by its choice of case studies, which focus on the most bureaucratic U.S. state agencies (such as the Department of Defense). But what is significant about the capital controls specifically, and about international monetary policy generally, is their relatively unbureaucratic political settings. International monetary policy is formulated and implemented with few intermediate layers of bureaucracy. This is one reason why monetary policy has to an increasing degree become the general medium for all economic policy. It is less visible politically and less restricted bureaucratically than are tax and fiscal policies. Bureaucratic politics analyses can be of use only to the degree that bureaucratic settings are relevant to the policy at issue.

The bureaucratic politics perspective on the U.S. state shares with statism a concern with intrastate aspects of policy generation. But it more strongly shares with American pluralism the assertion that power in the U.S. state is diffuse, that state organizations are highly specialized, and that, consequently, power is diffused according to the strength of bureaucratic political interests. In this view there is no sharp distinction between the institutional organization of state and society: political interests become the social-structural basis for bureaucratic politics. The bureaucratic politics paradigm becomes a form of intragovernmental pluralism. It is a special case of interest-group liberalism applied to the state.

The pluralist and interest group traditions encompass liberal, power elite, and simple ruling class models of state power as beholden to private interests.[62] Liberals tend to view private interests themselves as diverse and plural; thus government policy is a mixed response to these social interests. Radical critics, on the other hand, tend to see power as disproportionately residing in business circles, especially in large corporations and banks. Pluralist research has shown very little concern with foreign policy, unlike radical power structure studies which have devoted substantial research to it.[63]

In the classic pluralist work, *The Governmental Process*, David Truman attempts to deal with situations similar to the ones studied in this book. He argues that when no obviously mobilized interest groups exist, policy is the outcome of a consensus of ''significant publics''; this results in a potential interest group in the form of widely shared ideology.[64] Arnold Rose defines this, as do many realists, as constituting the national interest, by definition a "widely shared" ideology. The transmitters of this ideology may be business representatives, but even their domination of government does not indicate to Rose that they represent all of business nor even particular sectors of it. "The decision makers may have business backgrounds, but this is not conclusive or strong evidence they act to promote the interests of business. . . . They promote . . . their conception of the national interest in foreign affairs."[65] Pluralism shares statism's difficulty in defining national interests, especially in terms of the dynamics of the national and global economy, as well as its assumption that there are clearly defined "business interests."

A remarkable weakness in American social science has been its failure to pursue analyses that examine the specific intersection of bureaucracy and class. It has been suggested by organization theorists and some Marxists that this is because class theory and organization theory represent two conflicting paradigms. Yet it can be most productive, and in many areas it may be essential, to view state–capital relations in terms of both organization and class. A limitation of most statist, bureaucratic politics, and pluralist perspectives is that they pose questions too narrowly, excluding the dynamics of class, capital, and state bureaucracy.[66]

Elite, radical, and Marxist perspectives, to the contrary, often pose their questions broadly to focus exactly on those areas which mainstream theory has often slighted. Yet many variations of radical and Marxist analysis compartmentalize their analyses in ways similar to their mainstream counterparts. In the tradition of radical and Marxist power structure research, the instrumentalist perspective on state and class argues that the state represents and implements the will of the dominant sector or sectors of a ruling class. The state is seen as organically tied to the ruling class through personnel and social class linkages and links with nonstate or quasistate policy organizations, such as the Committee for Economic Development and the Council of Foreign Relations.[67] While instrumentalism thus shares with liberal pluralism a view of the state as penetrated by and directly responsive to social forces, it differs in its emphasis on the domination of large corporations and banks in particular. Instrumentalism, through stressing class domination rather than class struggle and conflict, attributes to the state a power and capacity similar to that claimed for it by statists. Further, most power structure research and elite studies do not consider the interplay of market innovation and state intervention.[68] I argue that the personnel in a power structure as such are not as important as the ways in which policy develops and is implemented, how policy makers respond to events, and how their actions affect and are affected by the workings of a political-economic system.

My perspective attempts to capture the dynamic relation between a state system of power and the global political economy. It owes much to Marx, the work of Karl Polanyi, and to the recent revival of a world system perspective by Immanuel Wallerstein, although, as will be indicated below, my views diverge from his in important respects. The world market and global division of labor constitute the basis for the structure of classes and other social strata within and among nation-states. Yet, exactly because class structure is globally based, classes cannot be expected to play their ideal-typical role as if they existed in a closed economy. A form of class displacement occurs, such that the "interests" of classes within states (and of regions of nation-states) are complex. State structure, class "interests," and politics consequently do not correspond to a pure capitalism. Marx captured this complexity when writing of the 1848 revolution in France:

> In France, the petty bourgeois does what normally the industrial bourgeois would have to do; the worker does what normally would be the task of the petty bourgeois; and the task of the worker, who solves that? No one. It is not solved in France; it is proclaimed in France. It is not solved anywhere within the national walls; the class war within French society turns into a world war, in which nations confront one another. The solution begins only at the moment when, throughout the world war, the proletariat is pushed to the head of the people that dominates the world market, to the head of England.[69]

The structure of the world market and division of labor is an important aspect of the basis for Bonapartism—the growth of state-bureaucratic interests which may come to rule over capital's economic interests.[70] While Bonapartism *in extremis* may be the exception rather than the rule in advanced capitalist states, it finds a structural basis in the global political economy, which creates new contradictions among the economic and political interests of transnational capital.

Given that capital's interests are contradictory, the representation of these interests in politics becomes closely linked with ideology. State policy cannot be understood without taking ideology and the problem of interests into account, along with the global structural basis for class and social strata formation.[71] Yet most of those writing within a world system perspective have attempted an analysis of the state without consideration of these factors. Immanuel Wallerstein defines the world system perspective as "a working social system larger than any state whose operations are themselves a focus . . . of social analysis. How states and parties, firms and classes, status groups and social institutions operate within the framework and constraints of the world-system is precisely what is debated." What is striking in the diversity of world systems literature is the lack of the development of state theory.[72] In Wallerstein's and others' work on the world system, there is little concrete analysis of class and other social configurations in relation to specific state structure and policy. There is a great deal of emphasis on what Wallerstein calls the interstate system, and on the basis for a state's relative strength within that system. But these writers have not confronted the problem of a state's relation to its ruling economic class, nor the related question of the impact of state action on the world system as a whole. Wallerstein suggests that states, especially strong advanced industrial core states, attempt to distort world commodity, capital, and labor markets in favor of the "interests it [the state] represents." But neither he nor others have clarified those interests, a clarification seemingly demanded by Wallerstein's acknowledgment that social conflict within states imposes "constitutional compromises" upon a dominant class.[73] Capital controls and international monetary policy in general have been important attempts to distort the world and national markets, yet they clearly have not operated in what could be called the interests of U.S. TNBs and TNCs. This hole in Wallerstein's work results from not taking the state seriously as an historical subject, from reducing it to an instrument of a national ruling class or class fraction operating in the world system. Wallerstein's state only reacts to social forces nationally and to the operation of the world system globally.[74] Furthermore, the world system approach views state action, whatever its sources, overwhelmingly in pure economic terms. Yet geopolitical and other noneconomic factors, as evidence in this study indicates, are not reducible to economic and ruling class "interests."

Recent structuralist Marxist theories of the state argue that the state's relative autonomy from capital is essential in order to maintain capital's domination in the economic sphere. Poulantzas' last writings on the state emphasize an institutional view which stresses that the state "acts in a positive fashion, *creating, transforming and making reality*." This action is seen, however, in functionalist terms. The state organizes a "power bloc" of several bourgeois class fractions in order to "represent" "long term political interests of the whole bourgeoisie . . . although it does so under the hegemony of one of its fractions."[75] Poulantzas maintains that state economic functions are "directly articulated to the specific rhythm of the accumulation and reproduction of capital." Thus "all measures taken by the capitalist state, even those imposed by the popular masses, are in the last analysis, inserted in a procapitalist strategy or are compatible with expanded reproduction of capital . . . [since] they may guarantee the reproduction of class hegemony and domination exercised by the bourgeoisie as a whole."[76] The problem of class interests and representation, though made explicit by Poulantzas, disappear into his functionalism. Many other Marxists, most significantly O'Connor and Offe, have tended toward a functionalist approach to the state's "role" in the economy.[77] Functionalist versions of neo-Marxist state theory differ from instrumentalism not in specifying result—the state is seen as reproducing capital and capitalism as a social system—but in explaining how this is achieved.

Another variant of neo-Marxist state theory places greater emphasis on contradiction, especially on the role of class and other social conflict within the state itself. Wright, for instance argues that most state policy can be explained by the impact of class struggle and therefore state policy is often contradictory. The origins of these contradictions, however, are attributed exclusively to social and class conflict, thereby limiting this vision in ways similar to more mainstream pluralist variants.[78] Consequently, even sophisticated class conflict perspectives have tended to ignore the significance of both intraclass conflicts and the contradictory nature of capital's interests, which result in conflict between business and the state.

Conclusion

This brief review of theories of the state has stressed the failure to synthesize the problem of interests with a fully developed global political-economic perspective. The case studies of U.S. capital controls in previous chapters have emphasized four theoretical themes: the contradictory interests of capital; state mediation and formation of capital's interests; the state's unique relation to the world system; and the dialectic of state intervention and financial and market innovation. The general propositions offered below begin the process of analyzing how the state may attempt to protect capital from itself. It raises new possibilities for theoretical considerations of state autonomy, the role of ideology in policy formation and hence in relation to structuring markets, and the general relation of state and capital.

The first two themes, the contradictory interests of capital and the state's role in the mediation and formation of interests, have been discussed earlier in this chapter.

The third theme, concerning the state's unique relation to the world system, suggests that the state has specific links with other states and international economic institutions and must respond to a different set of priorities than does transnational capital. An important source of state autonomy from capital lies in its location in the world system. In this study, the state's own geopolitical, economic, fiscal, military, and social priorities have been illustrated by its international monetary and financial commitments and choices. Under the fixed-dollar-exchange-rate Bretton Woods system, the U.S. balance of payments deficit acted as both a constraint on and an imperative for state policy. The deficits were embedded in a number of economic and political-military factors: among the latter, the NATO alliance and the Vietnam war, as discussed in the various case studies; among the former, private appropriation alongside foreign revenue shortfalls in the public sector. The U.S. payments deficit constituted what I call, following James O'Connor, a global fiscal crisis: U.S. overseas social capital and social expenses were threatening to deplete the gold stock and causing speculative attack on the dollar as the deficits grew. Under these conditions of growing crisis, while transnational capital was the beneficiary of social capital and expense, the U.S. state had to not only preserve its own fiscal solvency but maintain geopolitical and international monetary stability and mediate and form the interests of capital in an environment of international financial innovation.

The final theme of this work stresses the dialectic of state intervention and financial innovation. State intervention to form, structure, and regulate markets unintentionally but inevitably produces financial and market innovations circum-venting state barriers, as individual units of capital pursue profits and unimpeded growth. Each instance of U.S. capital controls, along with other national restric-tions on the free movement of international capital, only intensified the pace of the internationalization of finance, thereby further limiting the ability of the U.S. and other states to conduct monetary and fiscal policies as they had previously. The most recent examples of the financial innovations studied were the evolution of what I call the three-tied monetary system in the United States in the late 1970s and the establishment of International Banking Facilities in the United States in 1980. Two of the three tiers of the monetary markets and these on-shore Eurodol-lar markets constituted growing unregulated enclaves in what was formerly a highly regulated situation. These developments created enormous pressure on the state toward greater deregulation of all domestic money and credit.

This process constitutes what I call the state attempting to protect capital from itself. This dialectic is far from limited to the twenty-year period of this study but has recurred at least since the nineteenth century. Karl Polanyi, in his classic work, *The Great Transformation*, observed in 1944 that in the nineteenth century private enterprise needed protection

> . . . on account of the manner in which the supply of money was organized under a market system. Modern central banking . . . was essentially a service devel-oped for the purpose of offering protection without which the market would have destroyed its own children, the business enterprise of all kinds. Eventually, however, it was this form of protection which contributed most immediately to the downfall of the international system.[79]

My work, which supports Polanyi's thesis, suggests that contemporary state monetary policy tends toward growing fragmentation and is increasingly suscep-tible to pressures for massive deregulation, which, if successful, threaten the stability of the global economic system.

Notes

1. The Erosion of U.S. Hegemony

1. For domestic aspects of this approach see, for instance, Manuel Castells, *The Economic Crisis and American Society* (Princeton, N.J., 1980); Ian Gough, *The Political Economy of the Welfare State* (London, 1979); and James O'Connor, *The Fiscal Crisis of the State* (New York, 1973). For international aspects, see John S. Odell, *U.S. International Monetary Policy* (Princeton, N.J., 1982).

2. See Bureau of Economic Analysis, U.S. Department of Commerce, *Survey of Current Business*, 43, no. 8 (August 1963), 44, no. 8 (August 1964), 45, no. 9 (September 1965), 46, no. 8 (September 1966), 47, no, 9 (September 1967), 60, no. 8 (August 1980), 62, no. 8 (August 1982), Washington, D.C. and *ibid.*, "Selected Data on U.S. Direct Investment Abroad, 1966-78," Washington, D.C. On the competitive aspect of the shift, see Stephen Hymer and Robert Rowthorn, "The Multinational Corporation and International Oligopoly: The Non-American Challenge," in *The International Corporation*, ed. Charles P. Kindleberger (Cambridge, 1970) and Stephen Hymer, "The Multinational Corporation and Uneven Development," in *Economics and World Order*, ed. Jagdish N. Bhagwati (New York, 1972). See also Peggy Musgrave, *Direct Investment Abroad and the Multinational Corporation: Effects on the United States Economy*, U.S., Congress, Senate Committee on Foreign Relations, 94th Congress, First Session, Washington, D.C., 1975, pp. xi-xiii. See also Paul Blumberg, *Inequity in an Age of Decline* (New York, 1980), pp. 152-53; Frederick T. Knickerbocker, *Oligopolistic Reaction and Multinational Enterprise* (Boston, 1973), pp. 45-60, 101-2, 153; and Ronald E. Muller, "National Economic Growth and Stabilization Policy in the Age of Multinational Corporations: The Challenge of Our Post-Market Economy," in U.S., Congress, Joint Economic Committee, *U.S. Economic Growth from 1976-1986: Prospects, Problems and Patterns*. Vol. 12, 95th Congress, First Session, Washington, D.C., pp. 41-2, 49, 54.

3. U.S., Congress, Committee on Banking, Currency and Housing, *Financial Institutions and the National Economy*, 94th Congress, Second Session, Washington, D.C., June 1976, pp. 813, 818. See also Frank Mastrapasqua, "U.S. Bank Expansion via Foreign Branching: Monetary Policy Implications," *The Bulletin*, New York University, Institute of Finance, January 1973, pp. 23-24; and Frank M. Tamagna, "The Role of U.S. Banks in the Changing Pattern of International Banking," unpublished manuscript, The American University, Department of Economics, study paper (Washington, October 1973), (draft), pp. 12-15.

4. Andrew Brimmer and Frederick F. Dahl, "Growth of American Banking: Implications for Public Policy," *The Journal of Finance*, May 1975, p. 345. *Federal Reserve Bulletin*, 56, no. 12 (December 1970), p. A.19; 65, no.12 (December 1979), p. A.16; 68,

no. 12 (December 1982), p. A.18, A.56. See also Franklin R. Dahl, "International Operations of U.S. Banks Growth and Public Policy Implications," in *Banking Markets and Financial Institutions*, ed. Thomas G. Giles and Vincent Apilado (Homewood, Ill., 1971), pp. 61–62; and Stuart W. Robinson, Jr., *Multinational Banking* (London, 1972), pp. 276–90.

5. Charles-Albert Michalet, "Etats, nations, firmes multinationales et capitalisme mondial," *Sociologie et societes*, XI, no, 2 (October 1979), pp. 49, 46. (Translation mine.)

6. Alberto Martinelli, "L'impact politique et social des firms transnationales," *ibid.*

7. Immanuel Wallerstein, *The Modern World System II* (New York, 1980), p. 38.

8. *Ibid.*

9. Michael Hudson, *Super Imperialism* (New York, 1972), p. 61. See also Benjamin J. Cohen, "The Revolution in Atlantic Economic Relations: A Bargain Comes Unstuck," in *The United States and Western Europe*, ed. Wolfram F. Hanrieder (Cambridge, Mass., 1974), p. 106; Fred Block, *The Origins of International Economic Disorder* (Berkeley and Los Angeles, 1977), pp. 33–38; and Richard Cooper, *The Economics of Interdependence* (New York, 1968), pp. 29–36.

10. David P. Calleo and Benjamin M. Rowland, *America and the World Political Economy* (Bloomington, Ind., 1973), p. 87.

11. Calleo and Rowland, *America and the World*, pp. 87–91; Cooper, *Economics of Interdependence*, pp. 40–43. For a general analysis of the post-war system, see Georges A. Pariente, "Speculation, change et systeme international des paiements," *Economie et societe*, IV, no. 5 (May 1970), pp. 955–91.

12. Robert Triffin, *Gold and the Dollar Crisis* (New Haven, 1960), p. 9.

13. Calleo and Rowland, *America and the World*, p. 89.

14. See Charles P. Kindleberger and Walter S. Salant, "The Dollar and World Liquidity: A Minority View," in *International Economic Reform*, ed. Gerald M. Meier (New York, 1973), pp. 266–78; Sidney E. Rolfe and James L. Burtle, *The Great Wheel* (New York, 1975), chapters 5–9 and 12. For a critique of the above, see George N. Halm, "International Financial Intermediation: Deficits Benign and Malignant," *Princeton Essays in International Finance*, No. 68 (June 1968), p. 5.

15. See Odell, *U.S. International Monetary Policy*, pp. 129–30, 161–64, 362–67; and Giovanni Magnifico, *European Monetary Unification* (London, 1973).

16. Herbert G. Grubel, "The Distribution of Seigniorage from International Liquidity Creation," in *Monetary Policy of the International Economy*, ed. Robert A. Mundell and Alexander K. Swoboda (Chicago, 1969), p. 269.

17. Alexander K. Swoboda, "The Euro-dollar Market: An Interpretation," *Princeton Essays in International Finance*, no. 64 (February 1968), pp. 11–12.

18. See Robert Z. Aliber, "The Costs and Benefits of the U.S. Role as a Reserve Currency Center," in *The Quarterly Journal of Economics*. LXXVIII, No. 3 (August 1964). See also Fritz Machlup, "The Cloakroom Rule in International Reserves: Reserve Creation and Resource Transfer," *ibid.*, LXXIX, no. 3 (August 1965), p. 347.

19. The International Economic Policy Association, *The U.S. Balance of Payments: From Crisis to Controversy* (New York, 1973), pp. 69–70. My emphasis.

20. H. L. Robinson, "The Downfall of the Dollar," in *The Socialist Register 1973*, ed. Ralph Miliband and John Seville (London, 1974), p. 422.

21. *Ibid.*, p. 426. See also Henry C. Aubrey, "Behind the Veil of International Money," *Princeton Essays in International Finance*, no. 71 (January 1969), especially pp. 4–22; and the statement by Robert Roosa which emphasizes similar points in Odell, *U.S. International Monetary Policy*, pp. 98–100.

22. James O'Connor, *The Fiscal Crisis of the State* (New York, 1973).

23. Block, *Origins of International Economic Disorder*, pp. 164–202; Calleo and

Rowland, *America and the World*, pp. 87–117; and Rolfe and Burtle, *The Great Wheel*, pp. 164–202.

24. Block, *Origins of International Economic Disorder*, pp. 171–82; Calleo and Rowland, *America and the World*, pp. 118–127; and The American Bankers Association, *The Cost of World Leadership* (New York, 1968), pp. 22–25, 227–29.

25. Walter S. Salant, Emile Dupres, Lawrence Krause, Alice M. Rivlin, William A. Salent and Lorie Tarshis, *The United States Balance of Payments in 1968* (Washington, D.C., 1963), p. 230.

26. *Ibid.*, pp. 215, 221–24. See also Odell, *U.S. International Monetary Policy*, pp. 88–106 for a general assessment of academic and government opinion.

27. Block, *Origins of International Economic Disorder*, pp. 182–84; Calleo and Rowland, *America and the World*, pp. 17–20, 67–84, 118–42; Hudson, *Super Imperialism*, pp. 168–88; and Rolfe and Burtle, *The Great Wheel*, pp. 75–86.

28. Block, *Origins of International Economic Disorder*, p. 191; Hudson, *Super Imperialism*, pp. 189–207; Odell, *U.S. International Monetary Policy*, pp. 130–164.

29. Block, *Origins of International Economic Disorder*, p. 178; Odell, *U.S. International Monetary Policy*, 174–78; and Rolfe and Burtle, *The Great Wheel*, pp. 94–97. See also Eugene A. Birnbaum, "Changing the United States Commitment to Gold," *Princeton Essays in International Finance*, No. 63 (November 1967) and *ibid.*, "Gold and the International Monetary System: An Orderly Reform," no. 66 (April 1968); and George N. Halm, "International Financial Intermediation: Deficits Benign and Malignant," *ibid.*, no. 68 (June 1968).

30. Block, *Origins of International Economic Disorder*, p. 178. See also Aubrey, *Behind the Veil*, for a general discussion of the two-tier gold system and the power of international money.

31. Aubrey, *Behind the Veil*; and Emile Despres in *International Economic Reform: Collected Papers of Emile Despres*, ed. Gerald M. Meier (New York, 1973), pp. 97–130; and Odell, *U.S. International Monetary Policy*, pp. 189–99; Block, *Origins of International Monetary Disorder*, pp. 193–202, 356–57; and Rolfe and Burtle, *The Great Wheel*, pp. 97–130.

32. Odell, *U.S. International Monetary Policy*, p. 263, quotes Treasury Secretary Connor at a private meeting with several American economists on August 18, 1971: "I appreciate your coming today. And since you have shared your thoughts with me, I think I should give you an idea of where I am going. My basic approach is that the foreigners are out to screw us. Our job is to screw them first. Thank you, gentlemen."

33. Joan Adelman Spero, *The Failure of the Franklin National Bank* (New York, 1980), pp. 8–10, 76–95, 172–191.

34. Ralph C. Bryant, *Money and Monetary Policy in Interdependent Nations* (Washington, D.C., 1980), p. 387.

35. Edward L. Morse, "Political Choice and Alternative Monetary Regimes," in *Alternatives to Monetary Disorder*, Fred Hirsch and Michael Doyle (New York, 1977), p. 125.

36. The Group of Thirty (1982), p. 17; M. S. Mendelsohn, *Money on the Move* (New York, 1980), pp. 87–88; and Spero, *The Failure of the Franklin National*, pp. 175–77, 182–83. See also *The Economist*, October 16, 1982, pp. 23–26; and Felix G. Rohatyn, "The State of the Banks," *The New York Review of Books*, November 4, 1982, pp. 3–8. For Citibank's role in the interbank market, see *The New York Times*, September 13, 1982, pp. 1 and 25; and *Multinational Monitor*, October 1982, pp. 9–15.

37. Harold van B. Cleveland and Ramachandra Bhagavatula, "The Continuing World Economic Crisis," *Foreign Affairs*, 59, no. 3 (1981), p. 600.

38. Bryant, *Money and Monetary Policy*, p. 463.

39. Rimmer de Vries, "Jamaica, or the Non-Reform of the IMF," *Foreign Affairs*

(April 1976), p. 596.

40. Richard M. Cooper, "Monetary Reform at Jamaica," *Princeton Essays in International Finance: Reflections on Jamaica*, no. 115 (April 1976), pp. 58–59.

41. de Vries, "Jamaica, or Non-Reform," p. 595.

42. Alan Holmes and Scott Pardee, "Treasury and Federal Reserve Foreign Exchange Operations," *Federal Reserve Bank of New York Quarterly Review*, 4, no. 1 (Spring 1979), pp. 67–87; *ibid.*, 4, no. 2 (Summer 1979), pp. 56–59; Scott Pardee, *ibid.*, 4, no. 3 (Autumn 1979), pp. 47–63; *ibid.*, 4, no. 4 (Winter 1979–80), pp. 58–61.

2. The 1962 Revenue Act

1. "New Deal for the Dollar?," *The Banker*, December 1960, p. 779.

2. Sidney E. Rolfe and James Burtle, *The Great Wheel: The World Monetary System* (New York, 1973), p. 80; Theodore Sorensen, *Kennedy* (New York, 1965), chapter 16; and Arthur M. Schlesinger, *A Thousand Days* (New York, 1965), chapter 23.

3. The International Economic Policy Association, *The United States Balance of Payments; An Appraisal of U.S. Economic Strategy* (Washington, 1966), p. 167.

4. *Ibid.*, pp. 165–170; and Fred Hirsh, "Expedients for the Exchanges; An American Initiative," *The Banker*, May 1962.

5. *Business Week*, February 11, 1961, pp. 27–28.

6. Ernest H. Preeg, *Traders and Diplomats* (The Brookings Institution, Washington, 1970), pp. 44–47; Robert Roosa, "The Balance of Payments and International Financial Cooperation," speech by Under-Secretary of the Treasury before the American Bankers Association, February 7, 1962, in Federal Reserve Bank of New York, *Monthly Review*, March 1962, p. 46. See also Robert Solomon, *The International Monetary System, 1945–76* (New York, 1977), pp. 40–44.

7. "Mr. Kennedy and the Dollar," *The Banker*, March 1961, p. 157.

8. U.S., Congress, House Committee on Ways and Means, *Hearings*, "Tax Recommendations of the President Contained in His Message Transmitted to the Congress," 87th Congress, 1st Session (April 20, 1961), p. 5.

9. U.S., Congress, *Congressional Record*, "Balance of Payments—Gold Outflow—Message from the President of the United States," 87th Congress, 1st Session (February 6, 1961), p. 1791.

10. Fred Block, *The Origins of International Economic Disorder* (Berkeley and Los Angeles, 1977), pp. 35–37.

11. "Balance of Payments—Gold Outflow—Message . . . ," pp. 1791–92.

12. Ways and Means, *Hearings*, p.6. The tax credit would apply to 15 percent of all new plant and equipment investments in excess of current depreciation allowances; 6 percent of such expenditures below this level but in excess of 50 percent of depreciation allowances; and with 10 percent on the first $5,000 of new investment as a minimum credit. The proposal thus favored large corporate investment as against small business, as was pointed out by the National Association of Manufacturers who opposed the invesment credit as a "giveaway" to big business.

13. *Ibid.*

14. *The Wall Street Journal*, February 3, 1961, p. 8. Surrey was a powerful figure in the Treasury, subject only to Dillon and Kennedy on matters of policy and implementation (see *ibid.*, January 19, 1961, p. 3; *ibid.*, April 13, 1961, p. 1; and "New Developments in Foreign Aspects of Taxation," *The Journal of Taxation*, 14, no. 4, pp. 252–54.).

15. U.S., Congress, Senate Committee on Finance, *Hearings on the Revenue Act*, 1962 (HR 10650), 87th Congress, 2nd Session, p. 395; and Sorensen. According to Solomon, Dillon and Roosa in the Treasury Department served as a "counter-weight" to

the more "daring proclivities in economic policy of Walter Heller and his colleagues at the Council of Economic Advisers." (Solomon, *International Monetary System*, p. 41.)

16. Gilbert Bruck, "A Dillon a Dollar," *Fortune* (February 1961), pp. 93–94 and 225.

17. Sorensen, *Kennedy*, p. 408.

18. Ways and Means, *Hearings*, pp. 22–23, 68.

19. *Ibid.*, p. 32.

20. *Ibid.*, p. 327.

21. David P. Calleo and Benjamin M. Rowland, *America and the World Political Economy* (Bloomington, Ind., 1973), pp. 167–79. See also, Herbert Stein, *The Fiscal Revolution in America* (Chicago, 1969), pp. 389–95.

22. Ways and Means, *Hearings*, pp. 75, 77.

23. *Ibid.*, p. 33.

24. *Ibid.*, pp. 3527–28.

25. *Survey of Current Business*, March 1961, pp. 8–9.

26. Ways and Means, *Hearings*, p. 302.

27. *Ibid.*, p. 325.

28. Senate Finance, *Hearings*, p. 2570.

29. Solomon, *International Monetary System*, pp. 37–44; see also, Stein, *Fiscal Revolution*, pp. 412–421.

30. Senate Finance, *Hearings*, pp. 2281–84.

31. *Ibid.*, p. 2595.

32. Ways and Means, *Hearings*, p. 3103. For a list of the Board of Trustees, Officers, and Executive Committee of the Machinery and Allied Products Institute, see *ibid.*, pp. 3158–59.

33. *Ibid.*, p. 2670.

34. *Ibid.*, p. 2645.

35. Quoted in Senate Finance, *Hearings*, "Statement of Industry Committee on Foreign Investment," p. 2555.

36. Senate Finance, *Hearings*, p. 2557.

37. The administration opted for an investment tax credit rather than accelerated depreciation because the former allowed the state to be directive as to the nature of the capital investment. Overall accelerated depreciation allowances would not have allowed for this directive function, which is why business preferred the depreciation.

38. "The Administration's Proposal to Tax Foreign Subsidiary Earnings: A Response to the Treasury's Rebuttal on this Subject . . . ," Machinery and Allied Products Institute, *Bulletin* (mimeo) (April 4, 1962), pp. 7–11.

39. *Conference Board Business Record*, pp. 33–35.

40. See, for instance, Judd Polk, Irene W. Meister, and Lawrence A. Veit, *U.S. Production Abroad and the Balance of Payments* (The Conference Board, New York, 1966); G. C. Hufbauer and F. M. Adler, *Overseas Manufacturing Investment and the Balance of Payments*, in U.S. Treasury Department, *Tax Policy Research Studies*, No. 1 (n.d.), Washington; and Philip W. Bell, "Private Capital Movements and the U.S. Balance of Payments Position," in U.S., Congress, Joint Economic Committee, Subcommittee on International Exchange and Payments, *Factors Affecting the Balance of Payments*, 87th Congress, 2nd Session; and Walter S. Salant, Emiles Depres, Lawrence Krause, Alice M. Rivlin, William A. Salant, and Lorie Tarshis, *The United States Balance of Payments in 1968* (The Brookings Institution, Washington, 1963); Peggy B. Musgrave, *Direct Investment Abroad and the Multinationals: Effects on the United States Economy* (paper prepared for Subcommittee on Multinational Corporations of the U.S. Senate Committee on Foreign Relations, Washington, 1976), pp. 35–128.

41. U.S. Department of Commerce, Bureau of International Commerce, Office of

International Investment, *Policy Aspects of Foreign Investment by U.S. Multinational Corporations* (Washington, January 1972).

42. Polk et al., *U.S. Production Abroad*, p. 132–33.

43. Seymour E. Harris, "The U.S. Balance of Payments: The Problems and Its Solutions," Joint Economic Committee, *Factors . . .* , p. 22.

44. Sorensen, *Kennedy*, p. 405.

45. *The Wall Street Journal*, July 3, 1962; March 16, 1961; March 14, 1961; November 14, 1962; and November 26, 1962—editorials.

46. Machinery and Allied Products Institute, "A Response to the Treasury's . . . ," p. 13.

47. Machinery and Allied Products Institute and the Council for Technological Advancement, "Private Investment Abroad," reprinted in Ways and Means, *Hearings*, pp. 3133–60.

48. Robert R. Barker, "U.S. International Balance of Payments," *The Financial Analyst*, 16, No. 3 (May–June 1960), p. 54.

49. Malcolm S. Forbes, "Fact and Comment," *Forbes*, April 15, 1960.

50. Ways and Means, *Hearings*, pp. 2823–24.

51. David Rockefeller, speech to the Economic Club of New York, March 7, 1961, as reprinted in *The Commercial and Financial Chronicle*, March 9, 1961, p. 24.

52. *Ibid.*, p. 25.

53. Senate Finance, *Hearings*, p. 2404.

54. Ways and Means, *Hearings*, p. 2619.

55. Committee for Economic Development, Research and Policy Committee, *The International Position of the Dollar* (Washington, May 1961).

56. The Committee for Economic Development, Research and Policy Committee, *National Objectives and the Balance of Payments* (Washington, February 1960), p. 19. The Research and Policy Committee of the C.E.D. is its most important policy-making body. During the late 1950s it was chaired by T. V. Houser of Sears, Roebuck and Co. and in the late 1960s, by Emilio G. Collado, Director of Standard Oil of New Jersey. Most of the committee's members represent the largest U.S. TNCs. See G. William Domhoff, *The Higher Circles* (New York, 1970) and Karl Schriftgeisser, *Business and Public Policy: The Role of the Committee for Economic Development: 1942-67* (Englewood Cliffs, New Jersey, 1967).

57. CED, *National Objectives . . .* , pp. 20–21.

58. In the late 1950s the CED considered the deficit problem "serious." Its first statement dealing with the payments problem (*ibid.*) stressed reducing the deficit, and placed emphasis on a domestic anti-inflation program as the "first line of defense." The 1961 statement argued that "reducing" the deficit was not adequate; it had to be eliminated. (Schriftgeisser, *Business and Public Policy*, pp. 125–27; and *ibid.*, pp. 1–14.)

59. Herbert Bratter, "Foreign Aid vs. Trade in Showdown Clash," *Banking* (January 1960), *Business Week*, December 4, 1960, pp. 25–26. and *International Position of the Dollar*, pp. 9–15.

60. *Ibid.*, pp. 43, 50–51.

61. *Ibid.*, pp. 50–51.

62. *The Wall Street Journal*, June 10, 1961, p. 10.

63. *Ibid.*, February 1, 1962, p. 7.

64. *Ibid.*, February 2, 1962, p. 3; and February 27, 1962, p. 28.

65. *Ibid.*, February 28, 1962, p. 10; March 30, 1962, p. 3; and June 14, 1962, p. 1.

66. U.S., Congress, Joint Economic Committee, Subcommittee on International Exchange and Payments, *Hearings, Outlook for the United States Balance of Payments*, 87th Congress, 2nd Session, pp. 98–100.

67. "A New Attack on the Payments Deficit, Interview with Under-Secretary of the Treasury Roosa," *Banking*, July 1962.
68. Sorensen, *Kennedy*, pp. 438–40; *The Wall Street Journal*, September 7, 1962, p. 2; July 17, 1962, p. 4.
69. U.S., Congress, *The Congressional Record*, 87th Congress, 2nd Session, p. 17760.
70. *The Wall Street Journal*, August 27, 1962; *The Washington Post*, August 27, 1962, and *ibid.*, August 25, 1962, pp. 17785–86.
71. U.S., Congress, *Congressional Record*, 87th Congress, 2nd Session, pp. 17750–51; see therein, speech of Senator Douglas, pp. 17774–76, and speech of Senator Gore, p. 18172, who stated that the "pressures of the business community" were alone responsible for the defeat of the original 1961 proposals. *The Wall Street Journal*, September 26, 1962, p. 3; and *Congressional Record*, pp. 21745–64 and p. 21707.

3. The Interest Equalization Tax

1. Henry G. Aubrey, *The Dollar in World Affairs* (New York, 1964), p. 53.
2. Richard N. Cooper, "The Interest Equalization Tax: An experiment in the separation of capital markets," *Finanzarchiv*, Band 24, Heft 3 (December 1965), pp. 448–49; and John S. Odell, *U.S. International Monetary Policy* (Princeton, N.J., 1982), pp. 89–96.
3. "The President's Special Message on Balance of Payments," in U.S., Congress, House Ways and Means Committee, *Hearings*, 88th Congress, First Session, pp. 8–9.
4. *The Wall Street Journal*, September 4, 1964, p. 5.
5. U.S., Congress, Senate Committee on Finance, *Hearings on HR 8000: The Interest Equalization Tax*, 88th Congress, Second Session, p. 71.
6. *The Banker*, August 1963, p. 523; and *The Wall Street Journal*, July 23, 1963, p. 14.
7. Department of Commerce data quoted in Ways and Means, *Hearings*, pp. 73 and 113.
8. Aubrey, *Dollar in World Affairs*, pp. 178–82 and 280–81.
9. Oscar L. Altman, "The Integration of European Capital Markets," *Journal of Finance*, March 1963, p. 209; and Janet Kelly, *Bankers Borders* (Cambridge, Mass., 1977), p. 49.
10. Ways and Means, *Hearings*, p. 58.
11. *Ibid.*, p. 58.
12. *Ibid.*, p. 15.
13. Senate Finance, *Hearings on HR 8000*, p. 63.
14. David Williams, "The Development of Capital Markets in Europe," *IMF Staff Papers* (March 1964), pp. 40–41. See also Dr. Sidney E. Rolfe, *Capital Markets in Atlantic Economic Relationships* (Boulogne-sur-Seine, April 1967), pp. 26–27, 70.
15. Williams, "Development of Capital Markets," pp. 37 and 53.
16. [U.S. Treasury Department], "A Description and Analysis of Certain European Capital Markets," in U.S. Congress, Joint Economic Committee, *Economic Policies and Practices*, Paper No. 3 (Washington, 1964), p. 3.
17. *Ibid.*, p. 22; and Williams, "Development of Capital Markets," pp. 49–51.
18. Paul Einzig, *The Euro-Dollar System* (London, 1965).
19. Rolfe, *Capital Markets*, pp. 26–27; and Altman, "Integration of Capital Mar-

kets,'' pp. 210–212.

20. See Bank of England, *Quarterly Bulletin* II (December 1962) pp. 63–66 and Cooper, ''Interest Equalization Tax,'' p. 463.

21. Ways and Means, *Hearings*, pp. 236–37.

22. Altman, ''Integration of Capital Markets,'' pp. 211–212.

23. Richard N. Cooper, *The Economics of Interdependence* (New York, 1968), pp. 127–28. See also Giovanni Magnifico, *European Monetary Unification* (London, 1973), pp. 199–222.

24. Cooper, pp. 24, 130–32.

25. Janet Kelly, *Bankers and Borders* (Cambridge, 1977), pp. 49, 106–08, 116, 180.

26. *Business Week*, August 3, 1963, p. 92 and July 27, 1963, pp. 19–22.

27. *Ibid.*

28. *The Wall Street Journal*, October 22, 1963, p. 2.

29. *Business Week*, July 27, 1963, p. 20; and *The Banker*, August 1963, pp. 519–23.

30. *The Wall Street Journal*, July 23, 1963, p. 14 and December 12, 1963, p. 7.

31. Ways and Means, *Hearings*, pp. 408–37; and Senate Finance, *Hearings on HR 8000*, p. 329.

32. The top level leadership of U.S. financial capital articulated an intense opposition to the IET. For example, testifying for the IBA at the House Ways and Means Committee Hearings was Andrew N. Overby, Chairman of the First Boston Corporation, former Assistant Secretary of the Treasury, former Deputy Managing Director of the International Monetary Fund and of the International Bank. Overby also represented the leading investment houses of Kidder, Peabody and Co.; Goldman, Sachs and Co.; and Kuhn, Loeb and Co.

33. Ways and Means, *Hearings*, pp. 22–25, 219; and Senate *Hearings on HR 8000* pp. 189–90. The IBA relied especially on the 1963 Brookings Institution study which argued that by 1968 the basic deficit would be eliminated without resorting to capital and/or exchange controls. See Emile Despres, *et al.*, *The U.S. Balance of Payments in 1968* (Washington, 1963).

34. Senate Finance, *Hearings on HR 8000*, pp. 168 and 188.

35. *Congressional Record*, 88th Congress, 2nd Session, pp. 17790–91; *ibid.*, p. 239.

36. *The Wall Street Journal*, October 22, 1964, p. 2; and *Congressional Record*, 88th Congress, 2nd Session, p. 18008.

37. For example, see Amas Ames, President of the IBA and Andrew Overby, Chairman of IBA, ''Memorandum to Members of the U.S. Congress,'' in *Commercial and Financial Chronicle*, November 28, 1963, p. 21.

38. Editors, *Monthly Review*, ''Review of the Monthly,'' November 1972, pp. 2–4.

39. Senate Finance, *Hearings on HR 8000*, pp. 150–54; and Ways and Means, *Hearings*, pp. 321–23.

40. Ways and Means, *Hearings*, p. 323.

41. Senate Finance, *Hearings on HR 8000*, p. 160.

42. See David P. Calleo and Benjamin M. Rowland, *America and the World Political Economy* (Bloomington, Ind., 1973), pp. 118–61 for discussion of the problems of the Atlantic alliance.

43. H. L. Robinson, ''The Downfall of the Dollar,'' in *The Socialist Register, 1973*, ed. Ralph Miliband and John Seville (London, 1974), pp. 410, 422–423.

44. See James O'Connor, *The Fiscal Crisis of the State* (New York, 1973), Chapter III; and Ronald I. McKinnon, ''The Exchange Rate and Macroeconomic Policy: Changing Postwar Perceptions,'' in *The Journal of Economic Literature*, Vol. XIX (June 1981), pp. 531–57.

45. Ways and Means, *Hearings*, pp. 145–50.

46. See testimony of Nathaniel Samuels, Chairman of the Foreign Investment Com-

mittee of the IBA in U.S. Congress, House Committee on Ways and Means, *Hearings on HR 3813*, 90th Congress, First Session, pp. 72–74.

47. *Ibid.*, p. 74.

48. Speech before the National Industrial Conference Federation in *The Commercial and Financial Chronicle* (October 29, 1964), pp. 3, 24–25.

49. Ways and Means, *Hearings on HR 3813*, p. 34.

50. *Ibid.*, pp. 33–34; and Odell, *U.S. International Monetary Policy*, pp. 79–164.

51. *Ibid.*, pp. 200–11.

52. U.S., Congress, Senate Committee on Finance, *Hearings on HR 12829*, 91st Congress, First Session, p. 21.

53. *Ibid.*, p. 67; and U.S., Congress, *Congressional Record*, 91st Congress, First Session, pp. 22809–13, 29484.

4. The Voluntary Capital Control Programs

1. Evelyn M. Parish, "The U.S. Balance of Payments in 1964," U.S. Department of Commerce, Survey of Current Business, March 1965, p. 13.

2. U.S. Department of Commerce, *Survey of Current Business*, March 1965, p. 20, Table 5.

3. Parish, "U.S. Balance of Payments," p. 16.

4. "Message of the President of the United States to Review of International Balance of Payments and Our Gold Position," U.S., Congress, Senate Committee on Banking and Currency, *Balance of Payments, 1965, Hearings*, 89th Congress, 1st Session, pp. 4–5. (Document not paginated.)

5. Secretary of Commerce, "Address before the Economic Club of New York," March 15, 1965; reprinted in Banking and Currency, *Balance of Payments Hearings*, p. 660.

6. *Ibid.*, p. 886.

7. *Ibid.*, p. 872, see also U.S. Congress, House Committee on Judiciary, Subcommittee on Anti-Trust, *Hearings on HR 5280*, 89th Congress, 1st Session, p. 406.

8. *Balance of Payments Hearings*, p. 180.

9. *Economic Report of the President and Annual Report of the Council of Economic Advisers*, 1966; p. 150.

10. U.S. Treasury Department, *Maintaining the Strength of the United States Dollar in a Strong, Free World Economy* (Washington, 1968), p. 4. (Also know as the *Blue Book*.)

11. John S. Odell, *U.S. International Monetary Policy* (Princeton, NJ, 1982), pp. 130–52.

12. *Ibid.*, p. 49.

13. Committee for Economic Development, *Gold, the Dollar and the World Monetary System* (Washington, 1965), p. 45.

14. *Ibid.*, p. 44.

15. *Ibid.*, pp. 44, 47–48.

16. William McChesney Martin, testimony, in *Hearings on HR 5280*, p. 406.

17. *Balance of Payments Hearings*, p. 166.

18. *Business Week*, June 12, 1965, pp. 36–37; Odell, *International Monetary Policy*, pp. 150–51.

19. Odell, *U.S. International Monetary Policy*, p. 150.

20. *Balance of Payments Hearings*, p. 5 (emphasis in original). Harry O. Johnson commented: "The private confidential negotiations, together with stress laid on the personal responsibility of the company presidents for their companies' programs, constitute in their way a significant new departure in the relationship of government and business

in this country, toward the political concept of the corporate state" (Harry O. Johnson, "Balance of Payments Controls and Guidelines for Trade and Investment," in *Guidelines, Informal Controls and the Marketplace*, ed George P. Schultz and Robert Z. Aliber (Chicago, 1966), p. 173.

21. *Balance of Payments Hearings*, p. 6.

22. *Business Week*, February 26, 1965, pp. 34–35.

23. U.S., Congress, Senate Committee of Judiciary, Subcommittee on Anti-Trust and Monopoly, *Hearings, Anti-Trust Exemptions—Balance of Payments*, 89th Congress, 1st Session, pp. 133–34.

The other members were: Fred J. Burch, President, General Electric; Elisha Gray, II, Chairman, Whirlpool Corp.; J. Ward Keener, President, B.F. Goodrich; George S. Moore, President, First National City Bank, New York; Stuart J. Saunders, Chairman, Pennsylvania Railroad; Sidney J. Weinberg, Partner, Goldman, Sachs and Co.

24. *Ibid.*, p. 133. Connor in his initial letter of March 17, 1965, to the 600 largest industrial corporations subject to the voluntary program, indicated that the informality and "flexibility" of the program was a result of the Advisory Committee's judgment, "that the leaders of American industry will respond quickly and favorably to that kind of approach and, as a result of such leaders' taking personal responsibility for this effort, our voluntary program will produce significant reductions in the balance of payments deficit."

25. *Business Abroad*, February 7, 1966, p. 8.

26. *Ibid.*, pp. 884–86.

27. Private communication with anonymous observer.

28. *Balance of Payments Hearings*, pp. 181–83 and Table 2. These data exclude royalties and fees, which in 1964 amounted to about $700 million, for all areas (p. 185).

29. *The Federal Reserve Bulletin* (March 1965), pp. 299–304.

30. *Ibid.*, August 1965, p. 1078.

31. *Ibid.*, pp. 371–75.

32. U.S. Congress, Joint Economic Committee, *Hearings* (February 26, 1965), reported in *ibid.*, p. 397.

33. The guidelines were tightened slightly to 109 percent of loans in 1964 as the base year. ("Revised Guidelines for 1966," *Federal Reserve Bulletin* [December 1965], pp. 1693–1701).

34. Council of Economic Advisers, *Report* . . . , p.167. The voluntary program, and the mandatory program following it, defined direct investment to *include* net capital outflows from the U.S. *plus* earnings retained by U.S. TNCs' subsidiaries abroad *less* capital transfers made with the proceeds of long-term foreign borrowing by the direct investor. This permitted retained earnings abroad to substitute for U.S. capital outflows. Direct investment so defined is not 'direct investment' as shown in the quarterly reports on the balance of payments in the *Survey of Current Business*, line 33 of Tables 1 and 2. This category *does not* include retained earnings and *does* include capital transfers made with the proceeds of foreign borrowing.

See also, H. David Wiley, "Direct Investment Controls and the Balance of Payments," in *The International Corporation*, ed. Charles P. Kindleberger (Cambridge, 1970), p. 97, footnote.

35. Johnson, "Balance of Payments Controls," p. 180.

36. *Monthly Economic Letter*, First National City Bank of New York (February 1966), p. 23.

37. *Balance of Payments Hearings*, pp. 345–46.

38. *Ibid.*, pp. 28–30.

39. *Business Week*, February 20, 1965, p. 22.

40. *Ibid.*, March 20, 1965, p. 134.

41. *Balance of Payments Hearings*, pp. 519 and 525–26.

42. *Ibid.*, p. 527.

43. CED, *Gold, the Dollar . . .* , p. 26.

44. *Balance of Payments Hearings*, pp. 549–59.

45. *Ibid.*, p. 546.

46. See Herbert Stein, *The Fiscal Revolution in America* (Chicago, 1969), pp. 131–68.

47. *Balance of Payments Hearings*, pp. 981–86.

48. *Ibid.*, pp. 739–43.

49. John R. Petty, "A Banker's View of Restrictions in Industry," *Management Bulletin*, no. 68 (1965), pp. 23–24. He explained the choice: "These words come hard from one who believes that our foreign military commitments have made it possible for governments to gain a new life. . . . Foreign aid . . . has given tangible and worthy results to the aspirations of man" (p. 24).

50. *Balance of Payments Hearings*, p. 497. The IEPA argued specifically that: "The United States should become more aggressive in the protection of existing markets in our trade negotiations. To accomplish this, we must cease putting undefinable political objectives ahead of clearly defined economic ones" (p. 501).

51. *Ibid.*, pp. 469–93, 514.

52. Behrman, "Foreign Private Investment . . . ," p. 293.

53. *Ibid.*, pp. 293–95.

54. *Business Week*, October 9, 1965, pp. 53–56; and *The Wall Street Journal*, November 18, 1965, p. 32.

55. *Dun's Review and Modern Industry*, September 1965, pp. 37 and 86–87.

56. *Business Abroad*, December 13, 1965, p. 28.

57. *Ibid.*

58. *Ibid.*, p. 31.

59. *Business Abroad*, May 30, 1966, p. 9.

60. *The Wall Street Journal*, December 14, 1966, p. 3.

61. *Business Abroad*, May 30, 1966, p. 11. See also, CED, *Symposium*.

62. *Business Abroad*, May 30, 1966, p. 12.

63. *Ibid.* (See also the issue of November 28, 1966, pp. 9–11 for evidence on the split between the Treasury and Commerce departments.)

64. *Ibid.*, November 14, 1966, p. 16.

65. *Ibid.*, October 16, 1967, pp. 8–9.

66. The Committee for Economic Development, *The Dollar and the World Monetary System* (Washington, December 1966), p. 48.

67. *Ibid.*, pp. 18–19 and 48–53.

68. *Balance of Payments Hearings*, p. 887.

69. Council of Economic Advisers, *Report*, p. 166.

70. Walther Lederer and Evelyn M. Parrish, "The Balance of International Payments in Second Quarter, 1965," *Survey of Current Business* (September 1965), pp. 20–21.

71. *Business Abroad*, February 7, 1966, p. 7.

72. Lederer and Parrish, "Balance of International Payments," pp. 11–15 and 21.

73. *Ibid.* (December 1962), pp. 17–22.

74. Council of Economic Advisers, *Report*, p. 166.

75. *Balance of Payments Hearings*, pp. 890–91.

76. CED, *Gold, the Dollar . . .* , p. 41.

77. Samuel Pisar and Evelyn Parrish, "The U.S. International Balance of Payments: Firt Quarter 1966," *Survey of Current Business*, June 1966, Table 2, pp. 28–29; and *ibid.*, March 1966, "The Balance of Payments: Fourth Quarter and Year 1965," pp. 24–25.

78. *Survey of Current Business*, March 1968, p. 171; and, Walther Lederer and Evelyn M. Parrish, "The U.S. Balance of Payments in 4th Quarter and Year 1967," *Survey of Current Business*, March 1968, p. 23, Table 1. Direct investment is here defined as

exclusive of retained earnings.

79. Council of Economic Advisers, *Report*, pp. 186–87.

80. *Survey of Current Business*, March 1968, p. 25, Table 3.

81. Treasury Department, *Maintaining . . .* , p. 159.

82. J. Herbert Furth, "Barriers to Investment Abroad as Tools of Payments Policy," *Law and Contemporary Problems* (Winter 1966), p. 82.

5. The Mandatory Capital Control Program

1. Walter Lederer and Evelyn M. Parrish, "The U.S. Balance of Payments in Fourth Quarter and Year 1968," *Survey of Current Business* (March 1968), pp. 14–16.

2. U.S. Treasury Department, *Maintaining the Strength of the Dollar in a Strong, Free World* (Washington, 1968), p. 6.

3. Lederer and Parrish, "U.S. Balance of Payments," pp. 17–18, 172.

4. U.S., Congress, Joint Economic Committee, Subcommittee of International Exchange and Payments, *The Balance of Payments Mess, Hearings*, 92nd Congress, 1st Session, pp. 121–22; and Leonard Dudley and Peter Passell, "The War in Vietnam and the United States Balance of Payments," *Review of Economics and Statistics*, Nov., 1968, pp. 437–38.

5. See Council of Economic Advisers, *Report . . . 1968*, pp. 170–71.

6. Dudley and Passell, "War in Vietnam," pp. 438–42. See Douglas Bohi, "The War in Vietnam and the U.S. Balance of Payments," *Review of Economics and Statistics*, pp. 71–74 and, response to Bohi by Dudley and Passell, *ibid.*, pp. 74–75. See also the official Department of Defense estimate in Joint Economic Committee, Subcommittee on Exchange and Payments, *Hearings*, 91st Congress, 1st Session, pp. 123–26.

7. David Halberstam, *The Best and the Brightest* (New York, 1974), pp. 603–04; 605–06.

8. *Ibid.*, p. 610.

9. The war had become the critical issue in the discussions between U.S. and European officials. *The Wall Street Journal* commented that European "patience" with the war was problematic, and that it "cannot last too long" (March 12, 1968, p. 1).

10. *Maintaining the Strength of the Dollar . . .* , p. 78.

11. *Business Week*, January 13, 1968, p. 17–20; and, January 6, 1968, p. 13.

12. Sir Alec Cairncross, *Control of Long Term International Capital Movements* (Washington, 1968), p. 91; Karel Holbik, "United States Experience with Direct Investment Controls," *Weltwirschaftliches Archiv*, Band 108, Heft 3, 1972, p. 507; and William W. Lancaster, Jr., "The Foreign Direct Investment Regulations: A Look at *Ad Hoc* Rulemaking," *Virginia Law Review*, 1969, pp. 163–64.

13. President Lyndon Johnson, "Balance of Payments," statement, January 1, 1968, in *Maintaining the Strength of the Dollar . . .* , p. ix.

14. U.S., Congress, House Committee on Ways and Means, *Administration Balance of Payments Proposals, Hearings*, 90th Congress, 2nd Session, Part I, pp. 6–8.

15. *Maintaining the Strength of the Dollar . . .* , p. 93.

16. *Ibid.*, p. 99.

17. *Survey of Current Business*, June 1968, pp. 9–10, 23–24. In 1969 errors and omissions accounted for a new outflow of $2.8 billion; in 1970, a $1.1 billion outflow and in 1971 a $10.8 billion outflow (*ibid.*, March 1971, p. 44, Table 1; and March 1972, Table 1).

18. *Maintaining the Strength of the Dollar . . .* , pp. xii–xvii.

19. *Ibid.*, pp. 63 and 67.

20. Samuel Pisar, "Capital Restraint Programs," in *United States International Eco-*

nomic Policy in an Interdependent World (the "Williams Commission") (Washington, July 1971), Vol. I, pp. 93–94; and "OFDI Regulation of Foreign Direct Investment," pp. 133–37.

As in the voluntary program, the OFDI definition of direct investment differs from the payments accounting definition in that the former includes retained earnings. See below, and *Survey of Current Business*, September 1968, p. 28; Table F. For a detailed discussion of the complexities of the OFDI regulations, see Lancaster.

21. OFDI, *"Regulations . . . ,"* pp. 116–117.

22. Ibid, p. 117; and Lancaster, p. 148, fn.

23. OFDI, *"Regulations . . . ,"* p. 117.

24. John Ellicott, "United States Controls on Foreign Direct Investment: The 1969 Program," *Law and Contemporary Problems, op. cit.,* pp. 48–62.

25. OFDI, *"Regulations . . . ,"* p. 118.

26. *The Wall Street Journal,* April 17, 1969, p. 3.

27. Cairncross, *Control Long Term Movements,* pp. 40–41.

28. *Ibid.,* p. 43.

29. *Ibid.,* October 3, 1963, p. 4; November 20, 1968, p. 15; John S. Odell, *U.S. International Monetary Policy* (Princeton, NJ: 1982), p. 192.

30. Odell, *U.S. International Monetary Policy,* p. 187.

31. Walter S. Salent, *et al., The United States Balance of Payments in 1968* (Washington, 1963), Chapters III, V, VIII, and IX. See also Odell, pp. 180–99.

32. Statement of Charles E. Fiero, Joint Economic Committee, *The Balance of Payments Mess, Hearings,* pp. 45–47; see also pp. 149–51.

33. "Remarks by Don C. Cadle, Acting Director of OFDI," in U.S. Department of Commerce, *O.F.D.I. News,* February 20, 1969, p. 1.

34. U.S., Congress, House Committee on Foreign Affairs, Subcommittee on Foreign Economic Policy, *Foreign Direct Investment Controls, Hearings,* 91st Congress, 1st Session, pp. 1–2.

35. *Ibid.,* p. 216.

36. *Ibid.,* p. 224. Cadle's testimony specifically rebutted business arguments that the OFDI program had: 1) curtailed foreign expansion of direct investment; 2) curtailed foreign expansion of direct investment in less developed countries; 3) was an important factor in the rapid decline of the import surplus in 1968; 4) brought the "debt overhang" problem to seriously high levels (pp. 220–22). Cadle, as Fiero before him, stated: " . . . the control programs were designed to achieve such temporary gains while providing time for more fundamental improvements. In the interim, use of foreign borrowing as a substitute for U.S. capital outflows has improved the nation's international liquidity position" (p. 222).

37. *Ibid.,* p. 228.

38. *The Wall Street Journal,* January 10, 1968, p. 16.

39. *Ibid.,* January 9, 1968, p. 16. See also, Sidney E. Rolfe and James L. Burtle, *The Great Wheel* (New York, 1975), p. 95.

40. *The Wall Street Journal,* January 16, 1968, p. 16.

41. See, for instance, *Barron's,* January 8, 1968, p. 1.

42. *Business Week,* January 6, 1968, p. 16.

43. *Ibid.*

44. For examples of the government's pressure, see Halberstam, p. 609.

45. *Business Abroad,* February 5, 1968, p. 7.

46. *The Wall Street Journal,* February 23, 1968, p. 14.

47. *Ibid.,* January 2, 1968, p. 3; and *Banking,* February 1968, p. 55.

48. *The Wall Street Journal,* January 4, 1968, p. 2; January 29, 1968, p. 7.

49. *Dun's Review*, February 1968, pp. 27–28.

50. *Ibid.*, p. 28. Statement of president of Leeds and Northrup Corp., George E. Beggs.

51. *Ibid.*

52. First National City Bank of New York, *Monthly Economic Letter*, February 1968, pp. 22–23. See also, *The Commercial and Financial Chronicle*, January 18, 1968, p. 1; and *Barron's*, January 8, 1968, p. 1.

53. *Business Abroad*, March 4, 1968, p. 7.

54. *Ibid.*, pp. 7–8.

55. Committee for Economic Development, *The National Economy and the Vietnam War* (April 1968, Washington, D.C.), pp. 15 and 47–48.

56. For instance, Fred J. Borch served on the president's Advisory Committee and on the CED's Research and Policy Committee. He voted to approve the CED policy statement without reservation, but his other personal statements were much stronger and direct than the CED position.

57. *Administration Balance of Payments Proposals, Hearings*, Part II, p. 613.

58. *Ibid.*, p. 621.

59. *Ibid.*, p. 615.

60. First National City Bank of New York, *Monthly Economic Letter*, December 1968, p. 136.

61. *Balance of Payments Mess, Hearings*, pp. 187–89.

62. These corporations and banks included: Occidental Petroleum, United Fruit Co., Chas. Pfizer and Co., Kennecott Copper Corp., Westvaco Corp., Stauffer Chemical Corp., the 3M Corp., ITT, Bank of America, Hewlett-Packard, Champion Spark Plug Co., Weyerhauser Co., and Eastman-Kodak Co. A variety of smaller corporations and companies also testified against the controls. See *Foreign Direct Investment Controls, Hearings*, pp. III-IV.

63. *Ibid.*, April 1969, p. 7.

64. John J. Powers, Jr., "Government, Business and the Balance of Payments," *The Conference Board Record*, pp. 38–43.

65. *Business Abroad*, December 1968, p. 7.

66. *The Balance of Payments Mess, Hearings*, pp. 1–87; and *Business Abroad*, July 1971, pp. 7–11.

67. *The Economic Report to the President*, 1968, p. 10. Johnson proposed a 1 percent income tax surcharge as well as a more moderate tightening of monetary policy, but this only slowed the boom somewhat, especially given that it was an election year. (See *Economic Report . . . ,* 1969, p. 6.)

Nixon's administration encountered a moderate economic slowdown in 1970, but attempted to reverse that trend using only moderate monetary restraint (*Economic Report*, 1970, pp. 7–9). In short, through 1971 both administrations, while attempting to avoid large federal government budget deficits (unsuccessfully save for 1969), were not committed to classical solutions for balance of payments reasons.

68. CED, *National Economy and the Vietnam War*, pp. 10–11 and 30–42.

69. American Bankers Association, *The Cost of World Leadership* (Washington, 1968), p. 69.

70. *Ibid.*, p. 70.

71. *The Wall Street Journal*, April 22, 1969, p. 18.

72. Administration Balance of Payments Proposals, *Hearings*, pp. 802–03.

73. *Ibid.*, pp. 808–09.

74. *Ibid.*, p. 632.

75. ABA, *Cost of World Leadership*, pp. 250–51.

76. *Ibid.*, p. 291 (emphasis in original).

77. *The Balance of Payments Mess, Hearings*, p. 307.

78. *United States Economic Policy in an Interdependent World* (the "Williams Commission").

6. The Contradictory Consequences of the Capital Controls

1. Samuel Pisar, "Capital Restraint Programs," in *United States International Economic Policy in an Interdependent World* (Washington, D.C., 1971), Vol. 1, p. 120.

2. Karel Holbik, "United States Experience with Direct Investment Controls," *Weltwirtschaftliches Archiv*, Band 108, Heft 3, 1972, p. 494.

3. *Ibid.* p. 495.

4. *Ibid.*, p. 499.

5. U.S. Department of Commerce, OFDI, *Regulation of Foreign Direct Investment in United States International Economic Policy in an Interdependent World*, Vol. 1 (Washington, D.C., 1971), p. 1212, tables I and II.

6. The 1960–70 trend continued through 1971 from $13.0 billion to $14.8 billion worldwide and from $5.0 to 5.7 billion in Europe (*Survey of Current Business*, September 1972, p. 19, Table I). For a different, but limited estimate, see Peter H. Lindert, "The Payments Impact of Foreign Investment Controls," *Journal of Finance*, December 1971, pp. 1083–99.

7. OFDI, *Selected Statistics*, pp. 2–5. 1970 is the latest year for which OFDI computed data is available.

8. OFDI, "Regulations . . . ," pp. 121–22.

9. The Bank for International Settlements, "International Banking Developments— Third Quarter, 1981" (mimeo), 15 February 1982, Basle, Switzerland, Table 1, p. 2.

Data is measured on a gross basis. Net of interbank deposits the Eurocurrency system's available international credit in 1981 was $875 billion.

For a discussion of problems of measuring the market, see Hunter Dufey and Ian H. Giddy, "Measuring the Eurocurrency Market," *Journal of Bank Research*, Autumn 1978, pp. 151–160.

10. Computed from: *Survey of Current Business*, March 1970, p. 36, Table I and p. 44, Table 8; March 1972, p. 44, Table 2 and p. 52, Table 9. For a defense of this system see Thomas D. Willett, *International Liquidity Markets* (Washington, D.C., 1980).

11. Arthur F. Brimmer, "Multinational Banks and the Management of Monetary Policy in the United States," *Journal of Finance* (May 1973), p. 439.

12. The Bank for International Settlements, *42nd Annual Report* (Basle, 1972), p. 148, Chart I.

13. The Bank for International Settlements, *40th Annual Report*, June 9, 1969, p. 149; and *42nd Annual Report*, June 12, 1972, p. 154.

14. Ira O. Scott, "The Euro-Dollar Market and its Public Policy Implications," in U.S. Congress, Joint Economic Committee, *Economic Policies and Practices*, paper no. 12, 91st Congress, 2nd Session, Washington, D.C., p. 14, Table 4.

15. Fred Klopstock, "Use of Eurodollars by U.S. Banks," in *The Eurodollar*, ed. Herbert Prochnow (Chicago, 1970), pp. 71–72; E. Wayne Clendenning, *The Euro-Dollar Market* (London, 1970), pp. 25–27; 186–87; and Jane Sneddon Little, *Euro-Dollars: The Money Market Gypsies* (New York, 1975), p. 133.

16. U.S., Department of Commerce, Office of Foreign Direct Investment, *Foreign Direct Investment Program, Selected Statistics* (Washington, D.C., July 1971), p. 10, Table III. See also Charles-Albert Michalet, "La politique de financement de l'enterprise multinationale," *Economies et Societes*, June-July 1972, pp. 1255–60.

17. U.S., Department of Commerce, Office of Foreign Direct Investment, *The Finan-

cial Structure of the Foreign Affiliates of U.S. Direct Investors (Washington, D.C., April 14, 1974), p. 70, Tables 4–19. See also Tables 4–37 and 4–39, pp. 79–80, for TNCs' debt/equity ratio.

18. *Financial Structure of Foreign Affiliates*, pp. 19–20.
19. Eric Chalmers, *International Interest Rate Wars* (London, 1972), p. 33.
20. Clendenning, *Euro-Dollar Market*, p. 58.
21. *Ibid.*, pp. 60–61.
22. *Ibid.*, p. 58.
23. See Chalmers, *International Interest Rate Wars*, pp. 34–46; Clendenning, *Euro-Dollar Market*, pp. 69–91; Paul Einzig, *The Euro-dollar System* (New York, 1965), pp. 75–86; and Little, *Euro-Dollars*, pp. 214–16.
24. Clendenning, *Euro-Dollar Market*, pp. 90–91.
25. Chalmers, *International Interest Rate Wars*, p. 180.
26. See, for instance, Fred H. Klopstock, "The Euro-Dollar Market: Some Unresolved Issues," *Princeton Essays in International Finance* (No. 65, 1968), p. 18; and Edward M. Bernstein, "Eurodollars: Capital Flows and the U.S. Balance of Payments," in *The Eurodollar*, ed. Prochnow, pp. 125–26.
27. Fred H. Klopstock, "Impact of Euro-markets on the United States of Payments," *Law and Contemporary Problems*, Winter 1969, pp. 165–70.
28. *Ibid.*, pp. 163–70.
29. See Charles Kindleberger, "Measuring Equilibrium in the Balance of Payments," *The Journal of Political Economy*, November-December 1969, pp. 873–91; and François Perroux, Jean Denizet, and Henri Bourguinant, *Inflation, dollar et euro-dollar* (Paris, 1971), pp. 54–58.
30. Edward M. Bernstein, "Eurodollars: Capital Flows and the U.S. Balance of Payments," in *The Eurodollar*, ed. Prochnow, pp. 130–32; and Clendenning, pp. 154–56.

The following indicates the impact of Eurodollar transactions on the U.S. balance of payments, calculated on a liquidity basis and an official settlements basis.

Impact of Euro-Dollar Transactions on U.S. Balance of Payments

	Liquidity basis	Official settlements basis
1. Transfer of funds to Euro-bank by U.S. corporation	Capital outflow	Capital outflow
2. Transfer of funds from U.S. bank to Euro-bank by foreign resident	No effect	Capital outflow
3. Borrowing by U.S. corporation from Euro-market	Capital outflow	Capital outflow
4. Borrowing by U.S. bank from Euro-bank, including transfer from foreign branches of U.S. bank	No effect	Capital outflow
5. Deposit of Euro-bank with U.S. bank	No effect	Capital outflow

Source: Modified from Edward M. Bernstein, "Eurodollars," p. 134.

31. Perroux, Denizet, and Bourguinant, *Inflation, dollar,* pp. 70–73.
32. Council of Economic Advisers, *The Economic Report of the President*, transmitted to Congress, February 1970, Washington, D.C., pp. 126–27.
33. Clendenning, *Euro-Dollar Market*, pp. 160–161.
34. BIS, *40th Annual Report*, pp. 145–46; and *Economic Report of the President*,

1970, p. 128, and "U.S. Balance of Payments," *Survey of Current Business*, Department of Commerce, Vol. XLVIII, No. 12 (December 1969), p. 18; also June 1969, p. 24.

35. Perroux, Denizet, and Bourguinant, *Inflation, dollar*, pp. 70–71; and *Economic Report of the President*, 1970, p. 130.

36. Otmar Emminger, "The Euromarket: A Source of Stability or Instability?" in *Eurodollar*, ed. Prochnow, pp. 114–15.

37. Louis Camu, *La crise du dollar et l'Europe*, Paris, 1971, p. 23.

38. See, for instance, Henry G. Aubrey, "Behind the Veil of International Money," *Princeton Essays in International Finance*, No. 71, January 1969; and Paul Sweezy and Henry Magdoff, *The Dynamics of U.S. Capitalism* (New York, 1972), pp. 149–237.

7. U.S. Attempts to Regulate the Eurocurrency Market

1. For a discussion of the Eurocurrency system as financial innovation, see George W. McKenzie, *The Economics of the Euro-Currency System* (New York, 1976); Ronald I. McKinnon, "Currency Substitution and the Instability in the World Dollar Standard," *American Economic Review*, 72, no. 3 (June 1982), pp. 320–333; and Jurg Niehans, "Innovation in Monetary Policy," *The Journal of Banking and Finance*, 6, no. 1 (March 1982), pp. 9–28. For discussion from points of view within the Federal Reserve System, see Anatol B. Balback and David H. Resler, "Eurodollars and the U.S. Money Supply," The Federal Reserve Bank of St. Louis, *Review*, 62, no. 6 (June/July 1980), pp. 2–11; Edward J. Frydl, "The Debate Over Regulating the Eurocurrency Markets," Federal Reserve Board of New York, *Quarterly Review*, 4, no. 4 (Winter 1979–80), pp. 11–20; "The Eurodollar Conundrum," 7, no. 1 (1982), pp. 11–19; and Marvin Goodfriend, James Parthemos, and Bruce Summers, "Recent Financial Innovations," Federal Reserve Bank of Richmond, *Sixty-Fifth Annual Report*, May/June 1979, pp. 5–19.

2. *The Banker*, "Supervising the Eurocurrency Dinosaur," August 1978, pp. 677–79; Richard Dale, *Bank Supervision Around the World* (The Group of Thirty: New York, 1982); Jessica P. Einhorn, "International Bank Lending: Expanding the Dialogue," *Columbia Journal of World Business*, xiii, no. 3 (Fall 1978), pp. 128–130; *International Currency Review*, 12, no. 4 (nd), 1980, p. 13; *Ibid.*, 13, no. 2 (nd) (1981); and Joan Edelman Spero, *The Failure of the Franklin National Bank* (New York, 1980), pp. 186–89.

3. *The Banker*, "Supervising the Eurocurrency Dinosaur," p. 79; and Spero, *The Failure of the Franklin National*, pp. 189–90.

4. *The Banker*, "Supervising the Eurocurrency Dinosaur," pp. 79–81; and "Supervising American Banks' Foreign Lending," *ibid.*, September 1978, pp. 65–67; Einhorn, "International Bank Lending," pp. 125–27; Spero, *The Failure of the Franklin National*, p. 187; and Ingo Walter, "Country Risk, Portfolio Decisions and Regulation in International Bank Lending," *Journal of Banking and Finance*, 5 (1981), pp. 84–91.

5. *The Banker*, August 1978, p. 83.

6. *International Currency Review*, 12, no. 4 (nd), pp. 13–14. David F. Lomax and P.T.G. Gutmann, *The Euromarkets and International Financial Policies* (New York, 1981), pp. 15–52, 103–23.

7. *Business Week*, September 11, 1978, p. 57; October 9, 1978, pp. 116–18; October 23, 1978, p. 52; November 13, 1978, pp. 18–31.

8. *Business Week*, October 2, 1978, pp. 96–102; October 9, 1978, pp. 116–18; October 23, 1978, p. 52; *Euromoney*, October 1978, p. 11; and Robert O. Keohane, "The International Politics of Inflation," April, 1979 (mimeo), The Brookings Institution Project on the Politics and Sociology of Global Inflation, pp. 14 and 32. For U.S.-German conflict, see Ricardo Parboni, *The Dollar and Its Rivals* (London, 1981), pp. 118–40.

9. Quoted in George W. McKenzie, "Regulating the Euro-Markets," *The Journal of Banking and Finance*, 5, no. 1, p. 109.

10. Frydl, "The Debate," "Eurodollar Conundrum," Goodfriend, Parthemos, and Summers, "Recent Financial Innovations."

11. Alexander K. Swoboda, *Credit Creation in the Euromarket: Alternative Theories and Implications of Control* (New York: The Group of Thirty: 1980), p. 1. For a brief overview see Kusum A.N. Luther, "Eurocurrency Markets and Liquidity: The State of the Issue," *The Social Science Journal*, 18, no. 2, April 1981, pp. 41-54.

12. This is similar in method to Odell, *op. cit.*, pp. 58-66.

13. Michel Aglietta, "World Capitalism in the Eighties," *New Left Review*, no. 136, (November–December 1982), pp. 5-41; Jacques R. Artus and John H. Young, "Fixed and Flexible Exchange Rates: A Renewal of the Debate," *IMF Staff Papers*, 26, no. 4, (December 1979), pp. 654-98; Arturo Brillembourg and Susan M. Schadler, "A Model of Currency Substitution in Exchange Rate Determination: 1978-79," *IMF Staff Papers*, 26, no. 3, (September 1979), pp. 513-42; George W. McKenzie, "Economic Interdependence and the Eurocurrency System," *British Journal of International Studies* 3 (1977), pp. 22-38; and Ronald I. McKinnon, *Money in International Exchange* (New York, 1979), p. 230.

14. For instance, see Aglietta, "World Capitalism," and Parboni, *The Dollar and Its Rivals*.

15. Ronald I. McKinnon, "The Exchange Rate and Microeconomic Policy: Changing Postwar Perceptions," *The Journal of Economic Literature*, vol. xix (June 1981), pp. 531-57. See also, Brillembourg and Schadler, "Model of Currency Substitution."

16. McKinnon, "The Exchange Rate," 1982, pp. 320-32. See also Ralph C. Bryant, *Money and Monetary Policy in Interdependent Nations* (Washington: The Brookings Institution, 1980).

17. Ronald I. McKinnon, "Dollar Stabilization and American Monetary Policy," *The American Economic Review*, 70, no. 2 (May 1980), p. 385.

18. McKinnon, *Money in International Exchange*, 1979, pp. 112-21; 156-59.

19. Thomas D. Willett, *International Liquidity Issues* (Washington: American Enterprise Institute, 1975).

20. See Marian E. Bond, "Exchange Rates, Inflation and Vicious Circles," *IMF Staff Papers*, 27, no. 4, December 1980, pp. 679-709; and Brillembourg and Schadler, "Model of Currency Substitution," p. 517.

21. D.F.I. Folkerts-Landau, "Potential of External Financial Markets to Create Money, Credit and Inflation," *IMF Staff Papers*, 29, no.1 (March 1982), pp. 77-78.

22. Neihans, "Innovation in Monetary Policy," pp. 16-19.

23. Swoboda, *Credit Creation*, p. 28; McKinnon, *Money in International Exchange*, "Dollar Stabilization," "The Exchange Rate," and "Currency Substitution"; Willett, *International Liquidity Issues*.

24. Folkerts-Landau, "Potential of External Markets," J. Hewson and E. Sakakibara, "The Eurodollar Deposit Multiplier: A Portfolio Approach," *IMF Staff Papers*, 21, no. 2 (1974), p. 327; Jane Sneddon Little, "Liquidity Creation by Euro-Banks: 1973-1978," *New England Economic Review*, January–February 1979, pp. 62-72; McKenzie, *Economics of Eurocurrency System*; McKinnon, *Money in International Exchange*, p. 218; Neihans, "Innovation in Monetary Policy," Swoboda, *Credit Creation*, Robert Triffin, "The International Role and Fate of the Dollar," *Foreign Affairs*, 57, no. 2 (Winter 1978-79), pp. 269-86. Eugene Versluysen, *The Political Economy of International Finance* (New York, 1981), concludes that while the endogenous credit creation of the Eurocurrency system is minimal, especially compared to domestic credit creation, the expansionary effect of the markets is nevertheless significant.

For earlier debates about credit creation, see: Fred H. Klopstock, "The Euro-Dollar

Market: Some Unresolved Issues," *Princeton Essays in International Finance*, no. 65 (1968); Jane Sneddon Little, *Eurodollars: The Money Market Gypsies* (New York, 1975); Helmut Mayer, "Multiplier Effects and Credit Creation in the Euro-dollar Market," *Quarterly Review*, Banca Nazionale del Lavaro, September 1971; Alexander K. Swoboda, "The Euro-dollar Market: An Interpretation," *Princeton Essays in International Finance*, no. 64 (February 1968); Fritz Machlup, "Euro-Dollar Creation: A Mystery Story," *Quarterly Review*, *op. cit.*; and Machlup, "The Magicians and Their Rabbits," *The Morgan Guaranty Survey*, May 1971; Milton Friedman, "The Euro-dollar Market: Some First Principles," *The Morgan Guaranty Survey*, October 1969; and Charles Kindleberger, "The Euro-dollar and the Internationalization of United States Monetary Policy," *Quarterly Review*, March 1969.

25. Little, "Liquidity Creation," pp. 62–71. See also, Bank of England, *Quarterly Bulletin*, 21, no. 3 (September 1981), pp. 351–60; and The Group of Thirty, *Risks in International Bank Lending* (New York, 1982).

26. Versluysen, *Political Economy*, p. 131.

27. Bank of England, p. 131.

28. Folkerts-Landau, "Potential of External Markets," p. 99 and table on p. 103.

29. John Hewson and Jurg Niehans, "The Eurodollar Market and Monetary Theory." *The Journal of Money, Credit and Banking*, 7 (June 1979), pp. 13–15.

30. McKenzie, *Economics of Eurocurrency System*, pp. 78–80.

31. The Group of Thirty, "Risks in Bank Lending," p. 17; and M. S. Mendelsohn, *Money on the Move* (New York, 1980), pp. 87–88. See also Spero, pp. 182–83; *The Economist*, October 16, 1982, pp. 23–26; and Felix G. Rohatyn, "The State of the Banks," *The New York Review of Books*, November 4, 1982, pp. 3–8. For Citibank's role in the interbank market, see *The New York Times*, September 13, 1982, pp. 1 and 25; and *Multinational Monitor*, October 1982, pp. 9–15.

32. McKenzie, *Economics of Eurocurrency System*, p. 67.

33. Willett, *International Liquidity Issues*, Table 6, pp. 64–65.

34. Swoboda, *Credit Creation*, pp. 20–22. See also M. Perkin, I. Richard, and G. Zis, "The Determination and Control of the World Money Supply under Fixed-Exchange Rates, 1961–1971," *The Manchester School of Economics and Social Studies*, November 1976, pp. 293–316.

35. McKinnon, "Dollar Stabilization," p. 385.

36. *Ibid.*

37. *Ibid.*, p. 366.

38. McKinnon, "Currency Substitution," p. 331. See also Bryant, *Money and Monetary Policy*, for similar joint cooperation proposals under regimes of high monetary interdependence. See Parboni, *Dollar and Its Rivals*, on the political and economic difficulties and past failures of attempts at such cooperation.

39. Willett, *International Liquidity Issues*, pp. 87, 100.

40. Swoboda, *Credit Creation*, pp. 30–33.

41. Frydl, "Eurodollar Conundrum." This approach is advocated by Versluysen, *Political Economy*, pp. 249–54. See also statements by Deutsche Bank Director and West German Secretary of State, and Federal Ministry of Finance, in *Intereconomics*, March/April 1980, pp. 65–71.

42. See, William Jackson, "Depository Institutions, Financial Innovations, and Economic Activity: Cycles and Trends since the Accord," in U.S., Congress, Joint Economic Committee, *The Business Cycle and Public Policy, 1929–1980.* (Washington, D.C., 1980), pp. 282–98; Hyman Minsky, "Finance and Profits: The Changing Nature of American Business Cycles," in *ibid.*, pp. 209–244; Hyman Minsky, "Finance and Profits: The Changing Nature of American Business Cycles," in *ibid.*, pp. 209–244; and Hyman Minsky, "Financial Instability Revisited: The Economics of Disaster," in Board

of Governors of the Federal Reserve System, *Reappraisal of the Federal Reserve Discount Mechanism* (Washington, D.C., June 1982) vol. 3, pp. 95–136.

43. *International Currency Review*, 11, no. 3 (nd) (1979), pp. 8–16. Rene Larre, Managing Director of the Bank for International Settlements, commented on Henry Wallich's speech to the BIS on June 15 that this constituted a "complete change of direction for U.S. foreign financial policy" (*ibid.*, p. 8).

44. *Business Week*, August 6, 1979, p. 78.

45. Anthony Solomon, "Remarks," at the Royal Institute of International Affairs (London, January 12, 1979), Department of the Treasury, *News*, mimeo, pp. 3, 5–6, 8.

46. Hugo Colje, "Bank Supervision on a Consolidated Basis," *The Banker*, June 1981, pp. 29–34.

47. Anthony Solomon, "Remarks" (May 11, 1979), Department of the Treasury, *News*, mimeo, n.p. See also Henry C. Wallich, "Policies of the 1980's," remarks to the French-American Chamber of Commerce in the United States, Inc., New York City, March 3, 1980, p. 5, mimeo.

48. Henry C. Wallich, "Euro-Markets and U.S. Monetary Growth" (text of article which appeared in *The Journal of Commerce*, mimeo, May 1 and 2, 1979, n.p.).

49. *Ibid.*

50. See Henry C. Wallich, "Developments in International Banking." Remarks to the Association of Foreign Banks in Switzerland, June 15, 1979, mimeo, p. 14; Minsky, "Finance and Profits."

51. Henry C. Wallich, "The International Monetary and Cyclical Situation." Remarks at a meeting sponsored by the Lanseszertrabank in Berlin, mimeo, June 18, 1979, p. 16.

52. Henry C. Wallich, "Why the Euromarket Needs Restraint," *The Columbia Journal of World Business*, XIV, no. 3 (Fall 1979), pp. 21, 24.

53. Wallich, "International Monetary Situation," June 18, 1979, p. 17.

54. Wallich, "Developments in International Banking," June 15, 1979.

55. This contradiction is overlooked by Gerald Epstein's otherwise extremely interesting article on the Federal Reserve and Paul Volcker, "Domestic Stagflation and Monetary Policy: The Federal Reserve and the Hidden Election," in *The Hidden Election*, ed. Thomas Ferguson and Joel Rogers (New York, 1981), pp. 141–95. For a conservative bureaucratic and political interpretation of Federal Reserve actions, see Robert J. Shapiro, "Politics and the Federal Reserve," *The Public Interest*, no. 66 (Winter 1983), pp. 119–39.

56. These reserve requirements (the exact rates of which were to have been negotiated among the states) would have gone into effect once states responsible for 75 percent of all Eurocurrency holdings agreed. (U.S., Congress, House Sub-committee on Domestic Investment and Monetary Policy, of the Committee on Banking, Finance and Urban Affairs; and Monetary and Policy Sub-committee on International Trade, *Hearings*, "The Eurocurrency Control Act of 1979," 96th Congress, First Session, pp. 3–10, 178.) Euro-reserves would "equalize" interest rates in the now lower Eurocurrency system, thereby forcing borrowers and lenders into national markets. This proposal is the exact reverse of the 1963 Interest Equalization Act (IET) which was imposed on sales of foreign, primarily European, equities and bonds in the New York capital market. See Chapter Three.

57. Anthony Solomon, "Remarks," before the New York State Bankers Association, mimeo, June 2, 1979, pp. 11–12.

58. *The Wall Street Journal*, June 10, 1981, p. 4.

59. *International Currency Review*, 12, no. 4 (nd), 1980. The *Review* obtained relevant documents through a Freedom of Information Act suit. Anthony M. Solomon wrote in a letter to Paul Volcker on November 7, 1980:

"When a substantial share of what is now Eurocurrency business is done from a U.S.

base, it will be made transparent to those that the United States has tangible, unassailable interest in sharing a common approach to regulation. Sooner or later, a consensus will be built recognizing the need for negotiations to achieve uniform treatment of international banking markets.''

He added: ''Authorizing IBFs would send a clear message that we take seriously the need for new approaches to organizing and controlling the Euromarkets and that we are prepared to move ahead with new initiatives.''

60. Documents reprinted in *ibid.*, 12, no. 4 (nd) 1980, pp. 14–16. See also, Cynthia C. Lichtenstein, ''U.S. Banks and the Eurocurrency Markets: The Regulatory Structure,'' *The Banking Law Journal*, 66, no. 6 (June/July 1982), pp. 498–511 for detailed Federal reserve regulations. See *The New York Times*, September 13, 1982 for alleged violations.

61. In U.S., Congress, *Hearings*, p. 32.

62. Dennis Weatherstone, ''Euromarket, Born of Control, Now Capable of Looking After Itself,'' *The Money Manager*, March 19, 1979, pp. 11–12.

63. Weatherstone's argument is presented in greater detail in Morgan Guaranty Trust Company, *World Financial Markets*, March 1979, especially pp. 8–13.

64. U.S. Congress, *Hearings*, p. 41; 131–39; 281–84. For supporting data see the survey of bankers' opinions by the Group of Thirty, *How Bankers See the World of Financial Markets* (New York: Group of Thirty, 1982).

65. See, Henry Kaufman, ''Where the Fed Has Gone Awry,'' *The New York Times*, October 7, 1979, section 3, p. 1.

66. Harold Van B. Cleveland and Ramachandra Bhagavatula, ''The Continuing World Economic Crisis,'' *Foreign Affairs*, 59, no. 3 (Spring 1981), p. 600.

For a critique of this strategy from a ''reformed monetarist'' view, see Guy E. Noyes, ''The Multiple Flaws of the Monetary Base,'' *The Morgan Guaranty Survey*, October 1981, pp. 6–10.

67. Cleveland and Bhagavatula, ''The Continuing Crisis,'' pp. 609, 615.

68. Bryant, *Money and Monetary Policy*, p. 122 (emphasis in original).

69. *Business Week*, October 8, 1979, p. 87.

8. State Policy Formation and Business Interests

1. For a general discussion, see the Symposium of Interest, in *Political Theory*, 3, no. 3 (August 1975) pp. 245–287; Grenville Wall, ''The Concept of Interest in Politics,'' *Politics and Society*, 5, no. 4 (1975); and Christine Swarton, ''The Concepts of Interests,'' *Political Theory*, 8, no. 1 (February 1980).

For the subjective view, see Robert Dahl, *Modern Political Analysis* (Englewood Cliffs, N.J., 1963); A. F. Bently, *The Process of Government* (Chicago, 1908); David Truman, *The Governmental Process* (New York, 1951); J. D. B. Miller, *The Nature of Politics* (London, 1962); and H. D. Lasswell and A. Kaplan, *Power and Society* (New Haven, 1958).

For objectivist critiques of the subjectivist views, see Isaac Balbus, ''The Concept of Interest in Pluralist and Marxian Analysis,'' *Politics and Society*, Vol. 1, no. 2 (February 1971), pp. 151–177; and William E. Connolly, ''On 'Interests' in Politics,'' *Politics and Society*, Vol. II (1972), pp. 459–77.

2. See, for instance, Bob Jessop, ''Recent Theories of the Capitalist State,'' *Cambridge Journal of Economics*, 1 (1977), pp. 353–73; *The Capitalist State* (New York, 1982); Nicos Poulantzas, *Political Power and Social Classes* (London, 1973); and Poulantzas, *State, Power, Socialism* (London 1979); Eric Olin Wright, *Class, Crisis and the State* (London, 1978); James O'Connor, *The Fiscal Crisis of the State* (New York, 1973); and Jurgen Habermas, *Legitimation Crisis* (Boston, 1975).

3. O'Connor, *Fiscal Crisis*, and "The Fiscal Crisis of the State Revisited," *Kapitalistate* 9, 1981, pp. 41–62.

4. Fred Block, "The Ruling Class Does Not Rule," *Socialist Revolution* (May-June 1977), pp. 6–28; Claus Offe, "Structural Problems of the Capitalist State," in *German Political Studies*, ed. von Beyme (Russel Sage, London, 1974); and C. Offe and V. Ronge, "Theses on the Theory of the State," *New German Critiques*, 6 (Fall 1975).

5. Manuel Castells, *The Economic Crisis and American Society* (Princeton, 1980); Anthony Giddens, *A Contemporary Critique of Historical Materialism* (University of California, 1981), pp. 182–229; Jurgen Habermas, *Legitimation Crisis* (Boston, 1975); Poulantzas, and Alan Wolfe, *The Limits of Legitimacy* (New York, 1977).

6. John S. Odell, *U.S. International Monetary Policy* (Princeton, N.J., 1982), pp. 50–58; 268–89; 348–51.

7. See Antonio Gramsci, *Prison's Notebooks* (New York, 1971), pp. 175–184, 210–276.

8. Charles E. Lindblom, *Politics and Markets* (New York, 1977), pp. 178–94. Lindblom draws a parallel between contemporary leadership dualities in the U.S. and medieval church and state leadership conflicts.

9. This is dependent on the state's relative monopoly on legitimate violence. See, for instance, Stephen D. Krasner, *Defending the National Interest* (Princeton, 1978); and Theda Skocpol, *States and Social Revolutions* (New York, 1979). Giddens, *A Contemporary Critique*, p. 220, makes this point as well.

10. See Bruce M. Russet and Elizabeth C. Hansen, *Interest and Ideology* (San Francisco, 1975) and Franz Schurman, *The Logic of World Power* (New York, 1974), pp. 3–107.

11. See Krasner, *Defending National Interest*, Hans J. Morgenthau, *Dilemmas of Politics* (Chicago, 1958), pp. 50–70; *The Decline of Democratic Politics* (Chicago, 1962), pp. 79–91; *In Defense of the National Interest* (New York, 1951), pp. 34–35; 222–242; Skocpol, *States and Revolution*, Richard Flathman, *The Public Interest* (New York, 1966); David Truman, *The Governmental Process* (New York, 1951). See also William Connolly, "On Interests in Politics," *Politics and Society*, 2, no. 1 (Summer 1972), pp. 459–477; and, Isaac Balbus, "The Concept of Interest in Pluralist and Marxist Analysis," *ibid.*, 1, no. 2, 1971, pp. 151–172; and Phillippe Schmitter, "Introduction," *Comparative Political Studies*, 10, no. 1 (April, 1977), pp. 3–38.

12. For instance, Skocpol, *States and Social Revolutions*, pp. 14–18, 24–33, dismisses ideology as worthy of serious consideration as a constitutive historical force.

13. This argument is similar to Habermas, *Legitimation Crisis*.

14. Charles W. Anderson, "Modes of Political Design and the Representation of Interests," *Comparative Political Studies*, 10, no. 1 (April 1977), pp. 127–52; Raymond Bauer, Ithiel de Sola Pool and Anthony Dexter, *American Business and Public Policy* (Chicago, 1972); and Schmitter, "Introduction."

15. Bauer, Pool, and Dexter, *American Business*, pp. xi, xii.

16. *Ibid.*, p. 473.

17. Theodore J. Lowi, "American Business, Public Policy, Case Studies and Political Theory," *World Politics*, no. 16 (1964), pp. 677–715.

18. Schmitter, "Introduction," p. 36.

19. Anderson, "Modes of Political Design," p. 129.

20. *The Wall Street Journal*, October 13, 1980.

21. Fred Block, "Marxist Theories of the State in the World Systems Analysis," in *Social Change in the Capitalist World System*, ed. Barbara Hickey (Beverly Hills, 1978).

22. Leonard Silk and David Vogel, *Ethics and Profits* (New York, 1976).

23. See, for instance: R. S. Allen et al., *What is Profit?*, papers presented at the Summer Course, Churchill College, Cambridge, England, 1970; George E. Manners, Jr.

and Joseph G. Louderback II, *Managing Return on Investment* (Lexington, Mass., 1981); William A. Paton, *Corporate Profits* (Homewood, Ill., 1965); Robert A. Peters, *ROI: Practical Theory and Innovative Applications* (American Management Association, New York, 1979); M. N. Siddiqi, *Recent Theories of Profit* (Bombay, India, 1971).

24. Stanley M. Davis, *Matrix Organization* (Reading, Mass., 1977); and *Managing and Organizing Multinations* (Elmsford, N.Y., 1979). For other examples see, William J. Abernathy, *The Productivity Dilemma* (Baltimore, 1978) and Oliver E. Williamson, *Markets and Hierarchies* (New York, 1975). As well see, Lowi, "American Business"; Alfred D. Chandler, *The Visible Hand* (Cambridge, Mass., 1977); Richard Edwards, *Contested Terrain* (New York, 1979) and Harrison C. White, "Where Do Markets Come From?" *American Journal of Sociology*, 87, no. 3 (November 1981), pp. 517–47.

25. G. William Domhoff, *The Higher Circles* (New York, 1970), uses the notion of class cohesiveness to assess upper class attitudes toward selected large social, political, and economic policy issues. His treatment, however, is too general to confront the problem of interest formation and mediation.

26. Domhoff, *ibid.*; and Karl Schriftgiesser, *Business and Public Policy* (Englewood Cliffs, N.J., 1967). James Weinstein, *The Corporate Ideal in the Liberal State* (Boston, 1968).

For a different approach see Phillipe C. Schmitter and Wolfgang Streeck, *The Organization of Business Interests* (mimeo) (Berlin, Germany, International Institut fur Management und Verwaltung, 1981), pp. 1–11; 22–24; 30–33.

27. Schmitter and Streech, *Organization of Business Interests*, pp. 22–23.

28. See Block, "Marxist Theories . . . "; O'Connor, *Fiscal Crisis* . . . ; Habermas, *Legitimation Crisis*; Poulantzas, *Political Power and Social Classes*; Andrew Shonfield, *Modern Capitalism* (New York, 1969); and Herbert Stein, *The Fiscal Revolution in America* (Chicago, 1969). All present similar arguments from different perspectives.

29. Poulantzas, *Political Power and Social Classes* and *Classes in Contemporary Capitalism* (London, 1976) and Skocpol, *States and Social Revolutions*, pp. 14–18, 24–33.

30. Henry C. Simons, "Rules Versus Authority in Monetary Policy," *The Journal of Political Economy*, 44, no. 1 (February 1936), p. 13. See also Hyman P. Minsky, "Capitalist Financial Processes and the Instability of Capitalism," *The Journal of Economic Issues*, XV, no. 2 (June 1980), pp. 507, 519–21.

31. Simons, "Rules Versus Authority," p. 17.

32. Max Weber, *Economy and Society* (Berkeley and Los Angeles, 1978) pp. 169, 172.

33. For a different interpretation of the politico-military interests of state in relation to capital, see Otto Hintze, *The Historical Essays of Otto Hintze*, ed. Felix Gilbert (New York, 1975), pp. 178–215; Krasner, *Defending National Interest*; Schurmann, *Logic of World Power*; and Skocpol, *States and Social Revolutions*, pp. 14–32; 284–93. See Karl Polanyi, *The Great Transformation* (Boston, 1957), p. 2, 29, 76 for elaboration of the idea of the state protecting capital from itself.

34. Schurmann, *Logic of World Power*, pp. 8–13, 7–113, 114–200, and Krasner, *Defending National Interest*. Both bear a strong resemblance to Joseph Schumpeter's theory of imperialism in *Imperialism and Social Class* (New York, 1951).

35. Clarence H.Y. Lo., "Theories of the State and Business Opposition to Increased Military Spending," *Social Problems*, vol. 29 (April 1982), pp. 424–38.

36. David Gold, "The Rise and Decline of the Keynesian Coalition," *Kapitalistate*, 6 (1977), pp. 130–47; and Herbert Stein, *The Fiscal Revolution in America* (Chicago, 1966), pp. 131–309.

37. Martinelli, pp. 25–26, my translation.

38. Gold, "The Rise and Decline," pp. 130, 132–134; Ellis Hawley, *The New Deal and the Problem of Monopoly* (Princeton, N.J., 1966), pp. 270–83; and

Stein, *Fiscal Revolution*, pp. 160–164.

39. Stein, *ibid.*, pp. 160–61.

40. Gold, "The Rise and Decline," pp. 147–51. See also Simons, "Rules Versus Authority in Monetary Policy," p. 13. Hyman P. Minsky, "Capitalist Financial Processes and the Instability of Capitalism," *The Journal of Economic Issues*, XI, no. 2 (June 1980), pp. 507, 519–21. Simons argued that productive capital required protection from financial innovation in order to maintain competition. Thus, he proposed a form of social-state control of financial institutions.

41. John Maynard Keynes, quoted in Block, *op. cit.*, p. 8.

42. Ronald E. Muller, "National Economic Growth and Stabilization Policy in the Age of Multinational Corporations: The Challenge of Our Postmarket Economy," in U.S. Congress, Joint Economic Committee, 95th Congress, 1st Session, *U.S. Economic Growth from 1976–1986: Prospects, Problems and Patterns*, vol. 12, p. 42.

43. Gold, "The Rise and Decline," p. 150.

44. Leon Panitch, "The Development of Corporatism in Liberal Democracies," in *Trends Toward Corporatist Intermediation*, ed. Phillipe Schmitter and Gerhard Lehmbruch (Beverly Hills, 1979), pp. 131–34.

45. Ernest Mandel, *Late Capitalism* (London, 1975), pp. 438–73.

46. Gold, "The Rise and Decline," pp. 132–34.

47. See Stanley Hoffman, *Primary or World Order: American Foreign Policy Since the Cold War* (New York, 1978); Thomas Schelling, *The Strategy of Conflict* (Cambridge, Mass., 1960); Hintze, *Historical Essays*; Robert Gilpin, *U.S. Power and the Multinational Corporation* (New York, 1975); Calleo and Rowland, *America and the World Political Economy* (Bloomington, Ind., 1973); Krasner, *Defending National Interest*; Peter J. Katzenstein, *Between Power and Plenty* (Madison, 1978).

48. Hans J. Morgenthau, *The Decline of Democratic Politics* (Chicago, 1962), p. 222; *Politics Among Nations* (New York, 1978), p. 4; and *In Defense of the National Interest* (New York, 1951), p. 222.

49. Hans J. Morgenthau, *Dilemmas of Politics* (Chicago, 1958), p. 70.

50. *Ibid.*, 1962, p. 91. For a critique of these geopolitical assumptions see Graham Allison, *Essence of Decision* (Boston, 1971), p. 13 *et seq.*

51. Krasner, *Defending National Interest*, p. xi.

52. Calleo and Rowland, *American and World Political Economy*, pp. 254–55.

53. Gilpin, *U.S. Power and the Multinational Corporation*, pp. 7–8, 39.

54. *Ibid.*, p. 38.

55. Krasner, *Defending National Interest*, p. 6.

56. *Ibid.*, pp. 6, 333, 316.

57. *Ibid.*, p. 32, fn. See also Schurmann, *Logic of World Power*, and Skocpol, *States and Social Revolutions*, pp. 24–33. Skocpol stresses the role of the state as unique institutions of social control and for maintaining national sovereignty. She pays little attention—in her general formulations—to its economic or to its ideological impact. Her ultimate moving force is state bureaucracy. For both Krasner and Schurmann, to the contrary, state ideology is uppermost. What is striking in both approaches is the relative lack of an integrated view of both state ideology and bureaucracy and of the dynamics of state and markets.

58. See Allison, *Essence of Decision*, Graham Allison and Peter Szanton, *Remaking Foreign Policy: The Organizational Connection* (New York, 1976); I. M. Destler, *Presidents, Bureaucracies and Foreign Policy* (Princeton, N.J., 1972); I. M. Destler, *The Making of Foreign Economic Policy* (Washington, D.C., 1980); and Morton H. Haperin, *Bureaucratic Politics and Foreign Policy* (Washington, D.C., 1974).

59. Graham Allison, "Bureaucratic Politics," in *Bureaucratic Power in National Politics*, ed. Francis Rourke (New York, 1965), p. 223.

60. Allison, *op. cit.*, 1971, p. 162.

61. See Kay Trimberger, *Revolution from Above: Military Bureaucrats and Development in Japan, Turkey, Egypt and Peru* (New Brunswick, N.J., 1978).

62. David Truman, *The Governmental Process* (New York, 1964); Arnold Rose, *The Power Structure* (New York, 1967); Elmer Eric Schattschneider, *Politics, Pressure and the Tariff* (Hamden, Conn., 1963), pp. 286–87; and see also Lowi, "American Business," pp. 680–81.

63. Schattschneider, *Politics, Pressure and Tariff*, pp. 286–87, is an important early exception to the 1950s and 1960s pluralist tradition. See Lindblom, *Politics and Markets*, for a similar position.

64. Truman, *Governmental Process*, p. 85.

65. Rose, *Power Structure*, pp. 23; 92–93.

66. Trimberger, *Revolution from Above*; and Skocpol, *States and Revolution*, are important exceptions as they examine the interactions of class, state bureaucracies, and the global system.

67. Domhoff, *Higher Circles*; and G. William Domhoff, *Power Structure Research* (Beverly Hills, 1980). See Poulantzas, *Classes in Contemporary Capitalism*, pp. 92–189 for a discussion of state monopoly capitalism.

68. Wright, *Class, Crisis, and State*, p. 271. See also Reinhard Bendix, "Inequality and Social Structure: A Comparison of Marx and Weber," *American Sociological Review*, 39, no. 2 (April 1974); Paul Goldman, "Sociologists and the Study of Bureaucracy," *The Insurgent Sociologist*, VIII, no. 1 (Winter 1978), pp. 21–28; Alvin M. Gouldner, "Metaphysical Pathos and the Theory of Bureaucracy," *The American Political Science Review*, 49 (June 1955), pp. 496–507, and Kenneth Westhues, "Class and Organization as Paradigms in Social Science," *American Sociologist*, 11, no. 1 (February 1976), pp. 43–44.

69. Karl Marx, "The Class Struggle in France, 1848–50," in *Selected Works*, II (np, 1933) p. 276.

70. The complexity of interests is captured by Marx writing on the bourgeoisie's role in the 1848 revolution: "It declared unequivocally that it longed to get rid of its own political rule in order to get rid of the troubles and dangers of ruling." The bourgeoisie, " . . . proved that the struggle to maintain its *public* (bourgeois) interests, its own *class interests*, its *political power*, only troubled and upset it, as it was a disturbance of private business." Consequently, a bourgeoisie does not necessarily pursue its own interests, its 'public' hegemonic interests as a class-for-itself, that, in Marx's words, " . . . in order to save its purse, it must forfeit the crown, and sword that it is to safeguard it must at the same time be hung over its own head as a sword of Damocles." Karl Marx, *The 18th Brumaire of Louis Bonaparte* (New York, 1975), pp. 67, 106–107.

71. *Ibid.*, p. 51–62.

72. Immanuel Wallerstein, 1978, "Preface," p. 7 in *Social Change in the Capitalist World System*, ed. Barbara Hockey Kaplan (Beverly Hills). Related points are made by Aristide Zolberg, "Origins of the Modern World System: A Missing Link," *World Politics*, 33 (January 1981), pp. 253–281; and Skocpol, *States and Revolution*. For a more detailed discussion, see James P. Hawley, "Interests, State Foreign Economic Policy and the World System: The Case of the U.S. Capital Controls, 1961–1974," in *Foreign Policy and the Modern World System*, ed. Pat McGowan and Charles W. Kegley, Jr. (Beverly Hills, 1983), pp. 223–254.

73. Immanuel Wallerstein, *The Modern World System* (New York, 1975), p. 61 and *The Capitalist World Economy* (Cambridge, 1979), p. 20; see also Frederic C. Lane, *Profits From Power* (Albany, 1979), pp. 13, 22, 57–59, 85.

74. Christopher Chase-Dunn develops Wallerstein's implicit idea that class fractions dominate states rather than classes as a whole. Christopher Chase-Dunn, "Socialist States in the Capitalist World Economy," *Social Problems* 27 (April 1980), p. 506; and Waller-

stein, *Modern World System*, 1975, p. 61.

75. Nicos Poulantzas, *State, Power, Socialism* (London, 1979), p. 30, 127–28.

76. *Ibid.*, p. 185.

77. O'Conner, *op. cit.*; Offe, "Structural Problems." An extreme functionalist formulation the 'capital logic' approach sees the state as an ideal collective capitalist. See John Hollaway and Sol Piccitto, eds., *State and Capital* (London, 1978).

78. Wright, *Class, Crisis, and State*, pp. 20–29.

79. Karl Polanyi, *The Great Transformation* (Boston: 1957), p. 198.

Index

program, 52, 94–95

Walker, Charles E., 75
Wallerstein, Immanuel, 6, 167–168
Wallich, Henry C., 134, 136, 137, 138
Wall Street, 8, 55
The Wall Street Journal, 35, 54, 59, 97, 98, 104
Watson, Arthur K., 80
Weatherstone, Dennis, 140
Weber, Max, ix, 147, 148, 156
Western Europe, 47, 112, 124; capital markets, 54; capital outflow and income received on foreign direct investments, 44, 70; competition in, 56; competition with United States, 29; defense spending, 77; direct investment, 25, 42; discrimination against U.S. goods, 23; economic health, 37–38; effect of OFDI program, 92, effect of VFCR, 93–94; expansion, 4; exports, 69; growth rate, 24; infla-

tion, 64–65; investments, 31; postwar reconstruction, 7, 8; as provider of U.S. income, 26, 27; recession, 87–88; savings patterns, 49–50; self-financing, 49; and TNCs, 5; U.S. net capital outflow, 109
West Germany, 40, 51; debts to United States, 13; dollar support, 134–135; growth rate, 124; interest rate wars, 116; and military debt, 21, 73; payments surplus, 89; recession, 17; revaluation of the mark, 16; stabilization program, 141–142; trade barriers, 91–92
White, Harry Dexter, 7
Willett, Thomas D., 127, 128, 131, 132
Williams, Albert L., 105–106
Williams Commission, 105–106
Wriston, Walter B., 100

Zijlstra, Jelle, 143

For Product Safety Concerns and Information please contact our EU
representative GPSR@taylorandfrancis.com
Taylor & Francis Verlag GmbH, Kaufingerstraße 24, 80331 München, Germany

www.ingramcontent.com/pod-product-compliance
Lightning Source LLC
Chambersburg PA
CBHW070418270326
41926CB00014B/2840